Asian American Identities and Practices

Asian American Identities and Practices

Folkloric Expressions in Everyday Life

Edited by Jonathan H. X. Lee
and Kathleen Nadeau

LEXINGTON BOOKS
Lanham • Boulder • New York • Toronto • Plymouth, UK

Published by Lexington Books
A wholly owned subsidiary of Rowman & Littlefield
4501 Forbes Boulevard, Suite 200, Lanham, Maryland 20706
www.rowman.com

10 Thornbury Road, Plymouth PL6 7PP, United Kingdom

Poetry in chapter 6 is from "In America," by Soojin Pate. Published with the author's permission.

Song lyrics in chapter 8 are from "Hidden Truth, Open Lies," by praCh. © Mujestic Records.

British Library Cataloguing in Publication Information Available

Library of Congress Cataloging-in-Publication Data

Library of Congress Cataloging-in-Publication Data Available

ISBN 978-0-7391-4732-0 (cloth : alk. paper) -- ISBN 978-0-7391-4734-4 (electronic)
ISBN 978-0-7391-4733-7 (pbk : alk. paper)

♾TM The paper used in this publication meets the minimum requirements of American National Standard for Information Sciences Permanence of Paper for Printed Library Materials, ANSI/NISO Z39.48-1992.

Printed in the United States of America

Contents

Acknowledgments

First and foremost we wish to express our deep gratitude to our contributors whose patience, understanding, commitment, and support saw this volume through to completion. We also wish to thank Melissa D. Wilks who supported this project when we first approached her with our idea. More importantly, we thank Amy King, our editor at Lexington Books, for her steadfast support and grace as she kindly waited for us to complete our volume after multiple requests for extensions.

Jonathan H. X. Lee wishes to acknowledge funding from San Francisco State University's Presidential Award in Fall 2011, that made work on this volume possible. He also wishes to thank his students and colleagues in the Asian American Studies Department at San Francisco State University for their support.

Kathleen M. Nadeau wishes to thank her Asian American studies students and colleagues, especially colleagues in the Anthropology Department at California State University, San Bernardino, for their stimulating conversations.

Introduction

Disciplines and Discourses in Asian American Folklore and Folklife: Prospects, Patterns, Practices, and Problems in an Emerging Landscape

Jonathan H. X. Lee and Kathleen Nadeau

Asian American studies was founded four decades ago out of global struggles for liberation. Fueled by the civil rights movement, anti-Vietnam War protests, and the women's liberation movement, it demanded an alternative definition of what it means to be "American." Discussions centered on the fact that being an American was no longer limited to the so-called normative white, middle class, Protestant, heterosexual image and ideals. Instead, the Asian American movement demanded that Asians living in America have the inalienable right to express themselves, and to be fully American. Regardless of degree of acculturation, this demand rejected the totalizing model of assimilation. Each cultural group, each generation expresses themselves in manifold ways, and determines for themselves how they can be American. Their stories and struggles, once told and recorded, will become part-and-parcel of the folkloric traditions of Asian America, and, by extension, part of American folklore and folklife traditions. Asian American folklore and folklife is not "exotic" and "other," rather, it is American—naturally, comfortably, and rightly.

Since Asian American studies arose from the struggles of the 1960s and 1970s, activists and scholars largely ignored the role of folklore and folklife in the Asian American experience, favoring political, economic, and social empowerment. This penchant for Marxian ideologies produced Asian American studies scholarship that minimized the centrality and necessity of folklore and how it informs folklife (i.e., traditional religion, rituals, and customs). True to form, folklore is understood in a rigid and traditional way, as stories and legends, if not make-believe fairytales. This volume is inspired by Michel Foucault's concept of "discourse" as practice, wherein he shows how meaning and subjectivity are produced through the process of discursive practices, which is dependent on historical conditions and ideological epistemologies.[1] We apply Foucault's notion that discourse consists not merely of signs and symbols that inform knowledge and meaning, but, rather, a practice that informs the objects from which they speak. Therefore, folklore is not just "people" and their "lore," but "peoples' everyday practices" and the things that they do with and to their bodies and with others in the community.

Folklore is important. Folklore is central to the way Asian Americans live, express themselves, maintain social relationships, and understand their position and sphere of influence as Americans. By studying and investigating Asian American folklore, we can only conclude that we need folklore because it makes life meaningful. We need folklore to know who we are. These lore and practices define our experience and how we understand those experiences. They create meaningful places and shared memories. At this junction, we experience community and determine selfhood. Past, present, and future are not isolated temporal entities. We who live in the present are accountable for the folklore and folklife traditions located in Asian America.

In studying Asian American folklore and folklife, we must acknowledge that change is a given. Folklore changes. Folk practices are modified, adapted, reinvented, and changed. Folklore and folklife are subject to historical, social, economic, and political conditions. These changes, accommodations, and adaptations reveal the creativity and agency of Asian Americans to define and redefine their way of life and who they are for themselves.

DEFINING FOLKLORE AND FOLKLIFE STUDIES

Folklorists often invoke a common *cliché* that there are more definitions of the word *folklore* than there are folklorists. The word *folklore* was coined by William Thoms in an article published in *Atheneum* in August 1846. Thoms intended the word to be employed as "the generic stories, songs, sayings, and the like current among backward peoples or retained by the less cultured classes of more advanced peoples." Since that time, there has been much development in the study of folklore. Twenty-one competing definitions of folklore by influential American scholars are listed in *The Standard Dictionary of Folklore, Mythology and Legend*, published in 1949. Today, after much innovation, the word *folklore* has come to be defined by some as whatever folklorists are interested in. According to Barre Toelken,[2] things of interest are items, events, and other cultural forms of dynamic expressions of local social life. Folklore is no longer restricted to the word *folk*, says W. Edson Richmond.[3] No longer do folklorists confine their studies solely to those things that are perpetuated orally or by precept. Folklore is most certainly not restricted to "backward" cultures. Folklore is concerned with those things that appear and, more importantly, reappear, in varied forms whenever and wherever human beings interact.

In the 1960s, examining folklife emerged as a way to compliment the oral tradition of folkloric studies. Don Yoder[4] and Warren Roberts[5] maintained that the study of folklore must go hand-in-hand with the study of folklife, which includes the multifarious dimensions of human culture: material culture, community festivals, architecture, dances, music, proverbs, vernacular speech, foods and foodways, clothes and jewelry, rites of passage, rituals, religion, traditional medicine and healing, and so on. On January 2, 1976, the Library of Congress created *The American Folklife Center*, which defined "American folklife" as "the traditional expressive culture shared within the various groups in the United States: familial, ethnic, occupational, religious, [and] regional; expressive culture includes a wide range of creative and symbolic forms such as custom, belief, technical skill, language, literature, art, architecture, music, play, dance, drama, ritual, pageantry, handicraft; these expressions are mainly learned orally, by imitation, or in performance, and are generally maintained without benefit of formal instruction or institutional direction. . ." (Public Law 94-201).[6]

The word *folklore* can be an abstract term. Folklore can contain religious or mythic elements, but it equally concerns itself with the mundane traditions of everyday life. Folklore can serve to validate a culture, as well as transmit a culture's morals and values. Folklore can also be used to assert social pressures, or, as in the case of jokes and festivals, relieve them. Folklife is a way of life—the expression of folklore through commonplace actions, rituals, and other forms of social interactions. Folklore and folklife are embedded in human social relationships. Therefore, to study folklore and folklife is to reveal social relationships, and what it means to be human. Many rituals and beliefs can be considered folklore and folklife, whether formalized in a cultural or religious system (i.e., weddings, baptisms, religious festivals), or practiced within a family or secular context. For example, in certain parts of the United States (as well as other countries), one places a knife, or a pair of scissors, under the mattress to "cut the birth pains" after giving birth. In various Southeast Asian countries, the umbilical cord of a newborn baby is buried underneath the house or in the garden, forever connecting the person to the land, and cementing kin relationships for multiple generations.

THE LANDSCAPE OF ASIAN AMERICAN FOLKLORE AND FOLKLIFE

Asian American Identities and Practices: Folkloric Expressions in Everyday Life employs the broadest definition and discourses on its topic. We contend that Asian American folklore and folklife among some Asian ethnic and cultural communities, has already been firmly established, while others are emerging. However, the various ways these have been expressed has not been studied as extensively as have other regional and world traditions. More research needs to be done to understand the similarities in and differences between various Asian American folklore and practices, theoretically and ethnographically, in order to make a new contribution to comparative folklore and Asian American studies. Folkloric studies is an interdisciplinary field that draws on various methodologies for the study of cultural matters. Hence, Asian American folklore and folklife consists of more than Asian mythologies that are narrated within Asian American families and communities, or Asian ritualistic traditions performed in the private sphere of the home. Asian American folklore and folklife is an integral part of the culturally various and diverse *Asian American ways of life.*

Asian American folklore encompasses the narrative histories of Asians in America. Asian American folklife is the totality of Asian material cultures, religious traditions, performances, celebrations, social relations, and so on, used to produce individual and collective Asian American identities and communities. Folklore for Asian Americans can be the oral traditions of family histories, including romantic tales of the homeland and of the struggles of resettlement in a foreign land. Asian American folklore can be the historical experiences of Asian immigrants in America, who, since the 1840s, cultivated the lands of the American West, built the railroads, worked the plantations of Hawai'i, constructed the levies of California's San Joaquin Valley, suffered internment during World War II, became naturalized citizens, and served in U.S. military forces. Asian American folklore also includes epic tales that entertained Asian immigrants, both historically and today, such as *The Tale of Genji*; *The Ramayana*; *The Tale of Kieu*; and *The Romance of Three Kingdoms*.

Asian American folklore bridges Asia to America with tales employed by elders and parents to transmit cultural mores, ethics, and pride to Asian American youth. More importantly, these stories inspire. For example, oral histories of the flight of Laotian refugees after the Pathet Lao Communist Party swept into power in 1975, as well as the origin myth of the Lao peoples emerging from a giant gourd, re-enforce social solidarity among Laotian Americans. The Cambodian origin tale of Kaundinya and Soma reinforces, among Cambodian Americans, a timeless link to Cambodia, her history, and land. Asian American religious folktales teach children how to resist worldly vices such as selfishness, greed, jealousy, and the lust for power, thereby encouraging them to become more caring and nurturing human beings and community members.

Asian folklore opens a window onto the relationship between men and women, or relationships among people. For example, the "female undead" (vampires) that came to America vis-à-vis Filipino, Indonesian, and Malay folklore are usually disguised as beautiful women; their goal and function does not suggest that hypersexuality is an innate aspect of their attack. The male vampires in these traditions prey only on children, which is opposite to the way male vampires behave in Euro-American contexts, where they are hypersexual and prey on anyone they desire.

Asian American folklife also reveals the transition from Asian to Asian American. For instance, in Cambodia, tattooing is a form of spiritual art. In this cultural context, tattoos are considered magical, and it is believed that they supply the carrier with power and the ability to influence good fortune. In Cambodia, it is men who create tattoos and are able to possess tattoos. However, in America, this has changed as Cambodian American women are now acquiring tattoos that once were only available to men. The most common magical tattoos are words of the Buddhist scriptures, in Pali, which are believed to protect and empower the carrier of the words.

Asian American folklife is embedded in everyday life. Expressions of Asian American folklife are the assemblages that unite Asia and America. For example, among Southeast Asian Americans from Burma, Thailand, Cambodia, and Laos, and South Asian Americans from India and Sri Lanka, people greet each other with their hands together in front of them, and make a bowing gesture. In Laos, it is called *"nop"* or *"wai"*; in Cambodia it is called *"sampeah"*; in Thailand, it is called *"wai"*; and among South Asians it is called *"a ñjali mudrā/namasté."* These vernacular expressions reveal social relationships, social status, and community unity. In Asian America, youth are taught to "speak" and "perform" these cultural expressions as a way to honor their elders for their life experience and collective wisdom. In so doing, they express themselves as Asian, and reinforce their cultural, religious, and ethnic identities. In Laos and Lao America, there are three forms of "nop": with one's hands together placed at one's chest to greet strangers and friends; with one's hands together with thumbs placed at one's chin to greet elders, teachers, and people of respect; and with thumbs pressed at the third-eye (the space between the eyebrows), which is the highest form of respect reserved for the Buddha.

Asian American folklife is expressed when ethnic clothes (i.e., Indian saris, Muslim veils, Thai sarongs, Filipino barong, Vietnamese *áo dài*, Japanese kimono, or Chinese *qipao*) are worn, or when cooking techniques are transmitted from parent to child. Asian American folklife is expressed in the observance of festivals and holidays, in the celebrations of rites of passage, as well as in the way each specific community cares for and maintains relationships with their deceased ancestors. Folklife is recorded in Hmong American "story cloth." Story cloths are made of designs created by women that depict scenes from daily life, usually village life. During the Vietnam War, however, some men drew pictures of their wartime experiences on the cloths that were embroidered by women as way to remember. Later, in the refugee camps, these cloths became popular with tourists and were produced by men and women for sale as tourist art. Hmong American story cloths reveal these changing gender relations. They function mainly as a marketing tool, but are sometimes distributed as gifts and heirlooms. Hmong American women combine fine needlework tradition with new knitting and quilting techniques to create designs that depict everyday life in the United States.

Folklore and expressions of folklife are portable, situated, and changing. Asian immigrants have introduced many elements of their folklore and folklife to America. Over time, new folklore about a given group develops, while some folklife practices are appropriated and become quintessentially "American," such as yoga, or the Chinese American fortune cookie. Another example are balikbayan boxes ("boxes returning home") that are cargo containers of Filipino American folklore and folklife. Almost every Filipino American sends balikbayan boxes filled with gifts and goods back to family members and friends in the Philippines. Balikbayans boxes magically transform into carriers of gifts that are opened and displayed to signify a person's hospitality. Balikbayan boxes sometimes are sent even at the expense of the Balikbayan (returning person).

The transnational fluid boundaries of Asia and Asian America can also be gleaned in popular video games from Asia that transmit Asian folklore to Asian American youth. This high tech transmission is exemplified with *Dynasty Warriors*, a series of tactical action video games created by Omega Force and Koei. The game is based on the Chinese epic *The Romance of Three Kingdoms*, known in Japanese as *Shin Sangokumusou*. *The Romance of Three Kingdoms* and its heroes—Guangong, Liu Bei, and Zhang Fei—become part of the cultural literacy of Asian American youth through video games.

Asian American folklore and folklife is the consequence of transplantation, accommodation, transformation, and invention of cultural traditions, material and ideological, of Asian subjects and communities in America. Hence, among Japanese American communities, a uniquely Japanese American way of life can be seen in the accommodations made to the Jodo Shinshu Buddhist tradition in America, and the production of the Buddhist Churches of America immediately after World War II. Or, to take another example, while beautifully handmade and interwoven paper cranes continue to be associated with a long, healthy, and happy marriage in Japanese America, since World War II and the atomic bombs dropped on Hiroshima and Nagasaki, they have become reversely associated with the wish to heal the sick in Japan. More recently, the "Got Rice?" logo has become a sign and symbol of pan-Asian American pride, while the popular metaphor of the Twinkie, Banana, and Coconut—yellow and/or brown on the outside, white-washed in the inside—bespeaks the cultural identity struggles of growing up in Asian America.

The authors will argue that Asian American folklore, as a way of life and practice, has emerged and continues to emerge as Asian Americans lay claim to and take root in the American mosaic. As such, the contributors in this volume all show how the Asian American historical experiences and continued international migration inform the production of new folkloric practices and ideologies, which in turn strengthen specific Asian American ways of life, while normalizing folklore that are squarely produced in Asian America.

SCOPE OF *ASIAN AMERICAN IDENTITIES AND PRACTICES: FOLKLORIC EXPRESSIONS IN EVERYDAY LIFE*

This volume is guided by three interrelated themes: *prospects, patterns,* and *practices,* which each chapter discusses.

Prospects explores the potential positive contributions and negative consequences that Asian American folklore can exert upon the Asian American community and their way of life. Relevant questions are: (1) How can Asian American folklore increase the range of choices for individuals in determining ethnic, cultural, national, and civic identities? (2) How can Asian American folklore aid the promotion of pluralism and tolerance? (3) How can Asian American folklore contribute to stabilizing ethnic communities and, thereby, improve interracial relations, generational conflicts, cultural production, and economic consumption?

Patterns focuses on examining the making and remaking of Asian American communities and identity through historical and folkloric patterns. Some questions to think about are: (1) What is the inter-play between folklore, historical experiences, and Asian American history? (2) What are some of the historical patterns that Asian American folklore unveils in cultural production and community formation?

Practices identifies specific situations, scenarios, and agents that actively produce and employ Asian American folklore as a source of sociocultural, ethnic, political, artistic, and religious resources. Some of the issues are: (1) What are some of the ways in which Asian Americans have relied on, explicitly or implicitly, Asian American folklore in their artistic expressions and performances; and (2) where is "Asia," in its dialectical relationship to Asian American folklore and folklife, located in the dual processes of international migration and American racialization?

Overall, as each of the chapters illustrates, this book shows that Asian American folklore and folklife is interwoven into social relationships, the creation of various types of ethnic, cultural, and national identities, and adaptive strategies within the particular historical periods, communities, and shifting boundaries and demographics of Asian America. The global context of Asian American folklore and folklife, especially in the racially charged post 9/11 context, conveys how Asians, past and present, maneuver the cultural spaces of their host society and old traditions to create new sites and new opportunities for cultural folkloric production and expression.

ROADMAP: CHAPTER OVERVIEWS

Ayako Yoshimura's study of Asian American humor, in chapter 1, discusses how humor can be a form of protest or resistance, or a form of community building, and by extension, configurations of ethnic and cultural identities in Asian America. As she explains, Asians have long been the butt of jokes, but now comedians such as Bobby Lee, Margaret Cho, Kate Rigg, and Russell Peters, among others, are producers of humor. Not only can they make fun of themselves before non-Asian audiences, but also they can make fun of other racial and ethnic groups. Using examples such as Cal Stewart's "Uncle Josh in a Chinese Laundry" ("No Tickee, No Washee") and "Rice, Rice Baby" by Kate Rigg (a take-off of Weird Al's song of the same title, itself a parody of Vanilla Ice's debut), she, historically and specifically traces the rise of Asian immigrants and Asian Americans in the American humor industry by tracking changes in how Asians are portrayed within that humor. Yoshimura, thereby, offers original documentation on the changing status of Asians and Asian Americans in the United States.

In chapter 2, Winston Kyan examines the relationship between folklore and visual culture in Asian America by comparing Burmese American Buddhist practices in domestic settings with those organized in community monasteries. Kyan focuses on Burmese American domestic altars and novitiate ceremonies conducted in the homes of Burmese Americans living far from Burmese Buddhist monasteries as a way of passing down folklore. In addition, he explores how folklore has shaped various understandings of the founding of the Theravada Buddhist Society of America and the Dhammananda Monastery as the San Francisco Bay Area's first Burmese American monastery. Kyan considers how cultural and religious folklore of the Burmese homeland is passed from older to younger generations and from monastic teachers to lay believers through the annual summer school at the Dhammananda Monastery, now based in Half Moon Bay, California.

In chapter 3, Dawn Lee Tu considers folklore a component of modern pan-Asian American feelings about ethnic and cultural identities, albeit in ways that complicate and challenge notions about identity development as being locally produced. Tu's study of self-identified Asian American youth in higher education considers how college-age youth are reappropriating the folklore of the Asian American movement of the 1960s and 1970s to reconstruct their cultural identities. Tu explains that these students' negotiations occur in a rapidly changing and highly complex environment in which active forms of resignifications are neither necessarily acts of resistance against hegemony or internalizations of the dominant ideology.

In her survey and analysis of Asian American children's literature, Lorraine Dong, in chapter 4, shows how Asian Americans express and identify with their Asian and American heritage through children's storybooks. Although Asian folklore tended to dominate children's literature up until the 1990s, it was not necessarily always of Asian origin. Often these earlier tales were variants of common European lore, such as Santa Claus tales, with uniquely Asian American twists. After 1990, however, Asian American children's literature took on a distinctly Asian American style as in origin stories, for example, about how the first elephant arrived from India or how the pie was introduced in China by a Chinese American laborer; or, ghost stories stemming back to the, largely, seemingly indentured Chinese constructed transcontinental U.S. railroad and the World War II Japanese American internment experiences. Asian Americans, explains Dong, are deeply rooted in the United States as evidenced by the localization of their long and rich folklore heritage. Similarly, Jonathan H. X. Lee and Vivian-Lee Nyitray provide a case study of the local production of a Chinese American god in chapter 5. Over time, and through the process of "culture work," local communities construct a meaningful identity for themselves using information drawn from history and received interpretation; the community then continues to narrate this identity for themselves and outsiders. In the case of Chinese immigrant communities, cultural and linguistic barriers can produce misinterpretations that become naturalized. Drawing primarily on material evidence from a Northern California Chinese American temple and its enshrined images, the authors reveal the ways in which culture work has created a god, "Bok Kai," and an edifice, "the Bok Kai Temple," that are contrary to Chinese tradition, may typify Chinese American culture work, and are uniquely significant to the local context of Marysville, California.

Chapter 6, by SooJin Pate, examines what has become a new rite of passage for an entire generation of Korean American adoptees entering adulthood, who initiate a quest to find their birth parents and roots in Korea, as well as in the United States. Additionally, she analyzes the Korean nation's "presentation" in responding to their return, for example, by way of a popular broadcast show that invites them to individually share their stories on "live TV," on the chance that they will be recognized by their birth families in the viewing audience. This is a complex and interesting study on the whys and wherefores of invented ritual returns, which, in this instance, Pate, herself a Korean American adoptee, helps to appease Korea's collective sense of concern for the adoptees' plight, while, simultaneously offering Korean American adoptees an opportunity to reconcile their position of inhabiting Asian and white American "racial" identities.

Francis Tanglao-Aguas, in chapter 7, also writes about his innovative and creative responses to feeling betwixt and between two worlds, having migrated when young from the Philippines to America, and then back again. He writes from his position as an Asian American playwright, who, intentionally, uses folklore and mythology in theater to expose false stereotypes that have become pernicious in mainstream American society. Tanglao-Aguas analyzes his grandmother's folktales, which inspired and gave him a sense of well-being as a child during the period of contradictions and dangers of Marcos' Martial Law. By extrapolation, folklore and mythology have the potential of offering immigrants a sense of centeredness and rootedness, while encouraging the wider society to better appreciate its own diversity.

In chapter 8, Cathy J. Schlund-Vials explores how praCh Ly, a Cambodian American rapper strategically and transnationally fuses Asian (Cambodian) and American music genres to convey and negotiate the traumatic story of Cambodia's "killing fields." Integrating traditional Khmer music, 1960s Cambodian rock/pop, documentary film, and contemporary U.S. hip hop, praCh tactically uses lyric and sample to underscore Cambodia's genocidal past, make visible his parents' stories of survival, and highlight the experiences of contemporary Cambodian Americans in the United States. Continuing the exploration of the relationship between folklore and artistic expression, Brett Esaki uses the theory of embodiment developed by performance theorist Phillip Zarrilli to examine the way Japanese American artists appropriate folkloric symbols in chapter 9. Zarrilli investigates the relationship between different modes of the body's awareness and the creation of art. Zarrilli theory was designed to develop Western actors' relationship to their bodies, hoping to stretch the craft of acting to embrace more of what some consider an Eastern relationship to bodies. Here, Zarrilli's theory is applied to other crafts, namely origami and hip hop music, and to Japanese American artists. The theory applies well to the artistic process of Japanese American artists, without assuming an East-West dichotomy and asserting that Japanese Americans are bridge figures between the East (Japan) and West (America). Two artists have been chosen to represent Japanese Americans, origami artist Linda Mihara, and hip hop musician Mike Shinoda, in order to balance gender and breadth of contemporary Japanese American arts. By looking at these artists with an eye to embodiment, Esaki shows that they appropriate folkloric symbols with serenity, seen as a sense of wholeness and composure.

In chapter 10, Mark S. Leo and Jonathan H. X. Lee explore the (mis)appropriation of Igorot folk dances in popular Pilipino Cultural Night (PCN) variety shows. Leo and Lee explore the interplay among folk dance, performance, identity formations, and the vexing tension of ethnic and cultural identities between Filipino and Igorot American youth. They reveal a problematic aspect of PCN's mission of decolonization through cultural performance by focusing on the "paradox of decolonization" in relation to Filipino Americans and Igorot Americans. Their analysis ask: What are the boundaries of Filipino American culture and identity? How are Filipino America and Americans created? Where are Igorot Americans located in that process?

In chapter 11, Jonathan H. X. Lee explores cultural conflict and folklore among historic and contemporary Chinese American communities and the veneration of Guangong. He places the veneration and contemporary life of Guangong temples within the milieu of Chinese American history, anchored in the ebb and flow of U.S. immigration policies. Lee examines the shift in popular conceptions of Guangong, arguing that temples in the United States reflect a shift in the ideological "war" and "cultural" conflicts. This is anchored within the larger historical discussion of Chinese immigration and the "war" against them in the early nineteenth century.

Based on recent fieldwork among Vietnamese Americans in California, in chapter 12, Janet Hoskins explores the meanings of the mirror that spirit mediums gaze into, and why it is also a required object on altars to the Vietnamese "mother goddesses," whose worship has just had a great resurgence in diasporic communities in California. Hoskins looks at religious ways of mediating displacement and reforming an identity in the reflected glory of the imperial past. Working with the same community, Rossina Zamora Liu's analysis of Vietnamese fortune-telling and sorcery in chapter 13 begins with a discussion on her ethnographic fieldwork and interviews, conducted at Orange County's Little Saigon, California, about the brutal murder of Lady Ha, a well-known Vietnamese American diviner and healer. Liu is interested in the question of how fortune-tellers and sorcerers negotiate authenticity, in the contexts of commercialization. She reconstructs the crime scene and prior business life of Lady Ha, while extracting and articulating the rich and informative folklore of Vietnamese fortune-telling and sorcery. She describes how Lady Ha inherited her position as a sorcerer, as did her husband, who descended from a long line of sorcerer-warlocks, thus, Lady Ha was perceived by the local community to be an authentic practitioner. Since her business was an incredibly lucrative enterprise that could net thousands of dollars for casting a single spell, Lady Ha's aura of authenticity waned, partially because she also catered to tourists who frequented her shop, by way of an eclectic "catch-all" mass of paraphernalia, crystals, religious symbols, and icons.

In chapter 14, Korean American Christian minister and scholar Christine J. Hong explores and reveals tensions and contradictions in the interplay between Korean folklore about women and Confucian virtues/principles, and by extension, patriarchal traditions, social order, and conservative Christian values of gender and gender roles in the contemporary spiritual lives and identities of Korean American Christian women. Hong discusses a vexing interconnection between Korean folklore and Korean American women's agency that reveals a nuanced understanding between practice and ideology, one that at times is contradictory, yet reinforcing.

Finally, as in all of the chapters, Ronald Y. Nakasone's chapter 15 demonstrates that the Asian American experience has not lessened the importance of the role of family and culture in Japanese America, in particular, and Asian America, more broadly. This is evidenced by the respectful ways in which Japanese Americans continue to modify and transform folkloric practices by innovatively incorporating Indian, Chinese, and ancient Japanese ideas and practices to honor individuals and ancestors.

CONCLUSION

Earlier generations of folklore scholars have studied the production and transmission of folklore in ways that were super-organic and disconnected from real social life. Asian American folklore, for example, was often falsely subsumed under the genre of Asian folklore in a way that was devoid of any real sense of human agency. Asian Americans with their rich oral traditions and folk festivals, poetry, songs, and diverse ways of narrating their histories, from overlapping points of view, were being "silenced" because someone else was telling their "stories." In contrast, the scholars contributing to this collection have deliberately taken a dialogic and engaged bottom-up approach to the study of folklore and folklife. The former, now defunct boundaries that had been superimposed from above, between oral and written traditions, folk culture, and high culture, have exploded in this new millennium, allowing materials to flow back and forth between them. Asian American folklore is a way of life, past and present, in what is pan-Asian American and specific to the community and individual.

Finally, each of our contributors has partnered with their communities to learn more about their rich hybrid cultural identities and heritage through folklore and its many manifestations in the context of daily life. They are scholars who engage theory in practice at the community level from a bottom-up and hands-on perspective. Many are performing artists, playwrights, poets, and artists in their own right, who deftly incorporate folkloric expressions in their innovative and creative cultural productions in ways that relate to real community issues and concerns. Similarly, folklore emerges out of life itself, ever bridging the past and present, the seen in the unseen, changing, even as it is "being" appropriated, reinvented, and transformed. Just as the boundaries that once separated the humanities from social sciences have given rise to interdisciplinary research, so, too, we invite you, the reader, to step across the sky into the magical world of folklore.

NOTES

1. Michel Foucault, *The Order of Things, An Archaeology of the Human Sciences* (New York: Vintage Books, 1970); Michel Foucault, *The Archaeology of Knowledge and the Discourse of Language* (New York: Pantheon Books, 1972).

2. Barre Toelken, "The Folklore of Academe" in Jan H. Brunvand, editor, *The Study of American Folklore: An Introduction* (New York: W. W. Norton & Company, 1978); Barre Toelken, *Dynamics of Folklore* (Utah State University Press, 1996).

3. W. Edson Richmond, "Introduction" in Richard Dorson and Inta Gale Carpenter, Eds, *Handbook of American Folklore* (Bloomington: Indiana University Press, 1986): xi-xix.

4. Don Yoder, ed., *American Folklife* (Austin: University of Texas Press, 1976); Don Yoder, *Discovering American Folklife: Essays on Folk Culture & the Pennsylvania Dutch.* (Mechanicsburg, PA: Stackpole Books, 2001).

5. Warren E. Roberts, *Viewpoints on Folklife. Looking at the Overlooked* (Ann Arbor, MI: UMI Research Press, 1990).

6. The Library of Congress. The American Folklife Center. Washington, DC. Web. (Accessed October 30, 2013) http://www.loc.gov/folklife/.

ONE

Folklore and Asian American Humor

Stereotypes, Politics, and Self

Ayako Yoshimura

INTRODUCTION

I remember, upon landing in the United States as an international student, watching the film *Sixteen Candles* multiple times because one of my first ESL teachers assigned it to us to improve our listening comprehension skills. Little did I understand at the time what the character Long Duk Dong (a Japanese exchange student bearing a mock Chinese name) might represent for Asians and Asian Americans in American society. Perhaps I was culturally naive, or simply so busy trying to process the rapidly spoken English dialogue that I did not find the character offensive. Nor do I recall any of my fellow classmates expressing discomfort at hearing Long's awkward English or witnessing his obliviousness to the laughter and disdain heaped upon him by the other characters. In retrospect, I wonder why our teacher selected that film for us; I do not believe that she meant it as an insult; after all, the film was a cute romantic comedy aimed at the cultural majority to which she belonged, and Long played only a supporting role as the quintessentially goofy foreigner. How was the teacher to know how the portrayal of this minor character might make racial and ethnic minorities feel?

Gradually, as I studied racial and ethnic issues and became aware of my own position as an Asian female in American society, I began to wonder what it would have been like to have been born and raised a racial and ethnic minority in America. As I became more linguistically

1

and culturally competent, I came to recognize what a powerful role humor plays as an agent of social critique. And it was during my sojourn in North America that the contribution of Asian Americans to its humor scene blossomed. In this chapter, I examine, from the perspective of a North American–trained folklorist, the ways in which Asian American comedians employ humor to communicate their viewpoints and challenge stereotypes, thereby illuminating Asian American intra-group-dynamics.

HUMOR AS ACADEMIC SUBJECT

In the study of folklore, humor—as it appears in *blasons populaires*, jokes, and jocular tales—has been researched as a type of verbal lore. Folklorists have collected and indexed such lore in order to understand the geographical diffusion of motifs, cultural patterns in manners of telling, and individual performance styles, as well as to conduct psychological and contextual analyses that explore socio-cultural implications embedded in the humor.[1] Because humor can reveal a perceptual boundary between originator and target, it provides a rich locus for researchers to examine the ways in which one group perceives itself esoterically while judging others exoterically.

Ethnic humor employs elements of targeted ethnic groups deemed by others to be especially, even uniquely, characteristic of those groups. These include physical, behavioral, and cultural traits such as cuisine, clothing, beliefs, customs, and speech. Bumptious Jewish American mothers, garlicky Italian Americans, and fried-chicken-eating African Americans are some such examples. Overemphasized or distorted, these characteristics are developed into ethnic stereotypes that underscore the boundary between originator and target, which maximizes the humorous effect at the expense of the target's Otherness.

In American humor, it has been customary for minority groups to embrace ethnic characteristics previously put forth as stereotypes by others, in order to turn the tables for their benefit. Self-deprecation in humor is often regarded as a means of self-empowerment, and ethnic groups such as African Americans, Jewish Americans, and Norwegian Americans have employed this strategy in order to claim for themselves negative stereotypes previously advanced by others. The difference between being ridiculed by others and ridiculing oneself is enormous. Through self-ridicule the originator exhibits acceptance of and confidence in qualities that may be perceived by others as evidence of inadequacy or inferiority. In this way an ethnic group is able to foster a sense of ethnic pride and solidarity. Employing humor, a minority group can challenge social judgments and biases projected by the majority, and confront them with the minority's own perspective in order to expose the foolishness of such judgments and biases, and to poke fun at the majority for its shortsightedness.[2]

Asian American humor has won little recognition in academia. *New Directions in American Humor*, edited by the renowned humor scholar David E. Sloane, includes not a single article dedicated to Asian Americans. The *Encyclopedia of 20th-Century American Humor* contains entries for minority groups such as "African Americans," "American Indians," "Hispanics," and "Jews," but none for Asians or Asian Americans. And it was only recently that *Studies in American Humor*, the official scholarly journal of the American Humor Studies Association, began to feature articles devoted primarily to Asian and Asian American humor.[3]

Such under-representation is not surprising, because in the last two centuries Asians and Asian Americans have contributed to American humor culture more as targets of manistream caricature than as humor producers. From the portrayal of the Chinaman in Cal Stewart's "Uncle Josh in a Chinese Laundry" (a classic "No tickee, no washee" scenario)[4] to Long Duk Dong in *Sixteen Candles*, the image of Asians (and Asian Americans) in mainstream America has typically been one of a goofy and incompetent foreigner.

THE RISE OF ASIAN AMERICAN HUMOR

However, the current is shifting now that multiple Asian Americans have emerged as humor producers. Margaret Cho and Bobby Lee, both Korean Americans, are at the forefront of Asian American humorists, while others are following in their wake as standup comics, developing their own performance styles and routines. A pivotal moment in the history of American humor was the victory of the Vietnamese American Dat Phan in the first season of the comedy competition television series *Last Comic Standing*.

As have those from other minority groups, Asian American comedians have adopted the tactic of lampooning majority-prescribed ethnic stereotypes, as well as the intra-group dissent to which those stereotypes can give rise. For example, the majority has bestowed upon Asian Americans "model minority" status, and while this may work to the group's advantage overall, there are many ethnic Asian American subgroups that do not enjoy the socio-economic privileges necessary to gain membership in this "model minority."[5] Additionally, while the notion of pan-Asianness may be of some benefit in promoting solidarity and coherence when dealing with the white majority, it does not honor the group's diversity and neglects internal segregations based on class, religion, and culture. Similarly, the relationship between immigrants and Asian Americans is frangible—especially due to the American mainstream conception of Asians as perpetual foreigners that so irks American citizens of Asian descent, particularly American-born children of immigrant parents. Moreover, the mainstream media has portrayed Asian females as sexualized ingénues and Asian males as undesirable and asexual. These media constructions have haunted many Asian American youths as they struggle to develop their self-images.[6]

Because stereotypes can often create conflicts within minority groups, Asian American communities attempt to educate others so as to debilitate the stereotypes. The educational tool used by Asian American comedians is humor.

CHALLENGING STEREOTYPES

Speech Accent

Speech accent is a primary source of ethnic humor because it is one prominent characteristic of ethnic groups, and Asian American comedians frequently employ style-switching in their stage performances. In her standup act, Margaret Cho recounts funny anecdotes drawn from her experience as a first-generation Korean American, often imitating her mother by employing a speech pattern characteristic of Asian immigrants, with incomplete sentences, missing articles, an inability to distinguish "l" from "r," and the omission of words' terminal consonant sounds.

Asian American comics' onstage style-switching conveys something more than its purely phonological feature. Many Asian Americans still experience being mistaken for immigrants by non-Asians, despite their native English. That "Asian-looking" people must have come from other countries is a common mainstream misconception that many Asian Americans find offensive. Thus when Asian American comedians engage in style-switching, they draw a distinction between Asians in America and Asian Americans. Switching between native English and stereotypically accented English allows Asian American comedians to demonstrate that they are native speakers of English, and simultaneously that they find Asian accents as comedically fertile as do non-Asians.

An effective use of style-switching launched Dat Phan's opening performance on *Last Comic Standing*, in which he introduced himself as a goofy foreigner by speaking in a heavy Asian accent, then a moment later surprised the audience by declaring in perfect English his ability to speak the language. In this instance, Phan debunked not only the familiar misconception, but also the all-too-common mass-media portrayal of Asians as goofy foreigners.

Comedians mocking accents for their own humor-delivery in front of a mainstream audience is different from actors adopting accents for typecast roles (e.g., Gedde Watanabe as Long Duk Dong in *Sixteen Candles*, Pat Morita as "Arnold" Takahashi in the television series *Happy Days*). Such roles in mainstream entertainment are created for the white racial majority, and are designed to fit existing stereotypes, such that the characters remain within the majority's perceptual comfort zone. Although the ability to feign accents is considered part of an actor's craft, many Asian Americans find it offensive that Asian American actors must play foreigners by faking Asian-immigrant accents, because this simply reflects the majority's perception of Asians as foreigners. On the other hand, standup comedians can employ this skill to deliver their own views on this condescending perception. For example, Henry Cho (a Korean American comic from Tennessee) sometimes intensifies his own Southern accent to parody rural Southerners. Russell Peters (an Indo-Canadian comedian active in the United States) regularly parodies multiple ethnic accents; and on the television program *Comedy Now!*, after joking about the Indian accent, turns his attention to the white accent:

> I can prove to you, white folks, that you have an accent. That's a pretty bold statement for a brown man. But I can prove to you: white people, when you swear, you sound like donkeys. You *do*, because you say stuff like, "Fuuck it!" "Buull shiit!" "Hee-haw, hee-haw" [thrusting his leg backward in two asinine kicks]. You talk funny, man; it's okay![7]

When comedians adopt accents, they not only exhibit their competence in speaking standard English, but they also employ humor to remind us that white people, too, sound funny.

Effeminate Asian Males and Sexually Objectified Asian Females

Asian males have been portrayed in the mass media as effeminate because of their smaller physiques and lack of body hair. Paul Ogata (a Japanese American comic) turns this trait into a joke:

> I can't grow a full beard because I'm Asian. And if I do let it come out, it doesn't connect everywhere. People like you [pointing at audience] who can grow beards, you're always taunting me in your passive-aggressive way: "Hmmm [twirling an imaginary handlebar mustache], are you trying to grow a beard?" Trying? How do you try? What do you...? Just at home you [he mimes an attempt by tensing his facial muscles]. "How does it look?" "It's still a little patchy."[8]

By contrast, Asian females have been overly objectified in the mainstream media. The biracial performance artist Kate Rigg uses standup comedy, singing, and writing to advocate for women's rights and gay marriage. As vocalist for the performing group Slanty Eyed Mama, she sings "Rice, Rice, Baby"—a takeoff on Weird Al's song of the same title, itself a parody of Vanilla Ice's debut—to criticize American society's Eurocentric perceptions of the Asian and Asian American community. Rigg is especially assertive in her disapproval of the way in which Asian women are portrayed in the mass media as exotic objects of desire, something that has grown into a phenomenon called "Asian fetish."[9] While some Asian and Asian American women believe that "Asian fetish" works to their advantage, others find it offensive because it reflects a view of Asian women as submissive playthings (e.g., the China doll, the geisha girl). Rigg sings:

> Okay, you wanna see my dumpling?
> Slanty Mama gonna make you a rolled spring.
> Hi! Mr. round-eye white guy,
> how you like my straight hair and slanty eyes?
> Straight hair, even straight hair down there.
> If you look in my Hello-Kitty underwear.
> Call me, I'll set you straight
> When you take me on a racially mixed date.[10]

As a self-styled "fierce Asian gangsta poet," Rigg declaims that not all Asian and Asian American women play goody-goody Asians because "there's a whole other world in the hearts of these Oriental girls," who do not conform to the stereotype concocted by mainstream America.

Asians as Incompetent in American-Style Humor

There exists a notion that Asians are not able to tell jokes. After successfully entertaining his audience, Eliot Chang (a Chinese American comic), closes a show on *Comedy Central* with the following remark:

> And I know exactly how every single Asian in the audience felt when I came out here. 'Cause you all looked at me, and you're like: "Oh, God, please be funny, please be funny. Ohh, my God. Represent, mo-fo, represent! If this guy sucks, we are *so* out of here. Put your jacket on, put it on!" C'mon, that's exactly what you were thinking. C'mon![11]

The impression that Asians (including Asian Americans) are culturally incompetent foreigners when it comes to dealing with American society generates the idea that they cannot understand American humor, let alone produce it. With his remark, Chang not only registers his awareness of this assumption, but also communicates the effect that it has had on fellow members of his racial group.

Asians as Poor Drivers

In a standup show Jo Koy (a Filipino-White American comic), after chiding the Latino segment of his Southern California audience for not having car insurance, proceeds to comment on the stereotype about Asians' inability to drive:

> They fuck with us all the time, man! Can't drive?!? We can fuckin' drive! I drove here, I didn't hit a bunch of fuckin' people on the way

here! . . . Shit! We build the best cars, you don't think we can fuckin' drive 'em? You think the engineer at Lexus is bragging about what he built: "Oh, rack-and-pinion steering; 0 to 60, 4.9 seconds!" "Hey, take it for a spin!" "Oh, no . . . [mimicking an Asian] Are you crazy?"[12]

Here Koy, in confronting the (white) American "they," taps into the notion of a pan-Asian "we" by invoking the brand name Lexus, which—although emblematic of a specifically Japanese tradition of fine automobiles—is used to represent all of Asia.

Asian Homogeneity

Non-Asians often claim that all Asians look alike. But the skill of distinguishing among Asians is not inherited. After explaining that he does not speak Korean, Henry Cho tells this anecdote:

Back home in Knoxville we were the only Asians when I was growing up. The only ones. My dad's the only Asian man I had ever seen in my life before I went to Korea. So back home I could pick him out of any crowd like *that*. Well, this reversed on me in Korea. We got off the plane, he walked twenty feet away, and I just lost him—[looking around, confused] "Aaah!" I found him like an hour later: "Dad, don't leave me, man! They're talking to me."[13]

Cho's personal-experience narrative demonstrates how one's surroundings construct one's perceptions and comfort zones. By acknowledging the anxiety that he felt when surrounded by Koreans in Korea, Cho reveals that not only could he not tell his father apart from other Korean men, he was not comfortable in Korea because it differed radically from the surroundings of his hometown. Another preconception of the majority about the minority is that members of the minority all get along well under a single homogenous socio-cultural umbrella. But of course the minority group is as internally diverse as the majority.

THE POLITICAL TINT TO ASIAN AMERICAN HUMOR

Sensitive political matters can be addressed and social critiques delivered behind the shield of humor. Dat Phan, returning as a former winner to a subsequent season of *Last Comic Standing*, comments on the Vietnam War:

Still some people try to blame me for being a part of the Vietnam War. Frickin' jackass morons, you know what I mean? I was a fetus back then, man.

Into his joke regarding the stereotype of the always-apologizing Japanese, Paul Ogata slips reference to a historical event about which both the United States and Japan are still sensitive:

That's what we do, as Asians. We apologize, right? You bump into a
Japanese tourist: [imitating a Japanese accent] "Sorry, sorry, sorry."
They bomb the Harbor: "Ah, sorry, sorry, sorry." I dare you to find the
biggest one you can and give him a good right hook to the head, just,
pow: "Oh, sorry sorry. Didn't mean for you to hit me. My fault. Sorry.
How's your fist? Good? Okay. Sorry."[14]

As a mixed-race Asian American, the half-Japanese comedian K. T. Tatara, challenges the majority's expectation that non-full-blooded Caucasian
Americans should embrace their ethnic heritages, simultaneously touch-
ing upon a sensitive war issue between the two countries that he represents biologically:

White people want me to be more Asian, which I think is kind of weird.
They're like: "Oh, can you speak Japanese? Have you been to Japan?"
I'm like: "No, I was born in Virginia." "*Oh*, that's so *sad*! You should
learn your culture. It's beautiful." I'm like: "Oh, really? White people,
can you speak Czech, Slovak, German, wherever the hell your grandparents are from? No? Oh! Then, shut the fuck up! . . . If Japan's so
pretty, why'd you blow it up then, huh?" It was a war, I know, white
people, my white side is tellin' me. Calm down.[15]

Since some Asian countries were enemies of the United States in twentieth-century wars, Asian Americans associated with those countries may
experience taunting while growing up, or may feel uneasy in American
history classes at school. Although those wars have ended, their effects
still linger in the lives of immigrants and their descendants in contemporary American society. Again, humor can be useful to allow discussion of
war-related issues while at the same time camouflaging their gravity.

Margaret Cho also works political statements into her standup show.
Well known as an advocate for women's rights and gay rights, Cho often
rants about social injustices that she attributes to the Republican Party.
She recounts that during George W. Bush's administration, she was con-
demned by conservatives for stating that although the president was not
Hitler, "he *would* be, if he applied himself":

And for this I was deluged with hate mail from the right wing. Sooo
much hate mail. But none of it was about political discourse. None of it
was: "Miss Cho, I believe you are being unfair to our administration."
None of it was like that at all. It was all: "Gook, Chink, cunt, go back to
your country where you came from, you fat pig! Go back to your country, you fat pig! Go back to your country, you fat dyke, fat dyke, fat
dyke, fat dyke, fat dyke . . . Jesus saves!" Ooo, *enchantée*! Well, I can't go
back to my country because I was born here. I am already *in* my country. The only person who has the right to tell you to go back to your
country is a Native American.[16]

In this segment, in addition to communicating her liberal political stance,
Cho criticizes the majority's tendency to lump Asians and Asian

Americans into one generic category ("Asians"), and its concomitant failure to recognize the difference between Asians in America and Americans of Asian descent.

Asian American comedians tackle racial and ethnic stereotypes in order to offer new perspectives about their racial and ethnic groups. When reseasoned to Asian American tastes and served to the original projectors of stereotypes, jokes about these stereotypes become charged with new meanings. The stereotypes that once reflected the majority's exoteric view of Asians and Asian Americans are redefined to communicate to the majority the esoteric Asian American opinions of those stereotypes. Thus, minority comedians, through humor, challenge social expectations wrongly assumed by the majority in order to counter with their minority viewpoints.

ASIAN AMERICAN HUMOR AS PEDAGOGY

A tamer brand of humor can be useful for educational purposes. The Minnesota-based Hmong comedian Tou Ger Xiong visits schools as a diversity-education consultant to perform standup comedy and tell stories about his early life in Laos and Thailand, immigration, and experiences growing up in America. Switching between English and Hmong, he exhibits competence in both American and Hmong cultures and confidence in his ability to find humor in life's tribulations. The Hmong are still under-represented in the Midwest, despite the size of their population, and racial discrimination against them is a grim part of everyday reality. For minority children, it is encouraging to hear a public figure recounting personal experiences to which they can relate: coping with the hardships of growing up a young immigrant child; being greeted with ethnic slurs such as "Chink" and "Gook"; facing the dilemma of having to be American at school while trying to be Hmong at home; or needing to fend for himself because his parents neither spoke English nor understood what he was going through because they themsevles had not grown up in America. Immigrant children and minority children must learn to balance mainstream culture with their household cultures, as they often discover that their cultural values are incongruent with mainstream norms. Comedians like Tou Ger Xiong enlighten minority children about the importance of embracing their own backgrounds, while teaching majority children about the experiences of their new neighbors, and the diversity of people's lives.

ASIAN AMERICAN HUMOR RECONSIDERED

In order for ethnic humor to be delivered effectively, it is necessary that both producer and audience share an awareness of perceptions of ethnic characteristics, and it is because of this prerequisite that studying humor helps folklorists understand the ways in which group characteristics are perceived, and the ways in which group identities are constituted. In contemporary American humor culture, minority comedians practice the principle of self-projected ethnic humor: countering exoteric ridicule with esoteric reinterpretation thereof. In this regard, the twenty-first century is witnessing a sea change as more and more Asian Americans enter show business as comedians. Ultimately, their self-produced ethnic humor communicates to mainstream America that the viewpoints and life experiences of Asian Americans are as varied as those of other groups. In their humor, boundaries are drawn between Whites and Asians/Asian Americans, and furthermore between Asians and Asian Americans.

The future of Asian American contributions to American humor is promising, yet some sensitive issues still linger. Often embedded in humor are caricature and discrimination. Humor has historically aided in disguising hatred and hostility. Regardless of Asian American comedians' mainstream success, it is important to recognize that not every Asian or Asian American appreciates ethnic humor. When Asian American comedians mock Asian accents, it can be understood merely to pillory immigrants from behind a mask of humor. Asian American comedians often proclaim that they caricature races and ethnicities in order to illuminate the stupidity of stereotypes pervasive in the mass media. However, not everyone agrees with the practice of using racial and ethnic humor to tackle prejudice, because in the view of some, it only perpetuates stereotypes—or worse, legitimizes them.

Asian American comics are, after all, "American." They are native speakers of English who do not have typical Asian accents, whatever their ethnicities may be. When these comics adopt a stereotypically "Asian" accent, they can justify the parody through their biological associations with "Asia," yet they may in fact be understood to cast Asians as the "Other" by highlighting their deficiency in speaking standard English. When a comic employs the "Mock Asian" style of speech in making fun of whites, it may succeed in decentering them, but only at the expense of further alienating Asians.[17] Moreover, "Asian Americans" is such a broad category that a person of, for instance, South Asian background may not approve of the dominance of East Asian American comics in the Asian American comedy scene.[18]

Intra-group discord sometimes engenders harsh criticism. In her autobiography, *I Am the One That I Want*, Margaret Cho explains how hurt she was to receive disapproval and criticism from her "own people" (the Korean and Korean American community), and implies that it contributed to the cancellation in 1995 of her once much-anticipated Asian American sitcom, *All American Girl*. The fact that her show met resistance from inside the Asian American community reveals an aspect of the social reality that still exists: many Asian immigrants do not favor

American-style sarcasm and self-deprecation as a means of self-revelation, and not all Asian Americans believe in using self-deprecating humor to gain the understanding of the mainstream. Asian Americans have long struggled to differentiate themselves from Asian immigrants to prove to non-Asian Americans that they are indeed Americans, while Asian immigrants have long struggled to survive in a foreign land, no matter the degree of belittlement by the majority. When "Asians" are labeled a "model minority" (which some Asians and Asian Americans believe to be a positive stereotype), why dismantle this with self-ridicule? Cho notes that the most painful communication she received regarding her sitcom came from a twelve-year-old Korean (American?) girl: "When I see Margaret Cho on television, I feel deep shame." She reacts in her performance:

> Why? Why? I guess this was because they'd never seen a Korean American role model like *me* before, you know. I didn't play violin. I didn't fuck Woody Allen. I was not wholeheartedly embraced by all of the Korean community.[19]

While ethnic humor may allow Asian American voices to take part in the race and ethnicity discourse in American society, it may still register as derogatory to insiders trying to live up to the "model minority" status, or seeking to climb the social ladder in a white-dominated culture.

Humor is a vehicle through which Asian American comedians choose to communicate their perspectives to the public, but it must be handled with care because whether or not one enjoys the humor of one's own ethnic group depends upon how one positions oneself in society at a personal level.[20]

CONCLUDING REMARKS

Asians and Asian Americans constitute not one coherent group but a mix of people with varied personalities, in addition to differences in terms of race, religion, and culture. The success of Asian American humor will depend upon approval and support from inside as much as upon recognition from outside. But for now, the burgeoning success of Asian American humor on the mainstream comedy scene deserves celebration. The rest of the century has a lot to look forward to.

NOTES

1. Notable works by folklorists include Alan Dundes's *Cracking Jokes: Studies of Sick Humor Cycles & Stereotypes* (Berkeley: Ten Speed Press, 1987), and Elliott Oring's *Engaging Humor* (Urbana: University of Illinois Press, 2003) and *Jokes and Their Relations* (Lexington: The University Press of Kentucky, 1992). Both Dundes and Oring examine the psychoanalytical contexts of humor. *Humor and the Individual*, edited by Oring (Los

Angeles: California Folklore Society, 1984), is an anthology of essays that discuss humor as individual expression. James P. Leary compiles regional and ethnic humor in the Upper Midwest, including classic Norwegian "Ole and Lena" jokes, in *So Ole Says to Lena: Folk Humor of the Upper Midwest*, 2nd ed. (Madison: University of Wisconsin Press, 2001).

2. Elliott Oring, "Self-Degrading Jokes and Tales," in *Jokes and Their Relations*, ed. Elliott Oring (Lexington: The University Press of Kentucky, 1992): 122–34.

3. Frustration over the lack of scholarly attention given to minority humor spurred John McNally to compile *Humor Me: An Anthology of Humor by Writers of Color* (Iowa City: University of Iowa Press, 2002), which does contain a few selections by Asian Americans.

4. Cal Stewart, *Uncle Josh Weathersby's "Punkin Centre" Stories* (Chicago: Thompson and Thomas, 1905): 25–29.

5. In terms of educational achievement, the percentage of Asian Americans with college degrees is more than twice that of African Americans or of Latin Americans. However, among Asian Americans, for instance, a wealthy Chinese American from Hong Kong and a child of Chinese immigrants from the poverty-stricken countryside will not have access to the same kind of educational opportunities in the United States (Mary Yu Danico and Franklin Ng, *Asian American Issues* [Westport: Greenwood, 2004]: 31–32).

6. For more detailed discussions of these issues, see Danico and Ng, *Asian American Issues*.

7. *Comedy Now! Russell Peters LIVE* [video]. 2003. Retrieved May 30, 2010, from http://video.google.com/videoplay?docid=-2579833089500205658#.

8. *Paul Ogata – The Problem with Facial Hair* [video]. Retrieved September 3, 2009, from http://www. cranial.com/paul_ogata/5/.

9. So pervasive is this phenomenon of white males being attracted to Asian females that "Asian Girls" makes the list in Christian Lander's droll *Stuff White People Like: The Definitive Guide to the Unique Taste of Millions* (New York: Random House, 2008): 12–13.

10. *Asian American? Proud!! RICE RICE BABY (Kate Rigg)* [video]. Retrieved September 3, 2009, fromhttp://www.youtube.com/watch?v=2Z0rTNaykL8.

11. *Eliot Chang – Asian Sound* [video]. Retrieved September 3, 2009, from http://comedians.jokes.com/eliot-chang/videos/eliot-chang---asian-sound.

12. *Jo Koy – Latinos & Asians – Comedy Clip* [video]. Retrieved September 3, 2009, fromhttp://www.youtube.com/watch?v=Z0UXWTxDiCU.

13. *Going to Korea–Henry Cho* [video]. Retrieved September 3, 2009, fromhttp://www.youtube.com/watch?v=WH8E_nkDNDo.

14. *Paul Ogata – Sorry* [video]. Retrieved September 3, 2009, fromhttp://www. youtube.com/watch?v=8BtuOyygL44.

15. *K. T. Tatara–Mixed* [video]. Retrieved September 3, 2009, from http://www. youtube.com/watch?v=_QWWsSDd9qw.

16. *Assassin*, (DVD. Dir. by Kerry Asmunssen and Konda Mason. Port Washington: KOCH Vision, 2005).

17. Elaine W. Chun cites the example of Margaret Cho speaking Mock Asian while ridiculing whites for their excessive height and overly large eyes in "Ideologies of Legitimate Mockery: Margaret Cho's Revoicings of Mock Asian," in *Beyond Yellow English: Toward a Linguistic Anthropology of Asian Pacific America*, ed. Angela Reyes and Adrienne Lo (New York: Oxford University Press, 2009): 261–87.

18. In the introduction to her thesis, Tara Atluri discusses an incident in which, during her presentation of her analysis of Margaret Cho's performance style, the author's position as a South Asian woman invited a confrontational stance from her Korean American colleague: while Atluri did not feel that Cho should represent the entire Asian community in North America, her colleague was proud of Cho's success in the mainstream media and welcomed Cho as a pan-Asian icon (Atluri, "Lighten

up!?: Humour as Anti-Racism in the Work of Asian American Comic Margaret Cho," [MA thesis, University of Toronto, 2002]: 5–7).

19. *I'm The One That I Want* (DVD. Dir. by Lionel Coleman. New York: Winstar TV & Video, 2001). See also Margaret Cho, *I'm The One That I Want* (New York: Ballantine Books, 2001): 130–31.

20. Ultimately, whether or not one believes in humor as a tool for debunking stereotypes determines whether or not one favors the ethnic humor of one's own group. And it really depends on individuals' personal opinions. In researching the proverbial phrase "No tickee, no washee" and its potential racism, folklore scholar Wolfgang Mieder surveyed college students at the University of California, Berkeley. Their responses revealed a variety of views. One Chinese American student commented that she uses the proverb sarcastically to be politically incorrect, and another Chinese (American?) student noted that when her father had used it as a joke, her mother had not been amused (Wolfgang Mieder "'No Tickee, No Washee': Subtleties of a Proverbial Slur," *Western Folklore* 55.1 1996: 31–32).

TWO

Folklore and the Visual Culture of Burmese America

Domestic Buddhist Practices and the Dhammananda Monastery

Winston Kyan

The complex terrain of Asian American religions underscores the diverse components of visual culture as well as the varied practices of folklore. The resulting intersections of experience, tradition, and identity shed light on the intercultural, intergenerational, and transnational concerns at the heart of Asian American life. Within this context, the subfield of Asian American religions has rapidly developed since the 1980s, with outside-in studies on the appropriation of Asian religions by mainstream American culture leading to inside-out investigations of religious practices within Asian American communities.[1] In turn, these studies have generated critical examinations of immigrant religion from the perspectives of race and orientalism.[2] In particular, the growing importance of folklore and visual culture within Asian American studies not only suggests that these fields have emerged from the shadow of Asian American religion, but that more effort is made to understand the role of folklore and visual culture in the religious experience of underrepresented Asian Americans.[3]

Accordingly, this essay examines the relationship between folklore and visual culture in Asian America by comparing Burmese American Buddhist practices in domestic settings with those organized in community monasteries.[4] The first section of this essay focuses on Burmese

American domestic altars and novitiate ceremonies conducted in the homes of Burmese Americans living far from Burmese Buddhist monasteries as a way of passing down folklore. The second section of this essay moves from the private to the public and explores how folklore has shaped various understandings of the founding of the Theravada Buddhist Society of America and the Dhammananda Monastery as the San Francisco Bay Area's first Burmese American monastery. The third section considers how the cultural and religious folklore of the Burmese homeland is passed from older to younger generations and from monastic teachers to lay believers through the annual summer school at the Dhammananda Monastery, now based in Half Moon Bay, California. As a Buddhist monastery that primarily serves the Burmese Chinese community of Daly City and Fremont, the Dhammananda Monastery also provides perspectives onto the role of folklore and visual culture within the contexts of Chinese immigration to Burma as well as Burmese Chinese immigration to the United States.

FOLKLORE, VISUAL CULTURE, AND
DOMESTIC BUDDHIST PRACTICES

Burma is a multi-religious society that includes Theravada Buddhists, Muslims, Hindus, and Christians. Underlying these beliefs is the native animist worship of spirits (*nat*), viewed by some Burmese as irrational, but almost universally acknowledged as powerful. The domestic religious practices of Burmese Americans reflect this diverse religious heritage as well as the immigration history of these various groups to the United States. In general, the first significant group of Burmese immigrants began arriving during the late 1960s, when the elimination of quotas on Asian immigration in the United States coincided with the xenophobic policies of Ne Win's military regime that frequently targeted ethnic Chinese in Burma. Burmese Chinese, including those who would eventually establish important Burmese Buddhist monasteries on the West and East Coasts, were part of this initial wave.

Typically well-educated and multilingual in Burmese and one or more Chinese dialects, these Burmese Chinese remained faithful to Theravada Buddhist practices shaped by Chinese Confucian concerns for the family and filial piety. Between their arrival in the United States during the late 1960s and the systematic organization of Burmese Buddhist monasteries during the early 1980s, these immigrants spent over a decade continuing their educations and establishing themselves economically. Only then could they face the responsibilities and challenges involved in inviting and hosting eminent Burmese monks to visit the United States. Sometimes, this transition from private devotion to public worship was short lived. For example, my father, Dr. Chwan Kyan (his Burmese name is

Maung Maung Chwan), was elected to be the first president of the Theravada Buddhist Society of America. However, he accepted a new job in New Jersey shortly after the founding of the Dhammananda Monastery in San Francisco in July 1980.[5] Our family left a thriving Burmese Chinese community in the Bay Area and the promising foundations of a Burmese Buddhist monastery to move to a predominantly white southern New Jersey suburb far from other Burmese American Buddhist communities in Washington, D.C. and New York City. Nevertheless, this did not prevent our family from constructing a domestic space for key rites of passage and religious worship that transmitted Burmese cultural and religious folklore from the older to the younger generation.

An important place where folklore and visual culture overlap is the domestic altar of Burmese American households. Gilded sculptures of the Buddha, oil paintings of the *Shwedagon* pagoda in Yangon, photographs of Mount Popa (the volcanic home of thirty-seven great *nat* spirits), and ancestor portraits are arranged alongside daily offerings of water, fruit, and flowers. Inlaid betel nut boxes, lacquered harps (*saung gauk*), repoussé silver bowls, and carved ivory hairpins are also interspersed in between the sacred images and displayed with equal devotion as mementos of immigrant origin. For the first generation, these objects are a bridge that connects their lives in the United States with memories of the homeland. For the second generation, these objects are similarly significant as touchstones for cultural identity and family folklore that determine intergenerational conversations.

During her lifetime, my mother tended to the altar daily, accompanied by morning and evening prayers for the safety and good fortune of her family. The altar itself was situated in a second floor room and on a wall facing the front of the house. This way it occupied the most privileged place in the house, while serving a talismanic function that protected the house and the family. Notably, the blinds of the window facing the altar would be half opened in a gesture of assimilation to our non-Buddhist neighbors. My father would explain to us that this was to keep passersby who did not understand the Buddha's teachings from inadvertently disparaging the "strange" images on the altar. This anxiety toward revealing one's religious identity to outsiders is echoed in the signage of the current Dhammananda Monastery in Half Moon Bay, which only identifies itself through Burmese script and a street address (figure 2.1).

In many ways, the domestic altars in Burmese American homes provide a substitute daily ritual for Burmese Buddhists who would typically bring food to the monks before noon each day. This in turn, as Joseph Cheah has noted, is an American alteration in which the laity preparing and bringing food to the monastery replaces the daily solicitation of alms by monks.[6] Nevertheless, challenges arise when Burmese American Buddhists are faced with major rites of passage that are incompatible with a domestic setting. For example, the important initiation rite, or *shinbyu*, that marks the transformation of a boy from a layperson to a temporary monk, generates religious merit for the boy and for his parents. As such, it expresses both Buddhist devotion and filial piety by reenacting Rahula's decision to join his father's order of monks. Boys from Burmese American families that live near monasteries can participate in joint *shinbyu* rituals with other boys, and even undergo this rite several times as a youth.[7] These groups of boys also have the opportunity of integrating themselves easily into the routine of the monastery, with its structured periods of meals, meditation, and study already established.

For devout Burmese Buddhist families who do not live near a monastery, however, the key ritual of *shinbyu* must adapt to rules that render a private home suitable for monastic precepts. In addition to undertaking the five basic precepts to refrain from killing, stealing, sexual misconduct, lying, and intoxication, the young boy and his family must make domestic arrangements that accommodate the avoidance of luxurious beds, meals after noon, and the cohabitation of genders under the same roof. If a household is lucky, as in the case of my own *shinbyu*, an eminent monk is invited to preside over the ceremony. Rather than having the community at large bear witness, close family members gather to observe the boy's vow to uphold the Ten Precepts, the solemn shaving of his hair, and the somewhat embarrassing semi-public change of clothing from secular dress to monastic robes. Taken together, these ritual acts make profound visual impressions that prepare the family for the dramatic rupturing of family hierarchies within the home itself. During the *shinbyu* period, parents show daily obeisance to their son, who is now a novitiate (*koyin*), while the boy distances himself from his parents, who are now laypeople (*dagajee*).

The *shinbyu* ceremony also provides opportunities for the display of folklore and visual culture on the body itself. Attending family members use this occasion to show religious devotion as well as to display cultural pride through the wearing of elaborate sarongs (*htamein* for women and *pahso* for men). Frequently aromatic from storage with decades old mothballs, the wearing and viewing of these textiles provide a sensory link between the country of origin and the country of residence. The bright colors and complex patterns of these garments become the source of polite compliments and cultural bonding. Parents might also use the wearing and viewing of these textiles to instruct children that cotton is preferable to silk in regard to Burmese Buddhist aversions to taking life, or they might impress cultural pride upon children by recounting that the shimmering wave-pattern (*acheik*) distinctive to Burmese silk weaving would shred with age before any of its color and luster would fade.

On another level, the gendered specificities of tying the sarong (at the side for females and centered in front for males) reiterate the patriarchal relationships of the homeland, in which girls are only allowed to engage in the *shinbyu* ceremony as decorative bystanders. Elaborately dressed as

Burmese princesses-for-a-day, the girls in the family mark their participation in this ceremony by getting their ears pierced for the first time rather than entering into a religious role, reflecting the inferior spiritual position of women in traditional Buddhist thought. Nevertheless, as Tamara Ho has demonstrated, women play an integral role in Burmese American monasteries as cooks and sponsors of offerings (*ahlus*).[8] In the case of the Dhammananda Monastery, a team of women prepares, serves, and offers free Burmese food on celebratory occasions. The cooking team even has a name (The Theravada Buddhist Society of America Culinary Group), as well as named leaders (Daw Yi Yi Thein, Daw Hla Hla Win, and Daw Tin Tin Win), which reflects the importance of food in creating religious community and in reinforcing ethnic identity.[9]

Taken together, the visual culture of domestic altars and domestic religious ceremonies in Burmese America also highlight the important role of folklore in transmitting class identity alongside cultural identity. The possession of finely crafted objects from the homeland, the maintenance of a separate domestic space for religious devotion, and the financial resources needed to commission a novitiate ceremony signal the capacity of a post–1967 professional class of Southeast Asian immigrants able to differentiate themselves from later refugees with fewer resources. It is not uncommon to hear Burmese Chinese immigrants lament the loss of drivers, maids, and cooks in the United States. Arguably, the intersections of folklore and visual culture are as important in establishing proper Asian American middle class formations as they are in drawing links between the United States and Burma.

DHAMMANANDA MONASTERY AND BURMESE AMERICAN BUDDHISM

The history of the Theravada Buddhist Society of America and the Dhammananda Monastery as the first Burmese monastery in the Bay Area is well documented by its original members as well as in a monograph devoted to this topic by Joseph Cheah.[10] However, the different emphases taken up by each of these authors shed light on the role of folklore in shaping an origin myth for the first Burmese Buddhist monastery in the Bay Area. In his essay, "U Silananda and the Birth of the Theravada Buddhist Society of America," Stanley Khoo (his Burmese name is U Hla Aung), who was the original secretary of the Theravada Buddhist Society of America and is its current president, attributes the growth of the monastery to the deep religious knowledge and charismatic outreach of the scholar monk U Silananda (December 16, 1927–August 13, 2005).[11] U Silananda, who was the resident monk at the Dhammananda Monastery from its founding in 1980 until his death in 2005, was one of two monks who traveled with the eminent monk the Mahasi Sayadaw to the United

States in 1979 at the invitation of the Insight Meditation Society in Barre, Massachusetts. Since it was beyond the financial means of many Burmese in the United States to arrange such visits, this was a rare opportunity for these immigrants to reconnect with their religious roots after a decade or more of leaving Burma. Having experienced this reengagement, the Burmese immigrants in the Bay Area did not want to experience another break with their religious heritage and asked the Mahasi Sayadaw whether U Silananda could stay behind to propagate Buddhism in the Bay Area. What began, then, as an effort by white American Buddhists to invite masters of Insight Meditation to the United States in the 1970s, led to the establishment of culturally and ethnically specific Buddhist monasteries in the 1980s.

Dr. Maung Tin-Wa, who served as an intermediary between the various Burmese Buddhist groups during the visit of the Mahasi Sayadaw, provides another perspective. In an unpublished paper that he delivered on July 17, 1987, at the Conference on World Buddhism in North America held in Ann Arbor, Michigan, he situates the "Burmese Buddhist Movement in North America" within broader historical, cultural, and political currents from the 1950s to the 1980s.[12] He notes that while there was a brief encounter between Burmese Buddhism and the United States in the 1960s, when U Thant as the Secretary General of the United Nations (1961-1971) set aside a meditation hall at the UN and Burmese Buddhist monks gave lectures in the United States, no permanent presence was established.

Dr. Tin-Wa also identifies the years 1978–1979 as a pivotal time for Burmese Buddhism in the United States. In 1978, Dr. Rina Sircar, a student of the renowned forest monk, the Taungpulu Sayadaw, organized a group of mainly white American meditation enthusiasts to fund the Taungpulu Kaba Aye Dhamma Center in Palo Alto Hills (which was later formally established in 1981 in Boulder Creek, California). The Taungpulu Sayadaw quickly gathered a large following of devotees from various ethnic backgrounds, foregrounding the potentially universal appeal of Burmese Buddhism in the Bay Area. After the Taungpulu Sayadaw's return to Burma at the end of 1978 (he had to oversee the building of a pagoda), the Mahasi Sayadaw arrived a few months later in 1979 through the help of Dr. Rina Sircar. Dr. Tin-Wa incisively notes that although the Taungpulu Sayadaw was a forest monk and the Mahasi Sayadaw was an urban monk, the successive arrival of two highly eminent Burmese monks in the Bay Area was a call to arms for Bay Area Burmese Americans to unite and create a permanent Burmese Buddhist monastery. It could be argued, then, that the arrival of these two eminent monks in 1978 and 1979 were as crucial for the formation of a cohesive Burmese American identity in the Bay Area as it was for the establishment of Burmese Buddhism in the Bay Area.

In his monograph on Burmese American Buddhism, *Race and Religion in American Buddhism*, Joseph Cheah adds another voice to the history of the Dhammananda Monastery. Cheah picks up where the previous authors leave off, and writes that the Mahasi Sayadaw's visit to the Bay Area was so successful that he agreed to let two of his disciples remain. However, the lack of any established monastery in California at the time forced U Silananda and U Kelatha to move into a small room in the home of an elderly Burmese couple, U Chit Tun and his wife, Daw Khin Htwe. The situation became more desperate when later that year, U Kelatha agreed to head what would become the Mingalaram Monastery outside of Washington, D.C. When U Silananda returned to the Bay Area, it became clear that a permanent monastery had to be created to keep this monk in the United States. This association was eventually called the Theravada Buddhist Society of America, and the state of California approved its nonprofit status in February 1980.[13] On July 27, 1980, U Silananda became the first resident monk of a rented two-bedroom house at 425 Staples Avenue in San Francisco. One year later in 1981, the Theravada Buddhist Society of America raised enough funds to purchase a residential house in Daly City at 68 Woodrow Street. This second Dhammananda Monastery was active for nearly fifteen years until the mid-1990s, when a city ordinance was passed that prohibited this monastery from religious and cultural celebrations due to complaints from neighbors about parking problems and noise issues. This experience would have a profound effect on the organizers of the Theravada Buddhist Society of America, who became extra sensitive and vigilant from this point on about maintaining good relations with its neighbors.

Faced with a city ordinance that restricted the monastery from its essential activities, the Theravada Buddhist Society of America sold the property on Woodrow Street in 1996, and established the current Dhammananda Monastery on a 6.7-acre ocean-facing parcel in Half Moon Bay at 17450 S. Cabrillo Highway. Strict zoning laws required that the monastery wait three years to renovate the existing farm buildings. Even today, the original façade of one of the farm buildings remains in its original appearance, while the renovations and expansions extend back from the street to be as inconspicuous as possible. After another three years, all the internal and external construction requirements for the city and the county were finally met and the meditation center was completed. Finally, the third Dhammananda Monastery was dedicated on March 14, 2004. Currently, two monks are in residence: U Jotalankara, who became the senior monk after the passing of U Silananda, and U Osadha, a younger monk who runs the daily affairs of the monastery and will most likely take over as head monk of the Dhammananda Monastery. In an interview conducted with these two monks on August 4, 2011, both stressed that the priorities of the monastery were not to expand, but rather to focus on maintaining orthodox meditation practices in the monastery in the face of generational change. Along these lines, the Dhammananda Summer School and the Aye-Thet Scholarship program has emerged as a crucial means for transmitting the cultural and religious folklore of Burma from the older generation to the younger generation.

THE SUMMER SCHOOL

Ever since the founding of the Theravada Buddhist Society of America in 1980, U Silananda was regularly invited to visit the homes of devotees to lead ceremonies such as housewarmings and birthdays. It was on these occasions within the domestic sphere that parents expressed their concern over the second generation. How could they pass on their values to their children? How could Buddhist teachings keep their children from going astray, both in terms of morals and in terms of embracing other religions? To respond to these questions, U Silananda decided to hold Buddhism classes for the younger generation. This eventually developed into a formal summer school supported by a scholarship program that has become the primary means by which the older generation familiarizes the next generation with Burmese religion, culture, and folklore. The Aye-Thet Scholarship is named after Dr. Lyn Swe Aye and Dr. Khin Nyo Thet, who felt that Bay Area Burmese immigrants in the 1990s were a small community, and unlike other ethnic and religious groups with organized language, religious, and cultural programs, needed to help their children maintain their cultural identity. From a total enrollment of five students in that first year of 1992, the summer school has improved and expanded to a residential camp with over one hundred participants. Some students come from other states such as New York, New Jersey, and Florida; others have to be turned away due to lack of space. In any case, parents are encouraged by the fact that students return year after year, with some becoming teachers themselves for the next generation.

On August 3, 2013, during the closing day of the summer school for 2013, I was able to interview Mr. Stanley Khoo (via phone), as well as Dr. Ronald Yang and his wife Dr. Katherine Tan (at the monastery). I asked them about their expectations for the Summer School and the following is a summary of their responses. All agreed that parents wanted to recreate a similar Buddhist education that they had in Burma. However, given the fact that their children might only have one week of such instruction per year, there was a need to systematize their study into basic, intermediate, and advanced levels that would encourage them to return year after year. They were also all in agreement that the Summer School offered an opportunity for youth to become involved in the Burmese American community and to learn how to pay back to this community, even if Buddhism was not involved. There was also a sense of collective pride that numerous graduates of the Summer School went on to attend Stanford or

University of California, Berkeley. All three parents agreed that the success of the Summer School centered on the excellent teachings of the resident monks and that the future growth of the monastery depended on the second generation carrying the flame forward. Stanley Khoo noted that a few students were already being groomed to take over the reigns as the first generation continues to age.

On the same date, I also had the opportunity to interview several students of the Summer School. These included Leo Myo, Jason Kung, Benson Kung, and William Yang and Yema Yang (who are the children of Ronald Yang and Katherine Tan). Contrary to Joseph Cheah's interviews with students, which indicated that they felt pressured by their parents to participate in the Summer School, the students that I interviewed emphasized the positive outcomes of the Summer School.[14] All students agreed that opportunities to develop and maintain friendships drew them back to the program year after year, and that it was not until they were in their high school years did they realize how to connect their Buddhist education with their lives outside the monastery. The only female student in the interview group, Yema Yang, noted that at the age of sixteen she had an epiphany that Burmese culture and Buddhism was worth preserving. The students also expressed sincere appreciation for the dedication and sacrifice of the monks and volunteers, without which the monastery would not exist. Breaking it down into three points, one of the students noted that the success of the monastery depended on (1) dedicated people; (2) the ability of these dedicated people to make Buddhist knowledge and Burmese culture relevant and relatable; and (3) a wide variety of good food.

The students also expressed a clear awareness of their systematic transition from student to teaching assistant to teacher. They were also aware of the power of visual culture in conveying certain Buddhist principles; for example, they brought up the well-known image of a candle, wick, and flame to communicate ideas of karma and transmigration. One student, William Yang, noted the indelible photoshop image of a beautiful woman's head that was half a skull as a representation of impermanence and the pitfalls of desire. Yema Yang mentioned the image of a flowing river as another representation of passing impermanence. With remarkable maturity, they also mentioned that as teachers, they preferred to teach abhidharma and Buddhist philosophy at the advanced levels since this was more applicable to their lives than the more sensational tales of self-sacrifice told through Jataka tales and Buddhist birth stories. Finally, they clearly articulated how they edited and graded essays on the basis of (1) originality; (2) focus; (3) comprehension; (4) depth; and (5) personal experience.

CODA

The position of folklore and visual culture as simultaneously occupying the margins of mainstream social values as well as a central place within cultural production blurs categories such a popular and elite, public and private. Taken together, folklore and visual culture also facilitate an understanding of images and objects as dynamic participants in lived processes and invented traditions. Folklore and visual culture thus resist categorization as remnants of cultural authenticity that require careful preservation, while highlighting their capacity for gestures of assimilation and counter-assimilation in immigrant narratives. By focusing on both the domestic and the communal environments of Burmese American Buddhism, this essay considers how folklore and visual culture modifies daily religious practice as well as major rites of passage, shapes narratives regarding the founding of Burmese Buddhism in the Bay Area, and directs the future transmission of Burmese American culture and identity.

Figure 2.1. Sign outside the Dhammananda Monastery, Half Moon Bay, CA. Courtesy Winston Kyan.

NOTES

1. For outside-in perspectives, see Thomas A. Tweed and Stephen Prothero, eds., *Asian Religions in America: A Documentary History* (Oxford: Oxford University Press, 1999). For inside-out perspectives see David K. Yoo, ed., *New Spiritual Homes: Religion and Asian Americans* (Honolulu: University of Hawai'i Press, 1999). Also, see Pyong Gap Min and Jung Ha Kim, eds., *Religions in Asian America: Building Faith Communities* (Walnut Creek: Altamira Press, 2002).

2. For perspectives on race and Asian American religions, see Jane Naomi Iwamura and Paul Spickard, eds., *Revealing the Sacred in Asian and Pacific America* (New York: Routledge, 2003). Also see Tony Carnes and Fenggang Yang, eds., *Asian American Religions: The Making and Remaking of Borders and Boundaries* (New York: New York University Press, 2004).

3. For a discussion of underrepresented Asian Americans, see Huping Ling, ed., *Emerging Voices: Experiences of Underrepresented Asian Americans* (New Brunswick: Rutgers University Press, 2008). Also see Joseph Cheah, *Race and Religion in American Buddhism: White Supremacy and Immigrant Adaptation* (Oxford: Oxford University Press, 2011).

4. Also see Winston Kyan, "Folklore and Asian American Visual Culture." In *Encyclopedia of Asian American Folklore and Folklife* (3 vols.), edited by Jonathan H. X. Lee and Kathleen Nadeau, (vol. 1) (Santa Barbara, CA: ABC-CLIO, 2011), 54-58.

5. In addition to family folklore, the sudden move of Dr. Chwan Kyan to the East Coast shortly after the founding of the Dhammananda Monastery is recounted in Joseph Cheah's monograph on the Dhammananda Monastery. See Cheah, *Race and Religion*, 97.

6. Joseph Cheah, "Cultural Identity and Burmese American Buddhists," *Peace Review* 14:4 (2002): 418.

7. Cheah, *Race and Religion*, 102.

8. Tamara C. Ho, "Women of the Temple: Burmese Immigrants, Gender, and Buddhism in a U.S. Frame," in *Emerging Voices: Experiences of Underrepresented Asian Americans*, ed. Huping Ling (Rutgers: Rutgers University Press, 2008), 189-90.

9. Joseph Cheah, "The Function of Ethnicity in the Adaptation of Burmese Religious Practices," in *Emerging Voices: Experiences of Underrepresented Asian Americans*, ed. Huping Ling (Rutgers: Rutgers University Press, 2008), 207.

10. Currently in the Bay Area, there are eight Burmese monasteries (six Theravada and two Mahayana), three Karen Baptist Churches, and a Burmese American Catholic Fellowship. See Cheah *Race and Religion*, 96.

11. Theravada Buddhist Society of America, *Homage to Sayadawgyi U Silanandabhivamsa* (Half Moon Bay, CA: Theravada Buddhist Society of America, 2005), 89-93.

12. Maung Tin-Wa, *Burmese Buddhist Movement in North America* (Unpublished paper delivered at the Conference on World Buddhism in North America, Ann Arbor, Michigan, July 17, 1987).

13. Cheah *Race and Religion*, 97.

14. Cheah *Race and Religion*, 105-6.

THREE

The "Movement" as Folklore

Asian American College Youth and Vernacular
Expressions of Asian Pacific American Heritage

Dawn Lee Tu

"... at this moment in history, 'Asian American cultural production' mobilizes and amplifies the circulating discourses of Asian America, neo-nationalisms, transnationalism, Orientalism, multiculturalism, foregrounding the contradictions animating racialized ethnic identity in the United States."[1]

The Asian American movement occurred alongside the black and brown power movements of the 1960s and 1970s and is a significant historical reference point for the cohort of Asian American college youth described in this study. Current undergraduates, as with many of their co-ethnic peers, did not come of age during a period of social upheaval or ethnic community activism. These youth struggle to articulate a sense of self that is rooted in Asian American panethnic identity by drawing on concepts, notions, and accomplishments of important figures in the Asian American movement. Thus, the movement serves as a point of reference because it provides a combination of rich stories, oral histories, and traditions transmitted by family and community elders for students to draw inspiration from, as well as historical "facts" to fill in curriculum gaps about experiences of Asians in the United States. Students are engaged in two-fold cultural work: the articulation of new forms of Asian American panethnicity and the creation of historical continuity within the Asian American movement.

This study provides a glimpse into how young Americans create narratives of Asian American culture through strategic rearticulation of the Asian American movement and the negotiation of specific Asian ethnic identities, and why a broader Asian American panethnic identity remains salient. Looking into this world of college youth provides new insight on the persistence of racial identity and reveals a more complex picture of American racial formation for Asian Americans. I argue that the Asian American movement remains active and can be found in cultural and performative spaces such as Asian Pacific American Heritage Month (APAHM). This discussion begins with a brief history of APAHM and the role it played in the early Asian American movement. In the second section I engage in discursive analysis of how students have appropriated key ideas from the Asian American movement as demonstrated in their daily discourse and constructions of narratives of Asian American activist culture. In the third section I consider how Culture Night, as a vernacular expression, considers the methods of appropriation of Asian American stories and histories transmitted by "elders" and how students' performances are simultaneously disciplined by pedagogies of youth identity and Asian American folklore. I conclude with some final thoughts on how these activities define the continuing trajectory of Asian American student activism.

BACKGROUND AND THE STUDY

This chapter is based on research conducted over a three-year period at two University of California campuses (UC-1 and UC-2). The Asian American college youth interviewed in this study came from a variety of backgrounds and were at different points in their academic careers. Their stories reflect the experiences of many other Asian American college youth I have worked with over the years as a former student affairs administrator. These youth engaged in comparable struggles and negotiated the similar margins of existence as Asian Americans. I conducted a series of in-person in-depth interviews with five women and four men I essentially got to know over a two year period of their respective undergraduate lives. These nine college youth were among a larger group of about thirty students I engaged in numerous informal discussions with during the same period of time. These students represent a range of Asian American college youth; several were involved in social justice activist initiatives while others were beginning to explore their racial and ethnic identity and had no desire to become involved in struggles for social justice. All participants were members of other student organizations or on campus activities *not* focused on Asian American community issues including student government, peer-advising for their major, and residential life. Of those involved in the student organizations and efforts to address Asian American issues, several worked in the Asian American studies program office or the Gender Equity Center and worked on addressing Asian American women's issues. In addition to interviews, I conducted participant observation in student committee meetings, and during private advising sessions with advisors.

During interviews, I asked about family histories and what motivated them to become involved in APAHM planning activities that occurred at their respective UC campus. Students self-identified as Asian American including ethnic identities such as Filipino, Chinese, Vietnamese, Southeast Asian, Japanese, and Hmong. Each of them held multiple memberships and commitments to other Asian ethnic organizations. When I asked why they devoted so much time and energy to organizing Asian American events, they explained that they had no choice; no organization provided the opportunities to explore Asian American *as well as* their ethnic identity through social interaction with the possibility of exploring more "political" issues. Thus, students were commonly committed to at least three Asian American activities—APAHM, a pan-Asian student organization, and an Asian ethnic organization—in addition to their other noncultural commitments. [2]

UC-1 and UC-2 are comparable to many California universities with a growing minority population. Such characteristics include: Asian American and Pacific Islander student populations that are approaching a numerical majority, Asian American studies courses are offered, and the campus has a vibrant and wide-range of active Asian American student organizations. Despite the exceptional demographic of Asian Americans in California, the circumstances by which APAHM events are implemented are generalizable with other college APAHM programs across the United States (the phenomenon of "heritage months" is also similar to other nationally recognized Heritage Months across the United States including Black History Month in February, Women's History Month in March, and Native American/Indian Heritage Month in November). The events usually occur during the months of April or May at most universities, and events focused on exploring aspects of Asian American culture, heritage, and identity are student-organized, conceived, and implemented with general oversight from administrative advisors. The events were funded by the university, but were not a part of any co-curricular efforts or institutional articulation of campus diversity. A small cohort of students, many of whom were also members of other Asian ethnic-specific organizations, organized the activities. The most common programs are lectures given by academics, authors, and other notable figures, who students believe have made significant contributions to the greater understanding of the Asian American experiences. The month-long celebration usually culminated with a closing program referred to as the Asian American "Culture Show" or "Culture Night" consisting of "traditional" and "contemporary" dance performances, an invited feature performer such as a comedian or singer, and sometimes these performances are interspersed between a skit or dramatic narrative usually challenging the model minority[3] stereotype or some other salient aspect of Asian American identity.

Both UC-1 and UC-2 campuses are large, public universities with significant Asian American and Pacific Islander populations totaling about 40 percent of the total student population. APAHM activities at both campuses began during the 1970s by Asian American students, when the ethnic studies movement in California was well underway. Early archival documents indicate that at both campuses, APAHM activities similarly emerged because of a growing interest in ethnic cultures as part of a broader national interest in multiculturalism. The educational emphasis was generally focused on sharing ethnic culture and dance as a means to learn about other cultures. The role of Asian American studies also contributed to the creation of APAHM programs at both campuses. While students did not consult faculty teaching Asian American studies courses, they viewed Asian American studies as a resource they could tap into if they needed a scholarly speaker or a facilitator for an event. Asian American studies courses were a source of knowledge and created a connection to historical memory of the Asian American movement in which students advocated for specific kinds of APAHM programs. Nazli Kibria refers to this learnedness as "official pan-Asianism" or the official history and notion of Asian American panethnic activism by using keywords and phrases from the early Asian American activist movement and the ability to reference historical and community figures who worked towards equality for Asian Americans.[4]

Another critical structuring factor to the creation of APAHM were university diversity policies that defined and justified the need for campus diversity. Policy in general included defining of values and allocation of resources based on those defined values.[5] Diversity policies are therefore a defining of values related to diversity and resources allocated to meet the goals set around diversity. These policies ultimately help shape the consciousness of students when it comes to understanding their identity. The lessons they learn about diversity in college are the constructs of diversity they will carry into the rest of their adult lives. For Asian American college youth this has particular implications because these constructs of diversity are framed by the racial "role" Asian Americans play as a "model minority" and a "foreigner" that inform what Dhingra refers to as "identity management." According to Dhingra (2007) the workplace and civil society are two mainstream arenas where Asian Americans are consistently treated as ethnic workers even though they strive for public profiles as "good citizens" rather than self-interested "foreigners."[6] This study focuses on the critical time of the undergraduate years that inform and shape how these students eventually negotiate their Asian American identity and the ever-present model minority stereotype during their post-college years.

This project also came out of my own experience as an activist during my undergraduate years as a former student affairs administrator in multicultural affairs. Many of the students I worked with during the time of this study often talked to me about their attitudes and views on issues such as campus climate, experiences with discrimination, and most of all, why identifying as Asian American was important for them. This chapter attempts to understand these students' claims to and performances of Asian American panethnicity as both simultaneously a part of, yet distinct from, the tradition of the Asian American movement.

APAHM AS ACTIVISM AND NATIONAL CELEBRATION

Within the context of what can be called the Asian American movement, APAHM represented one front in the struggle for empowerment and visibility during the early years of Asian American activism. Scholars such as Yen Le Espiritu traced the origins of Asian American radical activism to the development of Asian American panethnic identity during the late 1970s. She argued that "panethnic groups in the U.S. are products of political and social processes, rather than of cultural bonds . . . culture has followed panethnic boundaries rather than defined them."[7] Thus, Asian Americans began to reject "Oriental" as an identity as early as the post–war years, while civil rights and radical movements of the 1960s forced the U.S. government to recognize and expand the rights of minority groups. In the 1970s, issues concerning individual equality shifted to the rights of underrepresented groups through government-mandated policies, such as affirmative action programs.[8] Through interaction with co-ethnics, Asian Americans quickly understood that it was in the material and economic interest of all underserved groups to mobilize in solidarity to access resources. Increased intergroup communication and contact facilitated growing consciousness among Asian Americans that lead to the coalescence of a panethnic identity. College students appropriated the federally created term "Asian American," refusing to be called "Oriental" which they felt was a racist identity.[9] The students expanded the notion of Asian American as an oppressed U.S. racial group and identified with third world struggles against imperialism and colonization. The dissemination of the "official ideology of pan-Asianism" occurred through the institutionalization of Asian American services, programs, and student organizations on college campuses.[10]

While students were making claims to Asian American identity, activism happening in civic life led to the formation of a radical Asian American identity. Michael Liu, Kim Geron, and Tracy Lai explain a "new identity was never part of the primary goal . . . [but] part of strengthening . . . the Asian American Movement [that] was reimagining itself in a pan-Asian context and as part of a cross-racial struggle to throw off a history of oppression."[11] Sucheng Chan emphasized change that was created through community agencies, while Fred Ho highlights change that was created by radicals and revolutionaries who comprised the Asian Pacific American Left.[12] Though a seemingly disparate and sometime contradictory collection of efforts, Daryl Maeda retrospectively views the movement as a sometimes contradictory collection of efforts unified by two fundamental premises: all Asian ethnicities shared common racial oppression in the United States and the most effective way to resist racism was to build a multiethnic and multi-racial coalition.[13]

Intended to raise awareness about and celebrate the contributions of these racial and ethnic groups, the creation of an annual Heritage Month reflects what Claire Kim refers to as "official" multiculturalist discourse that recognizes the growing racial and ethnic diversity of the nation by formally acknowledging these groups, while simultaneously not naming the tensions and antagonisms produced by this "new" diversity.[14] In this context, Heritage Month celebrations are part of what James Banks refers to as "content integration" in which teachers attempt to address the "sins" of omission by incorporating data and information about a particular minority group.[15] Carl Grant refers to this multicultural strategy as *plural* tolerance but not *pluralistic* understanding of differences that foster the kind of cooperation and communication required of building a truly multicultural and democratic society.[16] Celebrating the achievements of exceptional Asian American individuals and sharing native culture, without any critique of the dominant culture, indirectly embraced the ideology of the model minority stereotype popularized during the 1970s. APAHM celebrations offer an opportunity to make Asian American accomplishments and contributions to society visible, and can be interpreted as assimilationist projects that showcase the integration of Asian Americans into American society, despite cultural differences; the display of native culture through food, dance, and artifacts has continued to reify the "otherness" of Asian Americans. In this way, new diversity obfuscates the ways in which Asian Americans continue to experience inequality and discrimination despite being consistently racialized and valorized as the model minority.[17] Asian American youth in particular are confronted with these concealments as they begin to explore their racial and ethnic identities during the college years. This is the context in which many Asian American college youth join organizing committees for APAHM.

Following two decades of national upheaval during the civil rights movement of the 1960s and the antiwar demonstrations protesting the Vietnam War in the 1970s, commemorative heritage celebrations such as the bicentennial celebration of 1976 were part of U.S. political elites' attempts to restore American patriotism. All ethnic Heritage Months began as Heritage Weeks and were expanded in the 1970s into months. National Hispanic Heritage Week was declared by President Nixon in 1968; President Ford urged Americans to celebrate Black History Week in 1975; and President Carter designated Asian Pacific Heritage Week in 1979. Beginning in the 1990s, weeks were expanded into Black History Month (February), Native American Awareness Month (November), Hispanic Heritage Month (mid-September through mid-October), and Asian Pacific American Heritage Month (May). Presidents used presidential proclamations and executive orders to recognize particular groups of citizens and exhort the American public, especially educational communities, to observe the month with appropriate ceremonies and activities.

Jeanie F. Jew, the president of the Organization of Chinese American Women in 1976, is credited by several unverifiable sources for being the "creator" and the primary writer of all legislation calling for the creation of Asian Pacific Heritage Week/Month.[18] Jew observed the lack of Asian Pacific American representation in the bicentennial celebration and enlisted the support of Representatives Frank Horton (R-NY) and Norman Mineta (D-CA) to introduce legislation that called for broader national attention to the concerns, contributions, and history of Americans of Asian and Pacific Islander descent. The first ten days of May coincided with two significant moments in Asian Pacific American history: the first Japanese to arrive in the United States on May 7, 1843, and contributions by Chinese laborers to the building and completion of the transcontinental railroad on May 10, 1869 (Golden Spike Day). In June 1977, Horton and Mineta introduced House Resolution 540, asking the president to proclaim the first ten days of May as "Asian/Pacific American Heritage Week." Senators Daniel Inouye and Spark Matsunaga followed by introducing Senate Joint Resolution 72 on July 19, 1977, making a similar request to the president. This resulted in the introduction of House Joint Resolution 1007 on June 19, 1978, which was approved on July 10, 1978, followed by Senate approval on September 19, 1978. On October 5, 1978, President Carter signed Public Law 95-419, designating that Asian Pacific Heritage Week occur from May 4-10, 1979. Presidential Proclamation 4650 issued March 28, 1979, was designated the first Asian Pacific Heritage Week in 1979. For the next ten years, through annual presidential proclamations, Presidents Carter, Reagan, and Bush renewed the designation. Congress did not ask the president to expand the week to the month of May until 1990 with Public Law 101-283 (amending Public Law 95-419). Through Presidential Proclamation 6130 issued May 7, 1990, President Bush designated May 1990 as the first Asian/Pacific American Heritage Month. Congress passed Public Law 102-450 in 1992, permanently designating May of each year as "Asian/Pacific American Heritage Month." Opportunities for minority recognition such as APAHM occurred as a result of the struggles of civil rights and liberation movements during the 1970s and 1980s. Multiculturalism and tolerance, two ideological shifts that came out of these early radical struggles, allowed minorities to publicly express racial pride while making apparent the ways American history that left out their ancestors' narratives.

Asian American activists used demographic information as another educational strategy to reveal the actual numerical diversity of Asian American ethnic groups. As early as the 1970s, Asian American panethnic organizations advocated for more choices in the U.S. Census for Asian and Asian ethnic subgroups. In this specific struggle for recognition, activists criticized the U.S. federal government for systematically making invisible Americans of Asian descent. While some Asian Americans wondered whether this activism would disunify and detract from the efforts to rally behind Asian American panethnic identity, activists believed that Asian American panethnicity depended on the ability of individuals to be able to self-identify ethnically as well as more broadly. The "Asian" choice was not added to the U.S. Census until the 1980s, and only after great pressure was placed on the Bureau by Asian American panethnic organizations.

KEYWORDS OF THE ASIAN AMERICAN MOVEMENT

Liu, Geron, and Lai argue that the movement's demise began during the consolidation of conservative trends in the late 1970s.[19] Ironically, growth of globalization and technology did not heighten the sense of international solidarity that characterized the early decades of the Asian American movement. Combined with moderate conservatism during the Clinton administration, globalization has instead led to the disbandment of many Marxist and revolutionary organizations. The leadership in these organizations grew weary of prolonged political hostility and struggle to secure funding from federal government sources. Liu, Geron, and Lai explain that organizations could not maintain their ideological views and thus lost cultural resonance and the ability to provide an alternative movement to developing global capitalism. Furthermore, many specific Asian ethnic organizations began to focus on specific issues in their own ancestral home countries and pulled away from panethnic Asian American activism.[20] While conditions continued to remain the same, if not worse for Asian Americans during the 1990s, activism shifted to "achieving equity within the contemporary social structure . . . and adopted the mainstream conventions of competitive, pluralistic interest groups and . . . the politics of identity became widespread within the communities, but the framework lacked the resonance that could passionately animate large segments of the population."[21] Indeed, even though identity politics was significant with this cohort of Asian American students, contemporary activism shows that Liu, Geron, and

Lai's conclusions about the demise of the Asian American movement are part of an unfinished chapter on the evolution of Asian American activism and the continuing salience of the movement's symbolic significance for Asian American college youth today.

Since Asian American activism has never been a prominent part of mainstream portrayals of progressive activism, we can only conclude that Asian American students become interested in Asian American panethnic activities for very specific reasons. What little students know about the Asian American movement and the ways they fill their knowledge gaps speaks to the legacy of the movement itself. The basic tenants of the movement survived as decades passed. Basic concerns from the earlier movement remain critical for this generation of Asian American youth, including the concepts of "self-reliance, self-determination, equal treatment, rectification of historic wrongs, and the belief that activists were changing fundamental aspects of their communities."[22] I specifically observed how this discourse remained salient with students. In this study, the first group was comprised of "politicized" students, many of who had taken some to many Asian American studies classes, were familiar with campus racial politics, and showed complexity in thinking about racial identity and racial formation of Asian American as a group. These students often viewed APAHM events as a means to strengthening pan-Asian unity and as ways to educate non-Asians about issues in the Asian American community. These students spoke reverently about "those who came before," "the elders" in the community, how "old school" activists "empowered the community" through "raising consciousness." They expressed a desire to have a similar affect through APAHM events. For these students, the discourse of the Asian American movement served a particular significant purpose: to anchor and connect their progressive desires in a past movement where Asian American activism could be described as glorious in contrast to present portrayals of Asian American peers as complacent and apathetic. Politicized students sought to create educational programs that were consciousness-raising, usually by inviting a speaker or performer who could speak about empowerment and political activism. I refer generally to the second type of student as "moderate." These students had taken few to none Asian American studies courses and spent significantly more extracurricular time involved with Asian ethnic student groups instead of pan-Asian activities. Moderates were very averse to any kind of political activism and often expressed desire to have events that were more "fun" and "entertaining" instead of gatherings that were "too political" or "radical." One of their main concerns was to educate the campus community about the diversity within the Asian American population through events such as food tasting and ethnic dance and sought to establish co-sponsorships with the university.

These two typologies are by no means stable. During the two years of fieldwork, I observed how moderate students became politicized and politicized students softened in their confrontational rhetoric and distrust of the university. Espiritu and Kibria emphasize that Asian American identity is constantly produced in dialectical tension to a variety of social realities. As much as Asian American panethnicity has been a unifying identity, it also has an equally disunifying effect. Espiritu and Kibria acknowledge that disidentification, or the rejection of ethnic group identity in order to create social distance, has been a common phenomenon. Kibria's participants explain that identity has an "artificial feel," that it can be "stifling (and) antithetical to individualism, freedom of choice in affiliation" and that many felt an "aversion to clannishness, group conformity, and gender traditionalism" associated with Asian cultures.[23] The discourse of disidentification is often curiously rooted in liberal ideals in which one's individuality is based on one's ability to make choices apart from other groups. Some reject pan-Asian ethnic identity because of its flattening effect on Asian ethnicities; all Asians are subsumed under this rubric and group-specific issues become lost. These sentiments are especially legitimate in education as significant disparities between Asian ethnic groups exist but cannot be accurately conveyed in aggregated data.[24] Instead, we can view Asian American panethnicity as an identification that creates unity out of liminality. Viewed another way, students may also disidentify with being only ethnically Asian and take up the broader panethnic identity to critique how they have been racialized. Therefore, while many students identify with many aspects of the Asian American Movement, they remain largely focused on the politics of identity while attempting to engage in political consciousness raising.

Regardless of the split, all students I interviewed were interested in identity exploration for various reasons. In the event planning process, both types of students drew upon the folklore of the Asian American movement derived from two distinct places: Asian American studies curriculum and the stories they had been told by the "elders" including family, recent alumni, community members and mid-level administrators' advising efforts. In their learning, however, knowledge was never complete and both political and moderate students who became political over time filled in the gaps by tapping into the mythos of the Asian American movement. Diane Fujino has shown that students develop a greater sense of political "consciousness" through a combination of experiential learning activities and personal and academic-oriented self-reflection.[25] Thus, peer-to-peer learning or *pedagogies of youth identity* reflected a process of exploring basic identity issues for students who had been inculcated in activist ideology, and that recalled the Asian American movement. Political students appropriated ideas and concepts from what little they knew about the earlier Asian American Movement that resonated with them and created a new set of meanings. Since Asian

American studies classes fill the knowledge gap produced by the demise of activist organizations in the 1990s, these spaces exist wherein students can engage in basic identity development issues and learn about Asian American history that was missing from high school history classes. Some students recounted how they got involved in APAHM activities as a way to explore their ethnic identity and apply what they learned in Asian American studies classes. For example, Thomas, a fourth year student at the time of the interview, explained how, despite the fact that he began taking Asian American studies classes and became involved in APAHM organizing late in his undergraduate career, he finally felt able to articulate what it meant for him to be Asian American through both activities.

> Actually one of my biggest regrets in school, [is not] taking [Asian American studies classes] and getting involved in [APAHM] until [my] senior year. [Both] helped me understand [what it meant to be] marginalized. [Growing up] I think you can always feel it, like you always understand and feel being marginalized . . . you have that sense your identity might be under attack and you can't put that into words. You don't know words like 'marginalize' but when I took these classes I finally began to understand . . . [26]

APAHM activities also provided a way for students to consider the broader context of what they were learning. Regina reflected,

> APAHM and the Asian American Leadership programs are precursors to mobilizing issues . . . having people come and work together and building relationships makes community stronger and from there, begin to work on issues. This perspective comes from a mixture of taking classes . . . talking to other students and realizing that a lot of issues that we face as Asian Americans are really similar to one another.

Annie also echoed Thomas and Regina's sentiments:

> The leadership part was what stimulated my thinking. I couldn't really work on my leadership skills anywhere else. Leadership in general wasn't my strongest thing. [APAHM] was something I could definitely learn from. There's a lot that I still don't know about my family and culture; that's why I joined [the APAHM committee].

Asian American studies classes gave them a background in the language of Asian American activism that became social capital they could use in the APAHM planning committee.

The political students made assumptions about their peers' varying degrees of a radical activist identity based on several factors. The more political and radical a student sought to identify themselves, the more keywords they used from Asian American studies classes. By developing a common language, through utilizing words and phrases popularly used during earlier decades of Asian American activism, such as "grassroots," "raising consciousness," and "empowerment," students signified varying degrees of activist identities. For example, one student explained to me that APAHM "is about trying to raise awareness . . . it's about empowerment." Will explained at one event that the sense of empowerment

> . . . felt more like a political consciousness . . . the fact that there is this community . . . it's just great that this sense of consciousness or being conscious about [being] Asian American and that's a normal, accepted thing.

Glenn Omatsu explains how keywords shifted from the 1970s to the 1980s. Keywords such as "advocacy," "access," "legitimacy," "empowerment," and "assertiveness" were significant and formed the activist vocabulary for the generation of Asian American youth activists coming of age in the 1980s. The 1970s generation, according to Omatsu, followed Malcolm X's urgent call for freedom "by any means necessary," Mao's challenge to "serve the people," and referred to "power to the people," "self-determination," and "united front" organizing.[27] For the current generation of Asian American college students, many of the salient concepts have returned to identity politics and building a sense of Asian American pride. In addition to being a transformative space for identity introspection, APAHM has the potential to empower students as they take up panethnicity for political activism. One student recounted how a former committee member reminded her about the significance of panethnicity by referencing a significant radical Asian American activist:

> I reaffirmed my attitude when I spoke with [the former director of APAHM]. She recommended Yuri Kochiyama's work . . . and what really inspired and amazed me was how [Kochiyama] went about organizing people and building relationships . . . using social events to build relationships . . . she would talk about her ideology to other people . . . afterwards she was able to put together people from so many different walks of life. This was really important part of the civil rights movement. So bringing together groups through [APAHM and the Leadership program] was important to me.

Following the student's statement, I waited to see if any of the more political students would point out this historical inaccuracy, but many of those students simply nodded in approval. This quote is a great example of how, despite this erroneous conflation of Kochiyama with the civil rights movement (Kochiyama worked closely with Malcolm X, a radical black nationalist who often criticized Martin Luther King Jr. for being assimilationist),[28] the association of radical Black activism with the nonviolent strategies advocated by Martin Luther King Jr. reveals the students' desire for mutual understanding and civil activism rather than change "by any means necessary." Later on, Thomas referenced the Civil Rights Movement again, and encouraged the committee to find a speaker who could "address 1960 activism, and ideally someone who was present during the civil rights movement." He qualified this suggestion by making it clear that he wanted "someone who is seriously an activist, wants to change society, rather than find a place for Asian Americans in society." When it came time to vote for everyone's top choices, Thomas's suggestion got resounding support and revealed the students' set of morals and values. While attempting to validate a history of activism, students struggle with pressure from the university for civil (controlled) engagement and inadvertently promote a tempered nonassimilationist and nonconformity stance more closely aligned to early Yellow Power activism. I saw this pattern reemerge the following year at an APAHM planning meeting when a student expressed desire for APAHM events to include "historical Asian American activists, [such as] a panel or a speaker, who can discuss what they did and what the problems were back then." [29]

This desire to reclaim Asian American activist history was also reflected in efforts to invite local speakers who were "working in" or "working with the community." Speakers such as Helen Zia (author of *Asian American Dreams: The Emergence of an American People*, 2001) and Angela Oh (attorney who was a spokesperson for the Korean American community after the 1992 Los Angeles riots) were perceived to have overly ethnic-specific commitments and were not short-listed. These discussions eventually led to deeper discussions about who could be considered "legitimate" Asian American activist voices. Once the students realized that prominent speakers such as Helen Zia were beyond their budget, they thought of individuals who had participated in local struggles for social justice. Another speaker was suggested and praised for her knowledge of and involvement in the queer and Asian American community and her days on campus in the late 1990s when, according to students, there was "racial strife and hate crimes. She was there during all that change." Students showed great interest in learning more about the development of Asian American activism on campus within a broader notion of the movement. Students wanted speakers to inspire their peers and spark an interest in activism that could dispel stereotypes of their population as "[politically] lazy and apathetic." During a debriefing session, Regina explained that the keynote speaker at the Asian American student leadership event,

> . . . should have been more empowerment and leadership-based. [It] felt like there wasn't anything that rallied people together other than organizing for social change workshop. There wasn't something that got students to go back and . . . find out what's been going on and do something with the skills that we were giving them.

A yearning for activist role models, who could recount the stories about early activism and teach the students how to engage in critical and contemporary activism, was very apparent throughout my field research.

I don't want to oversimplify my portrayal of these students and their interests in being involved in APAHM activities. Similar to any other ethnic group, an array of individuals from different backgrounds with various forms of knowledge and experiences reveal the often disparate approaches to defining ethnic identity. The radical ideas that united many of them also became contentious points of concern for other students as they struggled to define Asian American panethnicity. The split between these two groups was not always even or consistent. At the beginning of APAHM planning sessions, when the committee was not constrained by budget or approaching deadlines, students gave surprisingly candid and noticeably contradictory feedback on political and social views. For example, when discussing whether to invite a community group to campus to provide training on Asian American community activism, one moderate student new to APAHM organizing explained, "we should change the name from 'activism' to 'training' because it sounds too severe . . . maybe 'student organizing'?" In our interview she shared, "planning [APAHM] events has been fun [but] it has made me reflective [*sic*] a lot about my behaviors towards my family." Before I had a chance to ask if she thought her reflective moment had anything to do with what she was learning through the group about Asian American experiences, she quickly insisted that her reflection "doesn't necessarily have to do with being [Asian Pacific Islander]."

Another moderate student suggested the need to have a food event and proposed an "Asian food potluck." This suggestion was met with silence as discussion moved onto the next topic. This lack of acknowledgment confused and made the student wonder if she had said something wrong. During an interview I asked her why she had suggested the potluck and she explained the she initially joined the planning committee because she saw it as an opportunity to learn more about her family and culture, but that she also supported the idea of Asian American unity because of the subtle racist treatment she experienced while growing up. She explained that a program she had attended at APAHM the previous year, about how imperialism affected Asian Americans and broader issues of discrimination directed toward Asian Americans, was very "eye opening" and caused her to reflect on how "other kids treated me because I spoke Chinese in [elementary] school." For both of these moderate students, being involved in APAHM planning gave them a chance to think deeply about their family and childhood experiences.

Although it is not clear if the Asian American movement is indeed waning, students are making connections to earlier activism by drawing on the folklore of the movement while struggling to stay connected to contemporary progressive causes. These students search for spaces within APAHM to create new forms of diversity, sponsored by university funding and resources. They struggle to explore and create Asian American panethnic identities as cultural producers during leadership opportunities. APAHM remains a contradictory space where ideological sparks of the Asian American movement could catch at any moment. In the next section, I take a closer look at Culture Night, the culminating event of APAHM, as an example of a program where the Asian American movement has influenced the process of how students create vernacular expressions of Asian American panethnicity on stage.

BREAKING "TRADITION": CULTURE NIGHTS

Culture Night (CN) is the most significant APAHM event for students because it closes the month and usually draws the greatest number of people, both on and off campus. The events can be very high profile if local ethnic media report on special guest performers. CN is such a significant event in their undergraduate years that students invite immediate and extended family members to attend. CN serves as the best opportunity to showcase Asian American culture and folklore, but more importantly, the production is the result of imagining what it means and could mean to be Asian American. The CN phenomenon has developed in conjunction with the production of Asian ethnic-specific cultural shows where every weekend during the spring, the campus events calendar usually has a CN on it. At some UC campuses, some Asian American student organizations compete for best dates by booking venues a year in advance. The format of a CN can adhere to previous years' conceptualizations. They are generally organized in two manners. First, a storyline unifies the entire program with dance sequences interspersed between each scene. Some shows are organized like variety or talent shows with dancing and other artistic performances, interspersed with commercials or campy spoofs of popular mainstream commercials. Another variation includes performances such as dancing and singing (folk and modern), comedy provided by a stand-up comedian, etc., with no commercial breaks. Some consider Pilipino Culture Nights (PCN) the most vibrant Asian American cultural night genre. PCN began just like any other ethnically-focused cultural night as a ninety-minute program unified by a storyline, with dances (folk and modern) interspersed. PCN has developed into longer and more complex productions. At one WCU campus, PCN consists of two to three hour shows spanning two nights. Another PCN is performed several times at another campus because of community demand.

Theodore S. Gonzalvez's research on PCN is a clear example of how folklore (in this case dances, oral histories, and other traditions) serves a critical role in how Asian American college youth produce vernacular

expressions that reveal what it means to be American.[30] Gonzalvez refers
to PCN as an example of "active subjectivity," wherein students participate in something that is instrumental in shaping not only their Filipino
American identities, but also their general conceptions of self.[31] Similar
dynamics occur with other APAHM CNs, where, through the process of
self-authorship, students internalize narratives of ancestors' histories that
were passed down to them, and then retell them through story and plot
narratives and traditional dance. Gonzalvez asserts that PCNs (and I believe all APAHM CNs) are a symptom as well as a response to the political climate of the era. PCN is a unique performance genre and serves a
significant purpose for Filipino students, allowing them to negotiate the
nationalist imagery of America's immigrant communities.[32] Gonzalvez
demonstrates how PCN has been instrumental in shaping, as well as
constructing, Filipino American identity for the generation of Filipino
students who attended college during the post–Reagan years. At that
time, Asian American college youth were desperately trying to hold onto
gains won by the previous generation that institutionalized Ethnic Studies in general, and Asian American studies in particular, at many
American college campuses on the West Coast.[33]

Gonzalvez observed how student organizers began to research and
incorporate into their storylines the rich history of Asian American student activism that occurred during the late 1960s. He and his peers struggled with issues over the format (e.g., pressure to represent Filipino culture in one night), how to define Filipino culture (and what is meant by
culture), how to represent Filipino culture (the implications of choosing
to use certain symbols), and what to do with the fact that many students
in the organization were not asking these questions. When I was an
undergraduate and involved in the production of APAHM CN, the organizing committee struggled over these exact issues. However, much to
my surprise, these questions did not come up in my field research. Even
though the format was already somewhat established, and I knew partic-
ipating Asian ethnic student groups would provide historical references
and native dances, I expected students to be more creative with the core
of the show. In brainstorming discussions students were somewhat open
to headlining act/s representative of pan-Asian sensibilities. Advisors expressed frustration with their attempts to get students to think more
critically about the general significance of CN. Critical engagement with
these issues was different from what Gonzalvez found and I experienced;
students negotiated the ideas primarily as a matter of what they believed
would be ideal public representations of Asian American culture and
identity.

In contrast to PCN, APAHM CN serves as a symbolic representation
of Asian American culture as an inherently *modern* identity represented
by "contemporary" headlining act/s, expressed in contradistinction to the
"traditional" or *native* (ancient, folk, other) ethnic dances performed by

Asian ethnic groups. This differentiation came up frequently as students delineated the boundaries between APAHM CN and other Asian culture nights. Isabel explained, "We should invite other people to participate . . . showcase stuff from their culture nights . . . but we don't want to overlap with their culture nights . . . [CN] should be about Asian Pacific American culture." For example, when discussing headline acts, the committee liked suggestions for performers, such as Jasmine Trias (American Idol finalist) who sang contemporary songs, comedians such as Russell Peters (popularized for his frank jokes about his experiences growing up Asian in North America), and Jennifer An (a Korean American finalist on America's Next Top Model) who was outspoken about her body issues as a minority woman. Suggestions for more traditional performances, such as martial arts demonstrations, taiko drumming, and tinikling were provided by other Asian student groups. They allowed for "Asian" acts to be performed and be placed in relation to Asian American culture but it was simultaneously important to them to have a distinct, more politicized space to convey the experiences of Asian Americans.

When I asked MLAs about why Culture Shows were becoming more prevalent, they attributed the consistent growth to the students' sense of obligation to "those that had come before them." Students referred to CNs as a part of tradition and were reluctant to break from previous years. Younger members expressed a reverence for student leaders who they believed made noble sacrifices to create the annual Culture Show. They felt it was their turn to take on the responsibility of educating the campus community, and pay respect to the culture that had been passed onto to them by their families. Oscar explained,

> [Planning] is open to the campus community but it's also more about their own discovery . . . understanding that in the process they are learning and they want to show what they've learned to their friends and families . . . the show is the next generation's take on [the culture] . . .

Natalie described her reluctance to break from tradition as a result of how knowledge is passed on. Technology and social networking play a role for alumni to stay connected with student organizations and enables current students to get information about past shows. She told me expectations are set when students run for an elected position; if they are elected they are expected to carry on previous traditions. At the beginning of the school year, Natalie met with newly-elected officers to educate students about previous events, and encouraged them to "stick with tradition only if it makes sense"; "just as long as you create events with intention." She was reflective and ambivalent about her own role however: "Maybe if I hadn't prepared anything for them about what previous students used to do, they would have reasons for a fresh start." Darren believed that the process of organizing the event reinforced the sense of tradition.

> Students pull it together themselves without any real help from the university. They teach dances to each other, they spend hours learning about their histories together. There is a shared experience in pulling such a complicated event together themselves so when they become leaders, they have it set in their minds that this is what Culture Night is all about—it was a positive experience for them and they want to create that for others so they stick to the standard templates because they know that's how they can express culture and have others experience what they experienced.

Culture Nights, as the culmination and epitome of APAHM's expressive culture, reveal how Asian American folklore can be as disempowering as they are empowering for students. Within the trajectory of the Asian American movement, these cultural performances can limit the empowerment of Asian American college youth if they do not engage in critical reflection on the purpose of and reasons for the performances. This does not hold necessarily apply to other aspects of APAHM programs.

TRAJECTORIES

APAHM performances of Asian American panethnic identity should not and cannot be viewed as inherently activist. Just as Chin, Feng, and Lee observed in their introduction to a special issue of the *Journal of Asian American Studies* on Asian American cultural production, "the term 'cultural production,' makes us aware that 'culture' is not simply an epiphenomenal manifestation of a pre-existing culture, but rather the product of hybrid cultural trajectories."[34] APAHM is difficult to categorize in terms of how scholars understand community organizations and therefore, should be seen as a hybrid of many types of organizations and serving varying functions. For some, being involved can be a way for them to engage in cocurricular learning about Asian American history and culture. For others it is a space in which they can explore basic issues of identity and what it means to be an Asian in America. Others see APAHM as a venue to educate and "give a taste" to non-Asians about Asian American culture and folkways. For politicized students, it has been a space for them to produce programs designed to spark interest and politicize other Asian American students.

Students' vested interests are ultimately to construct a narrative of Asian Americanness through programs, events, and workshops. By understanding APAHM in terms of the localized context as discussed in this article, we can place these activities in relation to the trajectory of the Asian American movement. The fact that APAHM events have been created and legitimated by institutions such as colleges and universities across the United States has several implications when trying to understand where to place these activities in the spectrum of the Asian American movement. Liu, Geron, and Lai describe the institutionalization of Asian American organizations during the movement's "mature years" of 1976-1982 as characterized by more flexibility: "organizations began to adopt more comprehensive points of view to cope with more complex environments."[35] In that environment, activists saw that utopian views could only ensure the survival of their organizations to a certain extent. Many saw the need to structure their organizations for long-term survival, including securing funding, creating long-term goals and measures for accountability, and developing strategies to meet the needs of their constituencies. Espiritu describes how the transformation and professionalization of these activist organizations was necessary in order to qualify for and secure more public funding.[36] According to Liu, Geron, and Lai, as community organizations began to professionalize, activists began to argue about whether to strategically effect change from within the system by "embedding individuals within capitalist institutions long-term and then taking them over" versus constraining capitalist institutions from the outside.[37] Energy that was put into strategy debates would not only contribute to the movement's receding power, but also shift the focus from international struggles to one of defending local neighborhoods and working class issues.[38]

APAHM can be seen as the result of one strategy that activists took during the last part of the movement. Student organizing to defend affirmative action programs began to appear across college campuses during the late 1970s and early 1980s, after the 1976 Bakke Supreme Court ruling. Indeed, according to Keith Osajima, Asian American activists have succeeded in transforming higher education by establishing Asian American studies across the United States.[39] What has remained constant during the Asian American movement has been the articulation of Asian American culture, ideals, and affirmation of ancestral homeland heritage, language, arts, and folkways. These performances "became an important way to document past values and struggles."[40] With the institutionalization of Asian Pacific Heritage celebrations, beginning as early as 1977, the call for recognition of Asian American contributions was and continues to be a strategy of creating more space to question the dominant culture while increasing the visibility of Asian Americans.

Daryl Maeda wrote retrospectively about the legacy of the earlier Asian American movement. He lamented that "the political connotations of 'Asian American' have been eviscerated in the decades since its construction."[41] The term is more closely aligned with demographics such as race, ethnicity, and national descent, made evident by the proliferation of organizations that unite across ethnic lines for the purposes of personal gain and profit maximization. He cautions that with the disassociation of the term with political goals "demonstrates the power of the state and dominant society to co-opt racial definitions and dim radically alternative visions."[42] I am not as pessimistic as Maeda is with the generation of college-age youth who are working hard to make meaning of Asian American panethnic identity. What I have illustrated here is how and why youth struggle in their everyday contexts to make claims to Asian American panethnicity by tapping into the folklore of Asian American activism and tethering their contemporary struggles to the legacy of the Asian American Movement.

NOTES

1. Soo-Young Chin, Peter Feng, and Josephine D. Lee, "Asian American Cultural Production," *The Journal of Asian American Studies* 3 (2000): 269.

2. Other activities included being involved in the minority recruitment and retention program, being an intern at the Multicultural Center, being an academic peer mentor, and serving as an elected student representative in the student government. All Asian American college youth I interacted with had commitments beyond Asian American community activities. While I was able to talk to some of the participants at length about what their non-Asian American activities meant to them in relation to helping them define Asian American panethnicity, I was not able to address these questions in depth with all participants. I would like to continue exploring this area in future research.

3. While this study does not solely focus on deconstructing the model minority stereotype or the forever foreigner syndrome, a definition of both characterizations is necessary because they persistently frame the ways Asian American college youth are positioned in relation to other college youth. The model minority stereotype can be traced to media images that appeared in American popular culture during the late 1960s. Chinese and Japanese Americans were the first subjects of the model minority image in which their newfound immigrant success stories shared two assumed characteristics: successful assimilation in the American mainstream and "good" cultural values. Newspaper and magazine articles that appeared in *Time* magazine and the *U.S. News and World Report* praised Japanese and Chinese Americans for their ability to overcome racial discrimination by working hard and minding their own business. These articles appeared to provide convincing empirical evidence from U.S. Census data to factually explain why these two groups in particular were able to move into high-status occupations, had rising incomes, low rates of mental illness and crime, and high achievement in education (Lee Tu, 2011, p. 61). The stereotype emerged during the racial politics of the civil rights movement during the 1950s and 1960s as the conservative right's answer to black militancy of the 1960s. Portrayed by the mainstream media in contrast to their African American and Latino counterparts, Asian Americans were reported to refuse assistance from federal relief programs such as welfare, have strong morality and cultural values because of "traditional" Asian reverence for learning, and a natural inclination for hard work and thrift. The educational success of Asian American youth have become generalizations about all Asian immigrants who have overcome hardships such as poverty, political turmoil in their homelands, and limited English language proficiency (Osajima, 2000).

4. Nazli Kibria, *Becoming Asian American: Second Generation Chinese and Korean American Identities* (Baltimore: John Hopkins University Press, 2002).

5. Sylvia Hurtado, Milem, J. Clayton-Pedersen, A.R. & Allen, W. R. (1998). Enchancing Campus Climates for Racial/Ethnic Diversity: Educational Policy and Practice. *The Review of Higher Education*, 21(3), 279-302.

6. Pawan Dhingra. *Managing Multicultural Lives: Asian American Professionals and the Challenge of Multiple Identities* (Stanford, Stanford University Press, 2007), 240.

7. Yen L. Espiritu, *Asian American Panethnicity: Bridging Institutions and Identities* (Philadelphia: Temple University Press, 1992), 13.

8. Espiritu, 1992, 13.

9. Espiritu, 1992, 30.

10. Kibria, 107.

11. Michael Liu, Kim Geron, and Tracy Lai, *The Snake Dance of Asian American Activism* (Lanham, MD: Lexington Books, 2008), xvi.

12. Sucheng Chan, *Asian Americans: An Interpretive History* (Farmington Hills, MI: Twayne Publishers, 1991), i.

13. Daryl Maeda, *Chains of Babylon: The Rise of Asian America* (Minneapolis: University of Minnesota Press, 2009), x, 75.

14. Claire Jean Kim, "The Racial Triangulation of Asian Americans," *Politics and Society* 27 (2004): 988.

15. James Banks, "Multicultural Education: Historical Development, Dimensions, and Practice," *Review of Research in Education* 19 (1993): 5.

16. Carl Grant, "Multiculturalism, Race, and the Public Interest: Hanging on to Great-Great-Granddaddy's Legacy," in *Education Research in the Public Interest: Social Justice, Action, and Policy*, ed. Gloria Ladson-Billings and William F. Tate. (New York: Teachers College Press, 2006), 160.

17. Claire Kim, "The Racial Triangulation of Asian Americans," *Politics and Society* 27 (2004): 995.

18. Dawn Lee Tu, "Asian Pacific Heritage Month," in *Encyclopedia of Asian American Folklore*, ed. Jonathan Lee and Kathleen Nadeau (Westport, CT: Greenwood Press, 2010).

19. Michael Liu, Kim Geron, and Tracy Lai, *The Snake Dance of Asian American Activism* (Lanham, MD: Lexington Books, 2008), 148.

20. Liu, Geron, and Lai, 2008, 151.

21. Liu, Geron, and Lai, 2008, 153.

22. Liu, Geron, and Lai, 2008, 87.

23. Nazli Kibria, *Becoming Asian American: Second Generation Chinese and Korean American Identities* (Baltimore: John Hopkins University Press, 2002).

24. The call for disaggregated data has been a significant issue for researchers who study Asian Americans. Education scholars have advocated for disaggregation of Census data by testifying for various Senate Judicial committees. Most recently, students at UCLA launched the Count Me In! campaign in conjunction with State Assembly Member Ted Lieu's bill AB 295 to call for disaggregated data in California to mirror US Census categories. For more information on the Count Me In! campaign visit: http://www.universityofcalifornia.edu/news/article/16826. For more information on AB 295 visit: http://www.aacre.org/agenda/AB295/.

25. Keith Osajima, "Replenishing the Ranks: Raising Critical Consciousness Among Asian Americans," *Journal of Asian American Studies* 10 (2007): 60 (as cited in Osajima, 2007).

26. Names have been changed.

27. Steve Louie and Glenn Omatsu, *Asian Americans: The Movement and the Moment* (Los Angeles: UCLA Asian American Studies Center Press, 1994), 21.

28. Robert E. Terrill, *Malcom X: Inventing Racial Judgement* (East Lansing, MI: Michigan State University Press, 2004), 116.

29. Fetishization of the civil rights movement and Yellow Power activism is especially evident in the way students have responded to anti-Asian racism. For example, while conducting interviews with MLAs, Asian American students across the WCU system were mobilizing large rallies in response to a series of hate incidents that occurred at several campuses. The strategies that students of color took consisted of protests and then building occupations, where demands for change were made. Having gone through and given student activism training, I was familiar with these approaches as they were grounded in activist traditions of students who had participated in the Asian American movement. I asked MLAs why the preferred method of

expressing discontent was protest and building occupation. Patty explained that students drew strategies from what they learned in Asian American studies classes about prior student activism. Stephen, a senior-level administrator, believed that those histories were "the only well students [could] draw from." He concluded the lack of contemporary activist role models and the fact that current undergraduates did not come of age during a mass movement such as the civil rights era provided few examples of how to respond to these kinds of situations. Therefore, while the language of the Asian American and civil rights movements were being appropriated, so were the direct action methods of protest.

30. For a closer analysis of the historical content commonly addressed in PCNs, see Barbara S. Gaerlan (1999), "In the Court of the Sultan: Orientalism, Nationalism and Modernity in Philippine and Filipino American Dance" in *Journal of Asian American Studies* Vol. 2.3: 251-287.

31. Theodore S. Gonzalves, *The Day the Dancers Stayed: On Pilipino Cultural Nights* (Philadelphia: Temple University Press, 1997), 163-82.

32. Theodore S. Gonzalves, "Dancing into Oblivion: The Pilipino Cultural Night and the Narration of Contemporary Filipina/o America," *Kritika/Kultura* 6 (2005): 50.

33. Theodore S. Gonzalves, "Dancing into Oblivion: The Pilipino Cultural Night and the Narration of Contemporary Filipina/o America," *Kritika/Kultura* 6 (2005): 28.

34. Soo-Young Chin, Peter Feng, and Josephine D. Lee, "Asian American Cultural Production," *The Journal of Asian American Studies* 3 (2000): 273.

35. Liu, Geron, and Lai, 2008, 97.

36. Espiritu, 82.

37. Liu, Geron, and Lai, 2008, 100.

38. Liu, Geron, and Lai, 2008, 109.

39. Osajima, 60.

40. Michael Liu, Kim Geron, and Tracy Lai, *The Snake Dance of Asian American Activism* (Lanham, MD: Lexington Books, 2008), 120.

41. Daryl Maeda, *Chains of Babylon: The Rise of Asian America* (Minneapolis: University of Minnesota Press, 2009), 54.

42. Maeda, 2009, 156.

FOUR

Once Upon a Time in Chinese America

Literary Folktales in American Picture Books[1]

Lorraine Dong

FROM CHINESE FOLKLORE TO CHINESE AMERICAN FOLKLORE

Folklore originates from oral tradition that is transmitted from one generation to the next. In literature, folklore is manifested as mythology, legends, fairy tales, fables, ghostlore, nursery rhymes, songs, ballads, and more. Authorship is mostly unknown, but the stories are eventually collected and recorded by individuals, oftentimes known as literary folktales in their written form. Chinese folktales published in English for North American children are translations, retellings, or variants from China that have spread to America. Folklore from Chinese America with American origins has rarely been recorded, if at all. Nonetheless, a body of Chinese American literary folktales is beginning to surface for children.

The transmission of Chinese folklore in the English language began with American and European Sinologists who translated Chinese literature for an adult English-reading audience. Chinese poetry and novels with historical or fictional characters that became folklore legends among the Chinese for both adults and children have been translated for the study of Chinese literature.[2] However, these Chinese legends are nearly nonexistent in American children's literature. In addition, the body of works that evolved and retold for children or as popular literature and media in China has been largely ignored by Sinologists.

The story of Guan Yü or Guan Gong, known as the God of War and Literature, is the most popular historic-turned-folkloric legend in China.[3] His legend has crossed the Pacific Ocean to America, where he is often mentioned in Chinese American literature. In spite of this, his is a relatively unknown Chinese legend for American children because no popular picture book or animated film has been written/produced in English about him. On the other hand, the fifth/sixth dynasty poem about Mulan has been translated into many languages. However, there is hardly any study or acknowledgment of the many Mulan stories that evolved in China (in recent count, at least two plays, ten films, one opera script, three television series, eleven short stories, nine novels, and over twenty-two picture books and comic books[4]). All vary in characterization, plot development, and theme. A popular American audience took notice of Mulan's story in Maxine Hong Kingston's *Woman Warrior* (1976), a novel that is not written for elementary school-aged children.[5] Since then, at least nine picture books, two short stories, one novel, and five animated films have been published or produced about Mulan in the English language for youth, the prevailing version being Disney's 1998 animated feature, *Mulan*.[6] In the case of Mulan, her story is a Chinese legend known among American children as a result of transferences from Chinese to English and from poetry to animated film, but mainly because of aggressive marketing and commercialization on the part of Disney.

Chinese nursery rhymes and folktales were also translated and published in English before the 1900s.[7] Again, these works were not picture books for children and were meant more for an adult audience curious about the "Orient." Beginning in the mid-eighteenth century, Sunday School Literature recorded and preserved some Chinese children's songs and tales. One book published in 1916 by the American Presbyterian Mission contains not only stories and songs that teach Christian values to children in China, but also a section on Chinese nursery rhymes.[8] C. H. Kwock's translation published during the 1960s might be the first Chinese nursery rhyme picture book targeted for American children. While in the preface he acknowledges the scholars who have translated Chinese rhymes, he must have felt the need to introduce them to children as he clearly states that his "book is intended for children to read and enjoy, rather than for scholars to analyze."[9] It is a small book (3.5" x 5.5") containing forty poems and illustrations. Originating from the southern, southeastern, and southwestern parts of China, these rhymes are reflective of the Cantonese and southern Chinese origins of the early Chinese immigrants.

Around the world, children's first exposure to folklore generally comes from their elders and in school. Likewise, since the beginning of Chinese immigration, Chinese children growing up in American Chinatowns learned Chinese folklore not from Eurocentric America, but from their elders, community language schools, and Chinese operas/movies.

Variants of Chinese tales published in the United States have appeared since the early 1900s, some of which have become classic picture books, like *The Five Chinese Brothers* (1938) by Claire Huchet Bishop and illustrated by Kurt Wiese.[10] In the 1960s, English-language picture books of Chinese folklore and other stories arrived from China, most of them published by the Foreign Language Press of Peking (Beijing), thus providing American children with another source of Chinese storybooks in English. Gradually, American publishers increased their publication of picture book translations or variants of Chinese stories for children, while the importation of English-language children's books from China decreased.[11]

American versions of Chinese traditional literature have ranged from direct translations of the original stories to different retellings and variants of the stories. For instance, Ed Young wrote and illustrated *Cat and Rat: The Legend of the Chinese Zodiac* (1995) and David Bouchard wrote with Zhong-Yang Huang illustrating *The Great Race* (1997),[12] both of which narrate the Chinese "zodiac" animal story differently with their own themes that do not follow exact popular Chinese renditions of the story. There is also the example of American variants that are based on a Chinese folktale about identical brothers: the aforementioned *The Five Chinese Brothers*, *The Seven Chinese Brothers* (1990) by Margaret Mahy and illustrated by Jean and Mou-Sien Tseng, and *The Seven Chinese Sisters* (2003) by Kathy Tucker and illustrated by Grace Lin.[13]

"The Nightingale" (1843) by Hans Christian Andersen falls under a different category of Chinese folktales, those with a storyline that takes place in China with Chinese characters, yet not derived from China nor written by someone of Chinese descent. An American example of this imaginary type of Chinese story is the anonymous 1898 poem that describes how the top (the toy) derived its name from a Chinese man named Ah-Top.[14] Another American classic, *Tikki Tikki Tembo* (1968), is a Chinese folktale retold by Arlene Mosel and illustrated by Blair Lent to explain the origin of short Chinese names.[15] These stories are not folktales from or by the Chinese people, raising concerns among scholars and the community to any claim of them being Chinese folklore.

Tikki Tikki Tembo and *The Five Chinese Brothers*, in particular, are the most controversial picture books criticized over issues of authenticity and Orientalism. The former has been attacked for its cultural confusion or ignorance of what is Chinese and Japanese, and for its racist claims about Chinese names, "dismiss[ing] them as some type of gobbledygook."[16] Frank Chin calls the latter, "ugly little *The Five Chinese Brothers*," as he notes in a picture caption,

> Perhaps no single book has so insidiously stereotyped the Chinese as *The Five Chinese Brothers*. From this still popular "classic," published in 1938, generations of children have come to believe that all Asian and

people of Asian descent are a putrid yellow, have slits for eyes, look exactly alike and act the fool. *The Five Chinese Brothers* is an insult to Asian Americans the way *Little Black Sambo* is an insult to Black people.[17]

In an attempt to replicate the success that the African American community had with banning *Little Black Sambo*,[18] the Asian American community called for a ban in the 1960s-1970s of *The Five Chinese Brothers* for its inauthenticity and racist Orientalism. The movement failed, and the book, as well as *Tikki Tikki Tembo*, continues to be published and read to this day as a classic.

Chinese folklore in the English language purportedly has two goals: to promote good children's literature and to introduce American children to Chinese culture. The former highlights literature as art and the latter focuses more on literature's educational function for children. Complicating the appreciation of this literature are matters of authenticity and Orientalism, especially the former because folklore itself is derived from oral tradition where variants are inevitable in both oral and written form. To alleviate this issue of authenticity in the translation or rewriting of Chinese folklore, authors oftentimes provide an afterword or appendix to cite and identify the original Chinese source. Disney's *Mulan* is an example of how an appropriated Chinese legend raises questions of authenticity.[19] Most *Mulan* books that are based on the Disney version mention the original poem as the source, but in the film credits, Robert D. San Souci is given writing credit for the story.[20] This exacerbates the authenticity question when the animated feature is based on San Souci's interpretation of Mulan's story, which he claims is based on the original poem but with his own reading "between the lines."[21] Needless to say, the question of authenticity is totally ignored by writers when they provide no citation or source.[22] As for the issues of Orientalism and its effects on youth, that cannot be resolved with a simple "disclaimer" in an afterword or appendix, and the likelihood is slim that writers or publishers will explain or defend their works as "Oriental" to an audience of children.[23]

Compared to other non-Asian immigrant groups, Chinese Americans do not have a long historical past with its nineteenth-century beginnings in America; hence Chinese folklore has been the foundation of Chinese American folklore. This folklore with its roots and origins in China, like the Chinese people, has immigrated to America, transnational and integral to the ancestral and cultural maintenance of the Chinese American community. There are two types of Chinese American folklore in children's literature, the Chinese one that is passed down to American children by immigrant elders and a Chinese American one with its origins in America. Chinese folklore allows Chinese American children to see themselves as ethnic Chinese in the tradition of their ancestors, but in Chinese

American folklore they see themselves as distinctly Chinese American with their own American identity.

While folklore fulfills the function of pleasure or entertainment, it also contains themes that express basic values for children (and adults), such as honesty, love, friendship, humility, patience, hard work, and courage, and the belief that good triumphs over evil. Because folklore reveals the shared values and ethics of a community or society, Chinese American folklore provides an opportunity for readers to be familiar with the values and ethics of this particular community. For children, this folklore contains moral and social justice stories that portray Chinese Americans as ethnic minority people living in a mainstream Eurocentric society. Equally important is that this folklore affirms an American past for Chinese American children.

ONCE UPON A TIME IN CHINA

Chinese folklore in American children's literature is presented in two basic formulaic structures: one that begins directly with "Once upon a time in China" and one that begins with a Chinese elder who tells the story to American children with the phrase, "Once upon a time in China." In this paper, the former body of work is not considered Chinese American folklore but the latter is, where an immigrant elder educates Americans about China and transmits this to become part of America's multicultural folklore. This section focuses on picture books with characters that serve as Chinese storytellers in America. Such characters are wise cultural ambassadors with little or no character development. The elders provide cultural maintenance for American-born Chinese children who have so-called lost their roots. However, this storyteller motif becomes troublesome when the authoritative character is passing down inauthentic Chinese folklore to Chinese American children in search of understanding their ancestral heritage, as well as all American children in need of understanding China.

Chinese holidays or festivals provide the best opportunity for the transmission of Chinese folklore to America's youth. Elders usually describe the holidays based on reminiscences of their younger days in China, followed by the origins of the holiday. Functioning as cultural ambassadors, these picture books apply very few literary techniques, and have minimal characterization and plot development. Prime examples are the numerous storybooks on Chinese New Year where the characters go through the motions of celebrating the holiday to explain the "how," "what," and "why" of New Year. Two Mid-Autumn Moon Festival books also illustrate this point. In *Mr. Fong's Toy Shop* (1978), written and illustrated by Leo Politi, the writer uses one page to narrate the story of the Moon Goddess and a short paragraph to describe the Yuan dynasty origin of the moon cake.[24] These folklore snippets function to present information about the Moon Festival, as well as to demonstrate the author's level of research in writing on the topic. The bulk of the story has Mr. Fong introducing Chinese festival activities (e.g., juggling, shadow plays, and puppets) to the children of Los Angeles Chinatown. He expresses pride every time the Chinese American children finish a cultural activity, like the lantern parade or the ribbon dance. In-depth characterization and plot development are lacking, making this more an informational or resource book about Chinese culture than a literary piece of writing. In a recent Moon Festival picture book written and illustrated by Grace Lin, *Thanking the Moon: Celebrating the Mid-Autumn Moon Festival* (2010), the reader follows a Chinese American family on the evening of the festival with no particular plot, except to show family togetherness and what families do on Moon Festival. It is only in the afterword that there is a one-sentence reference to the Moon Goddess.[25]

Picture books are beginning to use Chinese holidays as a setting to highlight themes that do not focus on retelling a holiday-related folklore. For example, in *This Next New Year* (2000), Janet S. Wong writes on the theme of hope and a second chance by describing all the things the part Chinese, part Korean narrator needs to do in order to have good luck in the new year.[26] In Karen Chinn's *Sam and the Lucky Money* (1995), Sam has a difficult decision to make: how to spend his Chinese New Year lucky money. In the end, he gives it to a homeless man in Chinatown, focusing on the story's theme of giving and sharing.[27] Among the Moon Festival picture books, Hoong Yee Lee Kraukauer also does not mention any folklore when she describes how her Chinese American family celebrates the Moon Festival in *Rabbit Mooncakes* (1994).[28] In this book, the holiday provides the setting to the main theme of overcoming fear and a lack of confidence. In *The Moon Lady* (1992) written by Amy Tan and illustrated by Gretchen Schields, a grandmother tells two granddaughters how she almost drowned and was separated from her family during the Moon Festival in China.[29] There are elaborate descriptions of what a well-to-do Chinese family does during the holiday and one page is devoted to the Moon Lady/Goddess folktale, which is presented in the format of a shadow play. The theme in Tan's picture book is not focused on Moon Festival folklore, but on the consequences faced by a little girl who is selfish and self-centered. Again, the holiday serves merely as a backdrop for the story's main theme.

Three holiday-themed picture books written by David Bouchard and illustrated by Zhong-Yang Huang portray grandmothers introducing Chinese holidays to American children in a "once upon a time" format; these books belong to Brouchard's Chinese Legends series. The first publication, *The Great Race*, deals with the origin of the twelve Chinese zodiac animals.[30] At the beginning of the book, the grandmother notices that her granddaughter has placed the zodiac animals in the wrong order and says to her, "Remember, it is not who won [the race] that matters. It is the order in which they placed that is most important. Listen carefully so that you can come to understand why each animal placed where it did."[31] And thus she begins her story from "Long ago," when the Great Buddha summons twelve animals that he has selected for a race. They are to race toward a "city of perpetual caring, peace, and never-ending opportunity for all people," not to see who would be first and greatest or last and weakest, but to "determine the order of [their] appearance for all matters of earthly importance."[32] The rat reaches the city first because he is "cunning" and "crafty,"[33] and the "hardworking" ox comes in second because he is more concerned about the rat than himself.[34] The grandmother concludes, "a weary ox entered the Jade City with only the welfare of a small rat on his mind. And in so doing he sealed his fate for all time as the second of the twelve animals in the zodiac."[35] Bouchard's version of the folktale with its Buddhist motif differs from a majority of the Chinese zodiac folktales, which focus on the competition among the animals to win the race. His story does not end by highlighting the competition of who finishes as number one, but on why there is a certain order in life.[36]

Bouchard's next book of Chinese Legends is on the origin of *nian* or "year." In *The Dragon New Year* (1999), a Chinese grandmother calms her granddaughter's fear of firecrackers and cymbal sounds with the story of why loud sounds are necessary for the new year: A hungry sea dragon named "Year" appears annually to eat the villagers. One year, it eats a young fisherman and Buddha helps the mother to drive Year away permanently by using fire and loud banging sounds. The end of the book brings the reader back to the present, where the granddaughter is asleep and the grandmother is "content, knowing that once again she had shared this important story—a story that this child would someday share with her own granddaughter."[37]

In *The Mermaid's Muse* (2000), the third of his Chinese Legends series, Bouchard introduces the reader to the origin story of another holiday, Duan Wu or the Dragon Boat Festival. The picture book begins with a grandmother saying to her grandson that he should not be afraid of the dragon boat that she has given him for his birthday: "Listen carefully, and take care never to forget this story. It is yours to pass on to your grandchild."[38] In this book, Qu Yuan (ca. 340-278 BC), a loyal advisor to the King of Chu, is unjustly banished to a faraway island. A sea dragon is intrigued by Qu Yuan and transforms herself into a mermaid. The two become very close and Qu Yuan decides to live with her at the bottom of the sea. But the villagers want to rescue him from the "monster," throwing *zongzi* (rice balls), spears, and arrows at the sea dragon. As the sea dragon lays dying, Qu Yuan turns into a dragon, and, together, the two fly off into the "fading sun."[39] One of the villagers, who is the little boy's grandfather's great-grandfather, carves a dragon boat in honor of Qu Yuan. This is Bouchard's origin story of the Dragon Boat Festival, which contains a mermaid and a romantic theme, in addition to the traditional Chinese theme of patriotism usually associated with Qu Yuan's story.

The three Chinese legends, as retold by Bouchard, convey themes of fear and purpose, but raise questions about authenticity. *The Great Race* does not cite a Chinese source, except that the grandmother is passing down "just one of many stories of how [the zodiac animals] came to place in the order that we know them."[40] In *The Dragon New Year*, Bouchard calls his "just-so" story as one way of "retelling how the Chinese New Year celebrations came to be" and that the "real origins of the festival are shrouded in the mists of time."[41] He concludes that "it is just possible that, one year, back in the mists of time, the celebration of the Chinese New Year began just as I have told it."[42] Both stories have a Buddha character that is not found among popular New Year folktales in China. In the afterword of *The Mermaid's Muse*, Bouchard provides some accurate account of the historical origin of the Dragon Boat Festival, but suspecting that the sea dragon/mermaid character in his story might raise questions among the Chinese, he concludes, "Over the centuries, Qu Yuan's life became wrapped in legend. It became entwined with stories of the water dragon. . . . As for the mermaid . . . well, the sea holds *some* secrets that live only in legends . . . or do they?"[43] The last four words in the title of Bouchard's afterword indicate to the reader his stand on the authenticity of his folktale: "This Legend as I Tell It Is *Rooted in the Truth*" (emphasis added).

The storyteller motif provides a link between China and America through an elder transmitting Chinese folklore for Americans to embrace. The aim of the grandmother characters in Bouchard's books is to pass down this folklore to the youth in order to ensure cultural maintenance and values of family and community. Bouchard's artistic freedom to create a Chinese variant from his imagination is problematic specifically for folklore when the equally important necessity for folkloric authenticity is put aside for art's sake. His grandmother characters have passed down questionable folklore to future generations of Americans in search of knowledge and future generations of Chinese Americans who do not have an accessible and comparative means of knowing their ancestral heritage. Fortunately, not all elder characters in children's literature transmit inauthentic Chinese folklore and traditions.

ONCE UPON A TIME IN AMERICA

Folkloric elements can be found in stories that have been published for children to historically explain the origins or beginnings of Chinese America in both past and present time settings.[44] If biographical picture books about historical personages of legendary stature are included as folklore, then Ruthanne Lum McCunn's *Pie Biter* (1983) about a Chinese

American laborer named Hoi, who introduced the American pie to China;[45] Allen Say's *El Chino* (1996) about Arizona-born Bong Way "Billy" Wong, who became Spain's first matador of Chinese descent;[46] Marissa Moss's *Sky High* (2009) about World War II aviator Maggie Gee from Berkeley;[47] Ken Mochizuki's *Be Water, My Friend* (2006) about the early years of San Francisco-born Bruce Lee before his martial arts and acting days;[48] and Paula Yoo's *Shining Star* (2009) about Los Angeles-born Anna May Wong, who was Hollywood's first major Chinese American actress, would fit under this category.[49] There is also *Dragon Parade* (1993) by Steven A. Chin and illustrated by Mou-Sien Tseng, a picture book that tells the origins of the first Chinese New Year celebration and parade in America as started by Norman Ah Sing.[50] However, these stories are more biographical and historical in nature, so they will not be discussed in this paper as folklore or folktale.

The earliest known children's literature with Chinese American characters in the genre of literary folktale is *Sing a Song O'Six Taels*, published approximately in late nineteenth-early twentieth century.[51] It contains twelve Mother Goose nursery rhyme variants that clearly reflect the anti-Chinese sentiment of the time. All the characters are drawn with yellow-skinned, animal-like facial features and are referred to as a "Chinaman" or "chink." They are demonized as rodent-eaters, laundry workers, and addicts, and as people with "funny" names:

> A washeeman Chinese
> Ah Chew is his name
> You simply sneeze.
> To pronounce the same. [9]

Below are sample variants of Mother Goose nursery rhymes from the book:

"Sing a Song of Sixpence" variant:

> Sing a song o'six taels
> Pocket full o' rice
> John is off to market
> To get a dozen mice. [2]

John is drawn as a Chinese American man wearing a fedora hat with his queue flying behind him.

"Little Jack Horner" variant:

> Little J. Horner
> Sat in a corner
> Eating a rodent pie.
> He said "this is rummy
> I've a pain in my tummy,
> Really I don't know why!" [3]

Little J. Horner is clutching his stomach with his animated queue in the air, while a mouse is escaping and running away from the open pie, an American baked dish.

"Old King Cole" variant:

> Old Chang Kole
> Was a merry old soul
> A writer of jokes was he
> He would smoke his hop
> And in dreams he'd stop
> And write of things he'd see. [7]

Old Chang Kole is lying down on his side, writing nonsensical Chinese words with a brush in one hand and smoking an opium pipe with the other.

Such negative depictions contribute to the highly charged anti-Chinese movement of the time and were not the product of the Chinese American community.

The Prince and the Li Hing Mui (1998) by Sandi Takayama and illustrated by Esther Szegedy is another variant.[52] This is a fairy tale variant of Hans Christian Andersen's "The Princess and the Pea" (1835). In the original story, a prince searches for a real princess who must pass the princess test by being able to feel a pea under twenty featherbeds and twenty mattresses. Takayama's story takes place on "an island in the middle of the ocean" with a princess in search of a real prince.[53] The princess is nicknamed Princess Li Hing Mui because she loves eating Chinese preserved plums known as *li hing mui*, the Zhongshan dialectal pronunciation of *lüxing mei*. Li hing mui is literally translated as "travel plums," eaten by Cantonese/Zhongshan immigrants to alleviate motion sickness during their travels between China and America.[54] The prince turns out to be a young man who also loves li hing mui and whose *popo* (grandmother) makes the best li hing mui on the island. He passes the test because he can feel a li hing mui buried under twenty featherbeds and twenty mattresses. Unlike Andersen's theme that true nobility is not determined by birth alone, but also by one's physical sensitivity, Takayama's story shows that true nobility requires both physical sensitivity and good manners. Andersen's European princess complains that the pea prevented her from having a good sleep, whereas Takayama's Chinese American prince does not complain and sleeps on the bare floor instead of bothering or offending his gracious hosts, a reflection of Chinese expectations that royalty must also be benevolent and respectful of their subjects.

Variants of folktales with Chinese American characters are few in number; instead, there are more "original" literary folktales about Chinese America. *The Story of Chinaman's Hat* (1990), written and illustrated by Dean Howell, attempts at folklore by explaining the origin of Chinaman's Hat, a tiny Hawaiian island located east of O'ahu. The story begins with Lick Bean who is from Shin Hway (a dialectal pronunciation of Xinhui in the Guangdong province of China).[55] He receives a bamboo hat from a girl named Mei Mei, and is ashamed that he might not be able to impress her because he is so tiny. Mr. Fong, the herbalist, gives Lick Bean a box of magic tea powder to help him grow taller. But the latter consumes the entire box in one gulp and instantly becomes a giant. He falls asleep and floats on the ocean all the way to Hawai'i, where a friendly king and people welcome the giant Lick Bean. When Lick Bean gives Mei Mei's hat to the king, the people make him a giant bowl, chopsticks, and another hat. After the effects of the tea wear off and Lick Bean returns to his normal size, the giant hat is left floating in the ocean and becomes the island of Chinaman's Hat. By chance, a boat with Mr. Fong passes by and takes Lick Bean back to China, where Mei Mei says to him at the end of the story that size is not important and gives him a new hat.

The Story of Chinaman's Hat contains themes about home, self-esteem, the necessity to patiently follow and listen to instructions, and that size does not matter. However, it is not an origin story from China or from the Chinese American or Hawaiian community; in fact, no one in China or Xinhui heard of Lick Bean when this book was translated to the people of Xinhui by Ou Jilin in 2000.[56] Howell has admitted in MySpace that the story is his own literary creation,[57] so this folktale is written from a perspective that is not Chinese, Chinese American, or Hawaiian, which might explain why the word "Chinaman" is not questioned, but accepted as is. In short, this folktale is not from the Chinese, Chinese American, or Hawaiian community.

One form of folklore that barely exists in children's literature is Chinese American ghostlore. Ghost stories lead a child's imagination and senses to the world of the unknown. For Chinese Americans, ghost stories are additionally significant because ghosts reflect a community or society with a past or history in America. Paul Yee has written a ghost story about a Chinese immigrant boy who befriends a white American boy ghost in the attic. In this example, the ghost does not affirm a Chinese American past, but a past for white America.[58] However, there are two literary ghost stories that do affirm Chinese America's historical past. They are set in the 1860s railroad-building days: *The Iron Moonhunter* (1977) by Kathleen Chang and *Ghost Train* (1996) by Paul Yee and illustrated by Harvey Chan.[59] The former story begins "[m]ore than a hundred years ago" (3) and the latter begins with "[o]ne day long ago" ([5]).

The three main characters in *The Iron Moonhunter* are descendants of Kwan Kung (Guan Gong): Kwan Ming, Kwan Cheong, and Kwan Hop.[60] While on the job building the railroad, Kwan Hop dies, falling two thousand feet from a cliff, and Kwan Cheong is buried alive in a cave-in. Haunted by the ghosts of all the dead Chinese railroad workers, Kwan Ming and the other railroad workers gather discarded train parts to build a train in the shape of a dragon. The train is named Iron Moonhunter and it searches at night for the lost souls of Chinese ghosts in order to provide them with a home on the train.

The ghosts of railroad workers in *Ghost Train* also find home via a train. Choon-yi is left behind in China when her father goes to America, who then dies in an avalanche while working on the railroad. Appearing in a dream, he instructs her to go to America, where she continues to see him in her dreams. This time the father wants her to paint a train.[61] While riding on a train to experience it firsthand, she hears moans of anguish. The train appears in another dream with her father and other workers sitting inside and talking about their hardships, and how they long to go home. When Choon-yi wakes up, she sees faces on every window of the train that she had painted earlier, including her father's. She takes the painting back to China and burns it on top of a hill. Now all the lost souls are home and can rest in peace.

According to Chang,

> *The Iron Moonhunter* is based on an old legend that still circulates in Chinese America: that the Chinese American railroaders built a railroad of their own while they were building the Central Pacific Railroad. Perhaps it's a fairy tale our grandparents concocted so we would think of the bitter past with wonder and pride; perhaps it's an explanation of abandoned railroad tracks in the Sierras that seem to lead nowhere; and perhaps it's true.[62]

There is no similar source statement in Yee's book. Nevertheless, both ghost stories have the same result of affirming the heroic history of the Chinese building America's railroads. Their themes include the discriminatory injustice faced by the Chinese American railroad workers of the 1860s and the universal need for home, themes arising not from a Chinese experience, but from a distinct Chinese American experience.

Similarly, the Qing Ming Festival provides an occasion for elders to narrate the heroic origins of Chinese American families. Folkloric elements are found in two picture books with a Qing Ming setting that begins with an elder informing a child about the festival and its purpose—to honor and respect one's ancestors. Unlike the storytellers in the previous section who teach the audience about the origins of Chinese holidays and customs, the storytellers in these Qing Ming holiday stories inform the audience additionally about a Chinese American family's roots in the United States. Instead of retelling Chinese folklore that begins a long time ago about the Chinese in China, the elder storyteller in each story introduces a tale of Chinese American origin that begins a long time ago with the arrival of the family's first ancestors in America.

During the 1960s-1970s, the Chinese Bilingual Pilot Project, ESEA, Title VII, began a series of bilingual booklets to recognize major Chinese festivals celebrated by the Chinese in America. Among their publications is Gordon Lew's *The Story of Ching-Ming*. This story describes how Qing Ming was celebrated in 1950s-1960s San Francisco when family/clan associations chartered buses to take their members to the cemetery. Since remembering one's ancestors is the main purpose of Qing Ming, it is natural for the father of Little Ming to talk about Grandpa who "came to America many many years ago" and worked very hard, twelve to fourteen hours a day.[63]

Coolies (2001) by Yin and illustrated by Chris Soentpiet is a more elaborate origin story of ancestors arriving in America. The picture book begins with the narrator asking his grandmother why they are bowing to a bowl of oranges to honor their ancestors.[64] The grandmother proceeds in formulaic fashion with the phrase, "[a] long, long time ago in China." She explains that their ancestors were very poor and in order to support the family, they sent two brothers to America, both of whom worked for the Central Pacific Railroad Company.[65] The poor working conditions and the mistreatment endured by the Chinese railroad workers are vividly described and illustrated. In this picture book, Qing Ming provides a cultural setting for the real themes of the story, which are similar to those of *Ghost Train*—the injustice suffered by the Chinese railroad workers and the importance of family, the latter of which is closely tied to the Qing Ming Festival. The story concludes with grandmother and grandson burning paper money to make their "ancestors rich in the spirit world forever."[66]

Qing Ming opens the door for readers to talk about family ancestors and the origins of a Chinese American family. Usually, stories depict the Chinese coming to America in order to support the family in China, yet always yearning to return and reunite with their families. However, these two Qing Ming stories differ in their concept of where home is located. Despite hardship and injustice, both stories conclude that America is home. Instead of saving money for the family in China, money is saved for the family in America. Little Ming's father in *The Story of Ching-Ming* says Grandpa worked hard "in order to save money to bring us over here [America]."[67] Likewise, in the end of *Coolies*, Wong's letter to his mother says, "We are hopeful and excited that soon we shall be reunited with you and our brothers here in America, the land of opportunity," and he sends money to his mother for the family to join the brothers in America.[68] This shift in focus of locality for home from China to America establishes Chinese roots in America.

Recently in children's literature, two origin fairy tales have emerged to explain the existence of a new, growing population of Chinese Americans, that of transnational adoptees. These stories contain elements of the fantastic to describe the beginnings of two transnational adoption families in which Chinese girls have been adopted by white American couples.[69] One actually uses the term "fairy tale" in its subtitle: *The Red Thread: An Adoption Fairy Tale* (2007), written and illustrated by Grace

Lin.[70] The other uses simply the word "tale": *Sweet Moon Baby: An Adoption Tale* (2010), written by Karen Henry Clark and illustrated by Patrice Barton.[71]

The Red Thread begins with a Chinese girl wearing a crown and asking two white adults to read a storybook with a front cover that is identical to the front cover of *The Red Thread*. The first page of the girl's book begins in formulaic fairy tale tradition: "Once a king and queen ruled over a magnificent kingdom."[72] The white king and queen have an inexplicable pain in their hearts. An old peddler gives them a pair of magical glasses and they see that a red thread is pulling at each of them. They follow their threads and arrive in a Chinese village where the red threads are tied to each of the two feet of a Chinese baby girl. The king and queen take the girl back to their castle and she becomes a princess. On the last page of the picture book, the two white adults reading the book are now wearing crowns on their heads also and they say, "Yes, it's our favorite story, too."[73]

Rather than portraying a formulaic Chinese storytelling elder, *The Red Thread* has white, younger American elders reading a fairy tale to a Chinese American youth. The storytellers are still related, this time as the girl's adoptive parents. It is common in picture books for the adoptive parents to explain where their adopted child comes from, and why and how they love the child as much as his/her birth parents. In this fairy tale with its magical elements, love is described accordingly, as magical and inexplicable: "They [the king and queen] never felt the pain in their hearts again. Instead, they were filled with joy and happiness. They never found out how the red thread had connected them to their daughter, but they knew *why*. And that was all that mattered."[74] Here, Lin adds a Chinese literary motif to the fairy tale by using the red thread to symbolize a love connection. In the preface, Lin writes, "There is an ancient Chinese belief that an invisible, unbreakable red thread connects all those who are destined to be together."[75] In addition to the magic of love, destiny is what created and brought together this adoptive family, and that explains the origin of this particular Chinese baby girl who is adopted by white American parents.

In *Sweet Moon Baby*, the tale begins with, "On a summer night in China," where "a baby girl was born."[76] Although the Chinese parents love their daughter, they have to give her up because they cannot provide for her. They place the baby in a basket on a river, to be watched over by the moon. The baby sleeps, as a turtle, a peacock, a monkey, a panda, and three golden fish protect and guide her along a fantastic journey. She finally opens her eyes when a white couple finds her among water lilies and takes her home. At the end, the now-grown little girl is sleeping in her bedroom with a picture on the wall of her white parents and herself. She has three stuffed animals—a turtle, a monkey, and a panda—and on her nightstand are a peacock feather and a goldfish. Meanwhile, the moon is watching her through the bedroom window.[77]

In China, the moon is associated with family, as celebrated during the Moon Festival when families traditionally gather together to admire the full moon. Clark uses the moon motif effectively in *Sweet Moon Baby* to symbolize the strong presence of family throughout the girl's life, from the beginning with the Chinese parents holding the baby up to the moon, to the moon looking over the baby during the journey and guiding her white parents to her, and, finally in the end, with the moon watching over the sleeping little girl. The moon also dominates in the inside front and back cover illustrations of the book: in the inside front cover, the moon hovers over a Chinese landscape with bamboo and mountains but no human presence, while the inside back cover depicts the white parents and Chinese daughter standing alongside a river and looking at the moon, with the implication that they are facing China.

Like many picture books about adoptions, the theme in these two fantasy stories focuses mainly on love, family, and home. They are meant to help children realize that both birth and adoptive parents love their children. *The Red Thread* and *Sweet Moon Baby* use a folkloric and fantastical presentation to explain the origins of, or reasons behind, a transnational adoption from the white parents' perspective. Unfortunately, these adoption fairy tales, as well as adoption stories with animal characters using panda bears to represent Chinese adoptees,[78] simplify and ignore the many complex issues of transnational adoptions.

With the exception of the two variants mentioned in the beginning of this section, Chinese American literary folktales are heavily focused on origins and the historical past, some of which can also be classified as realistic or historical fiction. These stories, based in America, provide a sense of belonging, which is significant for Chinese American youth in search of permanency and roots. Also of note is that these stories do not emphasize only origin and history, they also include universal themes of home, family, and social justice. However, the issue of authenticity arises when all these folktales are creations of the individual and not of the community.

ONCE UPON A TIME IN CHINESE AMERICA

Folklore that originated from China is the ancestral heritage of Chinese America. The American writers and Chinese storyteller characters in picture books that serve as cultural ambassadors and transmitters of this folklore have varying degrees of authenticity in their transference of Chinese folklore. This complicates the dilemma of an America that is already lacking in knowledge about other cultures and people, and of a Chinese America that is in need of accurately learning about its ancestral heritage.

Published Chinese American literary folktales are rooted on unique American experiences and do not appear to derive from the oral tradition of the community. The only exception might be Chang's claim in *The Iron Moonhunter*, which requires further verification. For the most part, these folktales are the individual creations of various American writers. They fulfill some functions of folklore as they explore themes of origins, home, family, and social justice. However, because they are literary folktales with doubtful oral community-based origins, questions arise as to how widespread and common these folktales are in the Chinese American community, and whether the values expressed in these stories are from the community or from the imagination of an individual. Two issues of inauthenticity arise: "fake" or inauthentic Chinese folklore transmitted by the elder characters and "fake" or inauthentic Chinese American folklore constructed purely from the imagination of the writers. For the former, the concern is the extent to which the Chinese folklore has deviated from the original source folklore. For the latter, additional concerns are that this body of imagined folklore has yet to be proven as authentic to and coming from the people and community of Chinese America, and whether or not the various social and moral values expressed in these Chinese American literary folktales are authentic to the social and moral values of the community that they are representing.

The necessity for authenticity in folklore is different from that for creative stories. Folklore serves as source material to learn about communities specifically or the world in general. Folklore variants and literary folktales are the retelling of stories that reflect the oral tradition of a community or nation. Because of this, it is problematic to imagine a folklore or literary folktale, misrepresent it as deriving from an oral tradition, and then apply the social and moral values expressed in that folklore to an analysis of the people it claims to represent. It is not enough to simply say, "it is just possible that . . . [this is] just as I have told it." Instead of constructing imaginary Chinese American folklore, it is necessary and now possible for children's book writers and illustrators to create picture books based on the actual oral folklore traditions of Chinese America, some of which have already begun to be gathered, recorded, and studied.[79] Until then, the two types of literary folktales discussed here will serve as the beginning of Chinese American folklore in American picture books.

NOTES

1. This is a revised and updated version of an earlier publication: Lorraine Dong, "Once Upon a Time in Chinese America: Chinese American Literary Folklore in Children's Picture Books," *Asian American Folklore: Passages and Practices*, spec. issue of *Amerasia Journal* 39.2 (2013): 48-70. Reprinted with permission from UCLA Asian

American Studies Center Press. Henceforth, "America" will refer specifically to the United States and Canada.

2. The most popular of these novels are *Sanguo yanyi* [*Romance of the Three Kingdoms*] by Luo Guanzhong (14th century), *Shuihu zhuan* [*Water Margin*] by Shi Nai'an (14th century), and *Xiyou ji* [*Journey to the West*] by Wu Cheng'en (16th century).

3. Guan Yü's biography and popular story can be found in *Sanguozhi* by Chen Shou (3rd century) and *Sanguo yanyi* by Luo Guanzhong (14th century), respectively. The two works are popularly translated as *Records of the Three Kingdoms* and *Romance of the Three Kingdoms*, respectively. Three Kingdoms refers to a historical time period in China, AD 220-280.

4. This book count and the one following are based on the author's personal Mulan collection and library.

5. Maxine Hong Kingston, *The Woman Warrior: Memoirs of a Girlhood among Ghosts* (New York: Alfred A. Knopf, 1976).

6. *Mulan*, Tony Bancroft and Barry Cook, dir., Disney, 1998.

7. E.g., Guido Vitale, *Pekinese Rhymes, Chinese Folklore* (Peking: Pei-t'ang Press, 1896) and Isaac Taylor Headland, *Chinese Mother Goose Rhymes* (New York, Chicago, and Toronto: Fleming H. Revell Co., 1900).

8. Janie Rice Bigelow, *Songs and Games for Little Children in the Kindergarten School and Home (Cantonese Colloquial)* (Canton, China: American Presbyterian Mission, 1916).

9. C. H. Kwock, *Chinese Mother Goose: A Collection of Chinese Nursery Rhymes* (San Francisco: Jade Mountain Press, ca. 1960s). This book has a self-publication "look" that is common among many ethnic minority books that were self-published or community-published during the 1960s and 1970s, due to rejection from mainstream publishers.

10. Claire Huchet Bishop, *The Five Chinese Brothers*, illus. Kurt Wiese (New York: Scholastic Book Services, c. 1938).

11. Mingshui Cai has comprehensively studied fifty-one Chinese folktales in English-language children's picture books; see Mingshui Cai, "Images of Chinese and Chinese Americans Mirrored in Picture Books," *Children's Literature in Education* 25.3 (1994): 169-191.

12. Ed Young, *Cat and Rat: The Legend of the Chinese Zodiac* (New York: Henry Holt & Co., 1995); David Bouchard, *The Great Race*, illus. Zhong-Yang Huang (Vancouver: Raincoast Books, 1997).

13. Margaret Mahy, *The Seven Chinese Brothers*, illus. Jean and Mou-sien Tseng (New York: Scholastic, 1990); Kathy Tucker, *The Seven Chinese Sisters*, illus. Grace Lin (Morton Grove, IL: Albert Whitman & Co., 2003). The author grew up in San Francisco Chinatown with popular Chinese stories and movies based on ten Chinese brothers.

14. "Ah Top," *Childhood's Golden Days*, Bright Eyes Series No. 210 (Chicago and New York: M.A. Donohue & Co., 1898).

15. Arlene Mosel, *Tikki Tikki Tembo*, illus. Blair Lent (New York: Holt, Rinehart & Winston, 1968).

16. Sandra Yamate, "Asian Pacific American Children's Literature: Expanding Perceptions about Who Americans Are," *Using Multiethnic Literature in the K-8 Classroom*, ed. Violet J. Harris (Norwood, MA: Christopher-Gordon Publishers, Inc., 1997): 117.

17. Frank Chin, "Where I'm Coming From: A Noted Chinese American Playwright's Thoughts on Asian Americans in U.S. Literature," *The Portrayal of Asian Americans in Children's Books*, spec. issue of *Interrracial Books for Children Bulletin* 7.2-3 (1976): 24-25. For another early critique of the book, see Albert V. Schwartz, "The Five Chinese Brothers: Time to Retire," *Interracial Books for Children Bulletin* 8.3 (1977): 3-7.

18. Helen Bannerman, *Little Black Sambo* (London: Grant Richards, 1899).

19. There is much debate over the authenticity, Orientalism, and appropriation of Mulan's story by Disney. See Lorraine Dong, "Mulan Leaves China," Jeffery Paul Chan, et al., eds., *At 40: Asian American Studies @ San Francisco State* (San Francisco: Asian American Studies, San Francisco State University, 2009), and Lan Dong, *Mulan's*

Legend and Legacy in China and the United States (Philadelphia: Temple University Press, 2010).

20. See "Full Cast and Crew for *Mulan*," *Mulan* (1998), available online at: www. imdb.com/title/H0120762. Although San Souci is given story credit, but not screenplay credit, one can see parallel if not identical elements between Disney's *Mulan* and San Souci's *Fa Mulan*, that do not exist in popular Chinese versions of Mulan's story.

21. Robert D. San Souci, "Author's Note," *Fa Mulan*, illus. Jean and Mou-Sien Tseng (New York: Hyperion Books for Children, 1998): [30]. In this situation, Disney's version is not based on any Chinese version, but a version created by a non-Chinese individual who is reading "between the lines." Hereafter, page numbers in books without pagination are indicated by brackets.

22. For a comprehensive discussion on authenticity and citing sources in picture books, see Betsy Hearne, "Cite the Source: Reducing Cultural Chaos in Picture Books, Part One," *School Library Journal* (July 1993): 22-27; Betsy Hearne, "Respect the Source: Reducing Cultural Chaos in Pictures Books, Part Two," *School Library Journal* (August 1993): 33-37.

23. For a more thorough discussion of the importance (or not) of authenticity in children's literature, see Dana L. Fox and Kathy G. Short, eds., *Stories Matter: The Complexity of Cultural Authenticity in Children's Literature* (Urbana, IL: National Council of Teachers of English, 2003). This volume contains twenty-one well written articles on the subject of authenticity by leading scholars in the field of children's literature.

24. Leo Politi, *Mr. Fong's Toy Shop* (New York: Charles Scribner's Sons, c. 1978): [8], [18].

25. Grace Lin, *Thanking the Moon: Celebrating the Mid-Autumn Moon Festival* (New York: Alfred A. Knopf, 2010).

26. Janet S. Wong, *This Next New Year*, illus. Yangsook Choi (New York: Frances Foster Books, 2000).

27. Karen Chinn, *Sam and the Lucky Money*, illus. Cornelius Van Wright and Ying-Hwa Hu (New York: Lee & Low Books Inc., 1995).

28. Hoong Yee Lee Krakauer, *Rabbit Mooncakes* (Boston: Little, Brown and Company, 1994).

29. Amy Tan, *The Moon Lady*, illus. Gretchen Schields (New York: Macmillan, 1992). This picture book was adapted from a chapter in Amy Tan's 1989 novel *The Joy Luck Club*.

30. David Bouchard, "The Chinese Zodiac," *The Great Race*, illus. Zhong-Yang Huang (Vancouver: Raincoast Books, 1977): [30].

31. Bouchard, *The Great Race* [5].

32. Bouchard, *The Great Race* [7].

33. Bouchard, *The Great Race* [5].

34. Bouchard, *The Great Race* [24].

35. Bouchard, *The Great Race* [26].

36. In Ed Young's *Cat and Rat: The Legend of the Chinese Zodiac*, the emperor holds a race among all the animals in the land. This is an origin story that functions to answer two questions: how the ranking order of the twelve animals came about, and why cats and rats do not get along. *Cat and Rat* begins with the close friendship between a cat and rat, but ends with the two becoming bitter enemies when the rat wins first place and the cat does not even rank among the top twelve. Competition among the animals is one of the main themes in this Chinese American variant of the folklore.

37. David Bouchard, *The Dragon New Year: A Chinese Legend*, illus. Zhong-Yang Huang (Atlanta: Peachtree Publishers, 1999) [29].

38. David Bouchard, *The Mermaid's Muse: The Legend of the Dragon Boats*, illus. Zhong-Yang Huang (Vancouver: Raincoast Books, 2000) [5].

39. Bouchard, *The Mermaid's Muse* [27].

40. Bouchard, *The Great Race* [30].

41. Bouchard, "The Buddha, the Dragon, and the New Year," *The Dragon New Year* [30].

42. Bouchard, *The Dragon New Year* [31].

43. Bouchard, "This Legend as I Tell It Is Rooted in the Truth," *The Mermaid's Muse* [32].

44. Not quite fitting the definition of folktale is an interesting series of books entitled "Tales from the Chinese Zodiac" by Oliver Chin. The first volume of the series began in 2006 with *The Year of the Dog*, followed in subsequent years by *The Year of the Pig*, *The Year of the Rat*, *The Year of the Ox*, *The Year of the Tiger*, *The Year of the Dragon*, *The Year of the Snake*, and *The Year of the Horse*. Each story begins with the birth of a baby dog, pig, rat, ox, tiger, dragon, snake, and horse, respectively, to correspond to the zodiac year, and through the animal's experiences with a Chinese boy or girl, the reader is informed of values associated with a particular zodiac animal. The place setting for these stories is ambiguous, yet the time setting is clearly contemporary as the Chinese characters are dressed in contemporary clothes. See Oliver Chin, *The Year of the Dog*, illus. Miah Alcorn (San Francisco: Immedium, 2006); *The Year of the Pig*, illus. Miah Alcorn (San Francisco: Immedium, 2007); *The Year of the Rat*, illus. Miah Alcorn (San Francisco: Immedium, 2008); *The Year of the Ox*, illus. Miah Alcorn (San Francisco: Immedium, 2009); *The Year of the Tiger*, illus. Justin Roth (San Francisco: Immedium, 2010); *The Year of the Rabbit*, illus. Justin Roth (San Francisco: Immedium, 2011); *The Year of the Dragon*, illus. Jennifer Wood (San Francisco: Immedium, 2012); *The Year of the Snake*, illus. Jennifer Wood (San Francisco: Immedium, 2013); *The Year of the Horse*, illus. Jennifer Wood (San Francisco: Immedium, 2014).

45. Ruthanne Lum McCunn, *Pie-Biter*, illus. You-shan Tang (San Francisco: Design Enterprises, 1983).

46. Allen Say, *El Chino* (Boston: Houghton Mifflin, 1990).

47. Marissa Moss, *Sky High: The True Story of Maggie Gee*, illus. Carl Angel (Berkeley: Tricycle Press, 2009).

48. Ken Mochizuki, *Be Water, My Friend: The Early Years of Bruce Lee*, illus. Dom Lee (New York: Lee & Low Books, 2006).

49. Paula Yoo, *Shining Star: The Anna May Wong Story*, illus. Lin Wang (New York: Lee & Low Books, 2009).

50. Steven A. Chin, *Dragon Parade: A Chinese New Year Story*, illus. Mou-Sien Tseng (New York: Steck-Vaughn Company, 1993).

51. Anon., *Sing a Song O'Six Taels* (n.p., n.d.), Ching Collection CHSA-03376, Chinese Historical Society of America Museum, San Francisco, California.

52. Sandi Takayama, *The Prince and the Li Hing Mui*, illus. Esther Szegedy (Honolulu: Bess Press, 1998). In this story, the queen and king are inspired by reading Andersen's fairy tale.

53. Takayama [3].

54. The author thanks poet Wing Tek Lum for his help in finding the origins of li hing mui.

55. Dean Howell, *The Story of Chinaman's Hat* (Honolulu: Island Heritage Publishing, 1990).

56. Ou Jilin and Ou Shuxun, trans., *"Tangrenmao di gushi"* ["The story of Chinaman's Hat"], *Nanren nüren he haizi [Man, woman, and child]* ([Xinhui], 2000). The author and Marlon K. Hom introduced the original picture book to Ou Jilin in Xinhui, who then translated it as a curiosity piece for the people of Xinhui.

57. Howell said, "I wrote the book in response to the original oil painting which I had made into prints. The prints of the image were very popular and people would ask me what the story was. I knew there wasn't a story, as I had created this new image just based on the name of the island 'Chinaman's Hat,' so I created this new legend" (Dean Howell Art, 5 Sept. 2010, http://www.myspace.com/deanhowellart).

58. Paul Yee, *The Boy in the Attic*, illus. Gu Xiong (Toronto: Groundwood Books/Douglas & McIntyre, 1998).

59. Kathleen Chang, *The Iron Moonhunter*, Chinese tr. Chiu-Chung Liao (San Francisco: Children's Book Press, 1977); Paul Yee, *Ghost Train*, illus. Harvey Chan (Vancouver: Groundwood Books-Douglas & McIntyre, 1996).

60. See note 3.

61. Choon-yi is born with one arm missing; the other arm is gifted with the ability to paint.

62. Chang, *The Iron Moonhunter*, back cover.

63. Gordon Lew, *The Story of Ching-Ming* ([San Francisco]: Chinese Bilingual Project, ca. 1960s): 18. Like Kwock's book cited in note 9 above, this book falls under one of many ethnic minority books that were self-published or community-published during the 1960s and 1970s due to rejection from mainstream publishers. The difference is that this book received a grant to write for educational purposes.

64. Yin, *Coolies*, illus. Chris Soentpiet (New York: Philomel Books-Penguin Putnam Books for Young Readers, 2001) [2].

65. Yin [4].

66. Yin [36].

67. Lew 18.

68. Yin [34]. In a sequel to *Coolies*, a third brother arrives in America, see Yin, *Brothers*, Chris illus. Soentpiet (New York: Philomel Books-Penguin Young Readers Group, 2006).

69. The adoption theme is the most popular among all the themes found in Asian American children's literature. The author's personal library has at least forty-five adoption picture books published from the 1960s to 2013.

70. Grace Lin, *The Red Thread: An Adoption Fairy Tale* (Morton Grove, IL: Albert Whitman & Company, 2007).

71. Karen Henry Clark, *Sweet Moon Baby: An Adoption Tale*, illus. Patrice Barton (New York: Alfred A. Knopf, 2010).

72. Lin [7].

73. Lin [32].

74. Lin [31].

75. Lin [3].

76. Clark [4].

77. Clark [26-27].

78. See D.L. Fuller, *Who Are My Real Parents?* (N.p.: [Peaceful Sunrise Publications], 2007); Kevin Leman and Kevin Leman II, *My Adopted Child, There's No One Like You* (Grand Rapids, MI: Revell, 2007); Susan E. Lindsley and Tina L. Christiansen, *Maya's Journey Home*, illus. Wendy M. Cannon (Oakdale, NY: Suitemates Publishing Company, 2008).

79. One example is Alice Tam's thesis that analyzes a compilation of ghost stories from the San Francisco Chinatown community; see Alice Tam, "The Ghosts of Chinese America: A Study of San Francisco Chinatown Ghostlore" (Master's thesis, San Francisco State University, 2004). There is also the pioneer study and translation of the transnational nursery rhymes, lullabies, and children's ditties originating from Chinese American families living in the Cantonese region of China, see Marlon K. Hom, "Rhymes Cantonese Mothers Sang," *Chinese America: History and Perspectives* (1999): 62-70.

FIVE

Things Matter

Chinese American Culture Work and the Gods of Marysville

Jonathan H. X. Lee and Vivian-Lee Nyitray

INTRODUCTION

Neglected by most twentieth-century scholarship beyond the fields of art and archaeology, the study of humans' relationship with material culture was reinvented during the late twentieth and early twenty-first centuries by international anthropologists and has spread to a variety of fields, including folklore. Recent scholarship increasingly indicates that evidence from material culture complicates oral or textual statements about religious beliefs and practices. It also indicates that human relationships with material objects provide the infrastructure upon which social life is lived and through which it is experienced.[1] In this analysis, our interactions with other people are largely mediated through material objects, even though classical sociological theory long tended to ignore the materiality of society in favor of immaterial concepts (e.g., Durkheim's "social solidarity").[2]

Anthropologist Daniel Miller has argued that the theoretical significance of the things around us tends to pass unnoticed, and that the glossing over of thousands of objects through which we interact risks missing a crucial dimension of everyday life that is of fundamental ethnographic interest.[3] However, when scholars do investigate material culture, their inquiries often focus on the disappearance of traditional artifacts and the loss of associated knowledge: the intention is to document and preserve the vestiges of a vanishing heritage.

The present chapter takes a different tack. Rather than focusing on loss, the authors posit that the study of Chinese American religious practice can illuminate a process of innovation and gain—a process of continued cultural production wherein traditional objects cannot only be repurposed within the Chinese American community, but can also be appropriated by nonheritage populations as well. The immediate case study is based on fieldwork conducted at the historic Bok Kai Temple in Marysville, California. By examining local religion and its material representations, this investigation reveals that the Chinese god of the North was symbolically and socially re-created into a Chinese American god of water and flood—illustrating how this refigured god and his temple have affected social relationships between the Chinese and non-Chinese communities in Marysville.

THE BOK KAI TEMPLE

Early Chinese immigrants to Northern California, who came largely from Cantonese-speaking regions, built the North Creek Temple [*Beichi miao* 北溪廟] in 1879, seeking divine protection from floods while simultaneously hoping for the provision of bountiful water for farming. Today, among the descendants of first-generation Chinese immigrants to Marysville and the larger non-Chinese local populations, the commonly used unofficial English designation for the shrine is the Bok Kai Temple. Understanding the meaning(s) of *Bok Kai*, however, is not a straightforward endeavor.

In standardized Cantonese romanization, *bok* [北] should be pronounced and spelled *bak*, meaning north; *ka* [溪] refers to a creek or mountain stream.[4] Hence, one very probable meaning of *Bok Kai* reflects its actual location—at the northern end of a creek (now the northern bank of the Yuba River)—as implied by the official written Chinese name of the temple, *Beichi miao*. Naming their communal temple in generic and location-specific terms would have given the Chinese immigrant population in Marysville an uncontroversial space for devotion, serving also to bind them as a new community despite differences of geographical origin, clan affiliation, or dialect. In this analysis, the Bok Kai Temple itself, although largely conforming to traditional Chinese architectural requirements for construction and decoration—and thus resisting assimilation and accommodation—is nonetheless a new hybrid, offering an innovative material expression of localized religious concerns.

There is, however, another possible explanation for the name *Bok Kai*: it may have come from *Beidi* [北帝], where *di* is pronounced in Cantonese as *dai*, meaning emperor. In this case, *Bok Kai* could possibly refer to the Cantonese pronunciation of *Beidi* as *Bak dai*, meaning Emperor of the

**Figure 5.1.   Beichi Gu Miao 北溪古廟, the Old North Creek Temple, March 2003.
Source: Courtesy of Jonathan H. X. Lee.**

North, a deity widely known and worshipped in China as both Beidi and
Zhenwu [賑務] (True Warrior).

   According to legend, Zhenwu was, in a previous existence, a butcher
who was also a very filial son. In that life, the burden of having killed and

butchered so many living things began to weigh heavily upon the butcher's conscience as he aged, and he wished to put down his cleaver and quit his grisly trade. But he was afraid that if he merely cast his cleaver aside, someone else might use it to slaughter living creatures; he also feared that someone might be injured accidentally by stepping on it. Therefore, he cut open his own stomach, pulled out his bowels, and used them to wrap up his cleaver, which he then threw into the river where it could not again be used to harm any living thing. The Bodhisattva Guanyin [觀音], observing this behavior and moved by the butcher's compassion, led his soul to the Western Paradise. There he became a Buddha. However, the stomach and bowels he had cast into the river turned into monsters: his stomach became a great black turtle, and his bowels turned into a huge black snake. These monsters overturned and sank many boats on the river and drowned many people. When the butcher, now entitled the Emperor of the Dark [North] Heavens, heard what was going on, he descended to earth and conquered the turtle and the snake—which is why he is always depicted with his feet trampling a turtle and a snake. Traditionally, the Emperor of the North was venerated as a powerful exorcist, a superior military general, and protector of the state.[5]

If, in Marysville, the Beichi miao were explicitly dedicated to the Emperor of the North, it might have been called informally *Bakdai miu*—a sound combination in Cantonese that is easily misheard by non-Cantonese speakers due to the glottal stop *k* followed immediately by the initial consonant *d*. The result: *Bakdai* eventually becomes *Bokkai*. The temple, situated on the riverbank, is understood to house the Emperor of the North, a.k.a. Bok Kai, renowned for his ability to control dangerous waters and thus, by extension, to quell floods. Bok Kai, therefore, would have offered the Chinese community protection of various and particular sorts, as well as serving symbolically to reaffirm their shared values of compassion and filiality.

Further strengthening this possible double meaning of *Bok Kai* as referring to either/both place *and* deity is the observation that, although "Bok Kai" is understood to be the main deity of the temple, it is not, in fact, Zhenwu/Beidi's image that is centrally located among the five gods enshrined on the altar of the *Beichi miao*. Standing along with the Bodhisattva Guanyin are the god Guandi 關帝 (patron of war and literature), Tianhou (the Empress of Heaven and marine/river-rain goddess), and the image of Zhenwu/Beidi flanks an unusual central deity, namely, Tudigong 土地公, the Earth God or god of locality. In China or Taiwan, Tudigong is typically enshrined on the ground or in a small shrine external to a temple.[6] In short, the physical placement of the images of the gods would seem to indicate that the temple is not solely, or even chiefly, dedicated to "Bok Kai," despite local understanding.

The process whereby *Bok Kai*, a constructed designation for temple and deity, has been absorbed into the fabric of the Marysville Chinese

Figure 5.2. Icon of Bok Kai. Courtesy of Jonathan H. X. Lee.

American cultural sphere can be explained through localized Chinese American innovation, or what will be discussed here as "culture work."

CHINESE AMERICAN CULTURE WORK

In a recent ethnographic study of the rural Taiwanese town of Beigang, Elana Chipman describes "culture work" [*wenhua gongzou*] as the explicit production of local and cultural identity through a variety of activities, including the publication of historical, folklorical, and archaeological research by amateurs and professionals.[7] In Beigang, culture work focuses primarily on the ritual and religious spheres, especially in relation to the historic Chaotian Temple. According to Chipman, such culture work is financed by local and national governmental bodies with the aim of developing "nostalgia tourism" and, in the case of Beigang, a national culture unique to Taiwan.[8]

Similarly, in the context of Chinese American communities, understanding the process of culture work reveals the significance of locality for the construction of identity and religious practices, creating and naturalizing new representations of Chinese religions as they were (and are) expressed and experienced in Chinese America. One example of this process is evident in the central California town of Hanford, where the restored Hanford Taoist Temple and Museum displays an unhewn log as a

Figure 5.3.　Chinese and Chinese American visitors making offerings to the gods of the Bok Kai Temple during the Bok Kai Festival and Parade, March 2008. Courtesy of Jonathan H. X. Lee.

Figure 5.4. Whole roasted pig offering. March 2008. Courtesy of Jonathan H. X. Lee.

representation of religious Daoism. Hanford's culture workers were second- and third-generation Chinese Americans, non-Chinese local residents, and historic preservationists, all of them wanting to re-imagine and restore Hanford's Chinatown heritage. Unable to read Chinese and largely unfamiliar with Chinese religions, they relied on translated sources to acquire desired cultural literacy. In consulting various sources, they encountered multiple romanizations and translations for Chinese words, making the task all the more difficult and confusing.

The Hanford culture workers may have been familiar with the *Dao De Jing*, in which the metaphor of the unhewn log refers to the natural state of the dao; this familiarity with the text in translation could easily have resulted in a cultural translation wherein a display of an unhewn log in the temple was seen as intelligible and appropriate.[9] This material representation of the dao is unique to Hanford; however, Daoist temples in China or Taiwan do not display unhewn logs, but might instead display an image of Laozi (Lao-tzu), the Jade Emperor, or the Eternal Mother enshrined on the altar.

There are two ways to approach this "unhewn log" phenomenon: One is to approach it in terms of cultural authenticity, questioning local representation of Chinese religion and finding it inauthentic. Alternatively, one may approach it from the perspective of Chinese American culture work, that is, the process by which ethnic, cultural, and religious identities and practices are maintained either in their original form, or find new representation. Consider what Anthony Giddens suggests is the basis of identity formation:

> A person's identity is not to be found in behaviour, nor—important though this is—the reaction of others, but in the capacity *to keep a particular narrative going.*[10]

New actors may be produced, new events accommodated, and new circumstances negotiated, but the narrative continues. In the case of Hanford's unhewn log, we see a vernacular religious expression, material evidence of culture work that honors historical conditions, continuing changes and developments, and incorporating new symbolic representations of localized Chinese religion particular to the context of late twentieth-century America.

THE BOK KAI FESTIVAL AND PARADE

Every year, Marysville hosts a civic community festival celebrating Chinese American culture in the context of the town's diversity. The highlight of the annual festival is the Bok Kai Parade, the oldest ongoing parade in California; the Year of the Horse in 2014 marked the 134th year of its celebration. The parade begins with the cracking of fireworks and pounding of drums. Accompanying the Golden Dragon are lion dancers, martial arts performers, floats, fire trucks, antique cars, school marching bands, and local community organizations such as the Boy Scouts and Rotary Club International. The parade includes participants from all over

Figure 5.5. Bok Kai Parade, March 2008. Courtesy of Jonathan H. X. Lee.

the San Francisco Bay Area, in addition to visitors from Asia (e.g., Hong Kong, Taiwan, and China). The authors have been attending the Marysville Bok Kai Festival and Parade intermittently since 1992.

In March 2003, author Lee attended and was given a post–parade tour of Marysville's Chinatown and a brief history of the Bok Kai Temple by a high school student. During the tour the young woman said, "Today, Bok Kai is only worshipped in Marysville and a little remote village somewhere in China." Given what can be surmised about the origin of "Bok Kai," such a statement is surely erroneous. Or is it? If, by "Bok Kai," the student was referring to the Emperor of the North, then she was indeed completely mistaken because he is popularly venerated throughout China, Taiwan, Hong Kong, and among Chinese diasporic communities in Southeast Asia (e.g., Vietnam).[11] If, however, by "Bok Kai," she was referring to the unwitting conflation of a temple's name with a temple's god, and to the subsequent production of a unique Chinese American god, then she was partially correct, as it bespeaks a unique instance of Chinese American culture work. Bok Kai is only worshipped in Marysville, where he is a localized innovation and representation. It is also worth noting, however, that although the Bok Kai temple "somewhere in China" does not exist, the mention of it is in perfect keeping with traditional under-

standings of Chinese temple creation. Through a process of "incense divi-
sion" (*fenxiang*), incense from one temple is used to inaugurate the bra-
zier of a later, related temple located at some distance from the first. [12] In
order for the material manifestation of a Bok Kai temple to exist and have
valid cultural capital in Marysville, a mother temple somewhere in China
has to be assumed (or constructed) in the process of Chinese American
culture work.

Over time, Bok Kai has become codified and naturalized as a referent
for the Emperor of the North, as well as for the temple. This new identity,
new representation, and spatial practice has entered mainstream knowledge and customs, and continues to be reinforced by Chinese American
culture work, particularly in the form of amateur historical and folklore
research and its publication by the local media, government, and the
Chinese American community. [13]

One feature of Chinese American culture work that distinguishes it
from Chipman's observation of Taiwanese culture work in Beigang
points to the frequent lack of Chinese-language abilities among second-
and third-generation Chinese Americans and among amateur scholars
conducting research on Chinese American religions. Early on, this mis-
communication was the result of the unavailability of a standardized
transliteration system that accounts for the multiple personal translitera-
tions of Chinese terms. Early sources on the Bok Kai Temple, for example,
transliterated the god's name as "Beidi," "Bok I, " "Bok Eye, " or "Pak
Tai." Such inconsistencies pose a significant challenge to Chinese
American culture work, especially if the culture worker is not literate in
Chinese. Additionally, the continuous flow of publications representing
Bok Kai as the "god of water and controller of floods" in local newspapers (e.g., *Marysville, CA Daily Appeal*) and in publicity pieces for the
annual parade, have functioned to naturalize this meaning. The Emperor
of the North is venerated as a powerful exorcist and superior military
general in China, Hong Kong, Taiwan, and Southeast Asia. But in the
town of Marysville, the emphasis is on his ability to control floods. When
author Lee presented a public lecture on the gods of the Bok Kai Temple
at the Chinese American Museum of Northern California in Marysville,
Arthur Tom, a third-generation Chinese American whose grandfather
participated in the gold rush and later started a business in Marysville
during the 1860s, asked, "I grew up learning that the god in the middle of
the main altar is Bok Kai, and he's the god that controls floods. Isn't that
correct?" Even after the central deity was identified as Tudigong, Mr.
Tom commented, "I grew up thinking he was the god of floods, which is
why Marysville has not had a flood since the temple was constructed." [14]
Does this matter? Not a bit. As local earth god, Tudigong surely must be
concerned with local welfare and have jurisdiction over the local waters;
as powerful protector from watery dangers, Beidi surely must be concerned with the local welfare; as Bok Kai, god(s) and temple together

stand vigilant. Culture work enables them to encompass and surpass the vagaries of belief, custom, accommodation, misperception, and festival appropriation.

CONCLUSION

The phenomenon unfolding in Marysville illustrates how the signs and symbols of Chinese religion in America may be reimagined, rearticulated, and re-created.[15] Over time, miscommunicated identity and representation became normalized: this is the birth of Bok Kai, present but misidentified on the altar of a temple that mistakenly bears his name. As a result, subsequent Chinese Americans continue to reproduce this representation as part-and-parcel of Chinese culture in America. Accompanying the new representation of Bok Kai as a Chinese American god are Chinese American socio-spatial practices such as the Bok Kai Parade. Together, these phenomena perpetuate the new representation of a Chinese god in Chinese America and new social practices. Bok Kai and the Bok Kai Temple are, thus, both material products of Chinese American culture work that display a loss of heritage, but also presents a heritage gain; the residents of Marysville have given rise to a new form of vernacular Chinese religion as it is created, experienced, lived, and represented in a Chinese American community.

NOTES

1. Jonathan H. X. Lee and Vivian-Lee Nyitray's "Things Matter: Chinese American Culture Work and the Gods of Marysville" first published in *Chinese America: History and Perspective, The Journal of the Chinese Historical Society of America* (2012): 1-5. Reprinted by permission of the Chinese Historical Society of America. Arjun Appadurai, ed. *The Social Life of Things: Commodities in Cultural Perspective* (Cambridge: Cambridge University Press, 1986); Colleen McDannell, *Material Christianity: Religion and Popular Culture in America* (New Haven: Yale University Press, 1995).

2. Emile Durkheim, *Elementary Forms of Religious Life*, trans., Karen Fields (New York: The Free Press, 1912, 1995).

3. Daniel Miller, *Material Cultures: Why Some Things Matter* (London: University College Press, 1998).

4. *Jyutping* (sometimes spelled Jyutpin) is a Romanization system for Standard Cantonese developed by the Linguistic Society of Hong Kong (LSHK) in 1993. Hanyu Pinyin was adopted in 1979 by the International Organization for Standardization (ISO) as the standard Romanization for modern Chinese. The Hanyu Pinyin system was developed in 1954, when the Ministry of Education of the People's Republic of China assigned a committee to reform the written language (Committee for the Reform of the Chinese Written Language).

5. Gray Seaman, *Journey to the North: An Ethnohistorical Analysis and Annotated Translation of the Chinese Folk Novel Pei-yu-chi* (Berkeley: University of California Press, 1987); Ma Shutian, *Zhongguo Daojiao zhu shen / Daoist Divinities of China* (Beijing: Tuan-jie Press, 1996. Reprint in Taiwan, 2003); Hong Xingrong, ed., *Quanguo fosha daoguan zonglan: Xuantian Shangdi / Taiwan's Buddhist and Daoist Temples: Xuantian Shangdi* (Taipei: privately printed, 1987); and Zhiwei Liu, "Beyond the Imperial Metaphor: A

Local History of the Beidi (Northern Emperor) Cult in the Pearl River Delta" *Chinese Studies in History* 35: 1 (Fall 2001): 12-30.

6. Alessandro Dell'Orto, *Place and Spirit in Taiwan: Tudi Gong in the Stories, Strategies and Memories of Everyday Life* (London: RoutledgeCurzon, 2002).

7. Elana Chipman, "Our Beigang: Culture Work, Ritual and Community in a Taiwanese Town" PhD diss., (Cornell University, 2007): 106-141; Elana Chipman, "The Local Production of Culture in Beigang," *Taiwan Journal of Anthropology* 6:1 (2008): 1-29; Jonathan H. X. Lee, "Transnational Goddess on the Move: Meiguo Mazu's Celestial Inspection Tour and Pilgrimage as Chinese American Culture Work and Vernacular Chinese Religion," PhD diss., (University of California, Santa Barbara, 2009).

8. Elana Chipman, "Our Beigang: Culture Work, Ritual and Community in a Taiwanese Town" (2007): 108.

9. Victor H. Mair, *Tao Te Ching: The Classic Book of Integrity and the Way. A Entirely New translation based on the recently discovered Ma-Wang-tui manuscripts* (New York: Bantam Books, 1990): 81.

10. Anthony Giddens, *Modernity and Self-Identity* (Stanford: Stanford University Press, 1992): 54—emphasis original.

11. John Lagerwey, "The Pilgrimage to Wu-tang Shan" Susan Naquin and Chün-fang Yü, eds., *Pilgrims and Sacred Sites in China* (Berkeley: University of California Press, 1992); Shinyi Chao, "Zhenwu: The Cult of a Chinese Warrior God from the Song to the Ming Dynasties (960-1368)" PhD diss., (University of British Columbia, 2003); Hong Xingrong (1987); and Seaman (1987).

12. Chang Hsun, *Wenhua Mazu: Taiwan Mazu xinyang yanjiu Lunwenji / Constructing Mazu: Selected Papers in Mazu Culture* (Taipei: Institute of Ethnology, Academia Sinica, 2003); Jonathan H. X. Lee, "Creating a Transnational Religious Community: The Empress of Heaven, Goddess of the Sea Tianhou/Mazu, from Beigang, Taiwan to San Francisco U.S.A.," Lois Ann Lorentzen, Joaquin Jay Gonzalez III, Kevin M. Chun, and Hien Duc Do, eds., *On the Corner of Bliss and Nirvana: Politics, Identity, and Faith in New Migrant Communities*, eds., (Durham: Duke University Press, 2009): 166-183.

13. Paul G. Chace, "Returning Thanks: Chinese Rites in an American Community" PhD diss., (University of California, Riverside, 1992); Joan Mann, "Two Daoist Temples: The Baiyunguan (White Cloud Temple) in Shanghai and the Bok Kai Temple in Marysville, 1880s until Present" *Chinese America: History and Perspectives* 21, (2007): 137-148; and Reuben Ibanez, *Historical Bok Kai Temple in Old Marysville, California* (The Marysville Chinese Community, 1967).

14. Personal communication to J. H. X. Lee (March, 8, 2008).

15. The processes of god-transformation took place in China as well, but perhaps not as blatantly. See Terry F. Kleeman, *A God's Own Tale: The Book of Transformations of Wenchang, the Divine Lord of Zitong* (New York: State University of New York Press, 1994): 1–83. In *A God's Own Tale*, Kleeman discusses the history and story of the development of a local northern Sichuan thunder-deity first imagined as a viper who later becomes the national god of literary arts, Wenchang. Similar to the Tianhou/Mazu cult, the Wenchang cult started as a local cult that subsequently was appropriated by the state and made into a national cult: During this process both deities were modified. Wenchang's central modification is the telling anthropomorphic transformation of the representation of the deity from a snake. He notes that the god's representation in human form fulfilled a major condition for official sanction of the cult and was followed by the granting of official titles (4–5). By the late twelfth century the identity of Wenchang evolved again through a series of revelations that depended on spirit writing (7). Although the factors for god-transformation in the case of Wenchang and Tianhou/Mazu in late imperial China is different from the factors that led to the changing representation and roles of Bok Kai, all three cases reveal something about the nature of the divine in Chinese religion: They are changeable. For another example, see James L. Watson, "Standardizing the Gods: The Promotion of T'ien Hou ('Em-

press of Heaven') Along the South China Coast, 960-1960" David Johnson, Andrew J. Nathan and Evelyn S. Rawski, eds., *Popular Culture in Late Imperial China* (Berkeley: University of California Press, 1985).

SIX

Finding the Missing Pieces

Korean American Adoptees and the Production of Ritual

SooJin Pate

INTRODUCTION

Taking my cue from the editors of this anthology, I define folklore in its broadest sense: as a way of life. Asian American folklore not only encompasses myths and divine practices, but it also encompasses the narrative and material histories that produce individual and collective Asian American identities. One of the ways in which Asian Americans narrate their everyday experiences and construct identity is through ritual.

This chapter examines how Korean American adoptees participate in the emerging body of Asian American folklore by attending to the ways in which they use ritual to experiment with and construct their identities. Departing from conventional concepts of ritual that define it as ceremonies that are handed down from generation to generation or given as divine instructions, I, borrowing from prominent ritual theorist Catherine Bell, define ritual as practices and activities that emerge from everyday life. If folklore is a way of life, then ritual is an *expression* of that way of life. However, I would also add that while folklore informs the kind of rituals that are being produced, rituals also inform folkloric production. Put another way, the creation of ritual leads to the expansion and innovation of Asian American folklore.

The process in which folkloric expressions of everyday life shapes Asian American identities and practices is vividly illustrated in how Korean American adoptees invent and enact rituals. They use rituals to construct pieces of their personal history in an attempt to forge a sense of identity. Examining the ritual production of Korean American adoptees is significant because we come to understand how larger social, political, and cultural factors (e.g., migration, assimilation, and dislocation) have informed the making of Asian American folklore.

Since 1955, just two years after the Korean War (1950-1953) ended in a ceasefire agreement, more than 150,000 South Korean children have been adopted by Americans, the majority of whom are white. Because many of these children were adopted as infants or toddlers, Korean American adoptees have grown up with a common set of questions: Where do I come from? To whom do I belong? When was I born? For the majority of Americans, the answers to these questions are self-evident and taken for granted; however, for Korean American adoptees, these questions are central to their quest for identity. These questions, along with, "Why was I put up for adoption?" haunt them well into their adult years. So how do adoptees find answers to these questions when little or no information about their past is known? The answer lies in the invention of rituals.

Discourses surrounding ritual have traditionally taken place in the context of religious studies. However, scholars are taking the discussion of ritual beyond the walls of temples, churches, and mosques and into the realm of everyday activities and interactions of people. They are doing this by redefining ritual as not simply a ceremonial event, but as a meaningful action. Bell distinguishes the difference between activities that are ritualistic versus those that are not: ritualization is a way of acting that distinguishes one activity from another in the very way it does what it does.[1] It privileges one activity over another by attributing a special meaning that distinguishes it from other activities.[2] Borrowing from Bell, the authors of *Ritual and Its Consequences* put it another way: "'ritual' frames actions in certain, very specific ways. It is the framing of the actions, not the actions themselves, that makes them rituals."[3] Thus, the authors define ritual as "a frame that tells us how to understand actions."[4] It is within these theorizations of ritual that I designate certain actions performed by Korean adoptees—primarily those related to connecting back to their pre-adoption life—as rituals.

In Asian American folklore, performing rituals is a strategy that is used not only to tap into one's ancestral past, but also to connect back to one's roots. For adopted Korean Americans, ritual becomes a tool to find the missing pieces of the puzzle of their past, to recover a history that was severed during the process of dislocation and transplantation. Therefore, in this essay, I argue that adopted Korean Americans produce rituals in an *attempt* to retrieve a past, a past that is both real and imagined. In examining this attempt (which by all means is not always successful), contours of an emerging way of life is narrated by Korean American adoptees: one that reveals the complexities of being both transracial and transnational adoptees. In this way, ritual production becomes a response to their vexed position of inhabiting both Asian and white American racial identities.

INVENTING RITUAL, CREATING IDENTITY

The concept of inventing rituals may seem like a contradiction in terms because popular preconceptions of ritual see it as a matter of unchanging tradition; however, as Bell points out, ritual changes with the changing needs and conditions of the community.[5] New rites are being invented every day, and their creation is integral to the construction of both communal and individual identity. Inventing rituals is particularly necessary if extant rituals cannot contain certain experiences and identities. Creating new modes of ritual action allows for new identities to be formulated and expressed, identities that are impossible to conceive within extant forms of ritual practice.[6] I suggest that Korean American adoptees have their own unique set of experiences that cannot be conceived within the traditions of previous ritual activity and, thus, is why they have invented their own rituals. Inventing rituals becomes a way to organize and unite the Korean American adoptee community around a common set of traumas, issues, and questions. Furthermore, the rituals they have produced help to (re)create the missing pieces in their history in an attempt to make sense of their past and their sense of self. Through ritual invention, Korean American adoptees are even able to create history out of no history, or what Marianne Hirsch calls postmemory.[7] This is the power and seduction of ritual invention.

By recalling their personal history and past through ritual, Korean adoptees are fundamentally working to formulate their identity. After all, as previously noted, inventing and performing ritual is tied to the construction of both communal and individual identity. As such, the cultural production of Korean adoptees, their literature and film, is an apropos site to examine the formation of Korean adoptee ritual and identity because it is precisely here where this is taking place. Eleana Kim describes Korean adoptee films as "performances of the search for identity" and can be read as a "journey of the self."[8] The same can be said of Korean adoptee literature. Indeed, the vast majority of Korean American adoptee literature and film are classified as personal narratives: from memoirs (literature) to auto-ethnographies (film).[9]

Two prominent rituals that appear in Korean American adoptee literature and film are the "birth ritual" and the "ritual of return." These rites of passage are codependent, with the ritual of return relying on the enactment of the birth ritual. In other words, the return ritual cannot exist without the birth ritual. The birth ritual causes the adoptee to lose his or her preadoption past, while the ritual of return provides the adoptee with the opportunity to reclaim it. As journeys of self-exploration, both Korean

American adoptee literature and film are motivated by the desire to find answers to questions about memory and their severed biological ties.[10] As such, the ritual of return becomes a key strategy to reinvent a way of life that considers Korea and what it means to be Korean.

The rituals of birth and of returning to one's homeland may seem like conventional rituals; however, I want to emphasize that the way Korean American adoptees go about enacting these rituals is highly unconventional and may, for some, not even look like rituals. This is because their unique status as Korean children adopted by primarily white Americans necessitates a unique ritual style. If an action becomes ritualized by acting in a way that privileges what is being done compared to other mundane activities, then these activities—being born and returning to one's birthplace—become privileged because of their significance to the adoptee's formation of identity. The production of ritual becomes a way to document a way of life and narrate an identity that is unique to Korean American adoptees. In this way, Korean American adoptees participate in the emerging phenomenon that is Asian American folklore.

THE PARADOX OF ADOPTION

Embedded in my analysis of how Korean American adoptees utilize ritual to retrieve the past is the underlying assumption that that past is missing or lost. It assumes that there is a past to recover. Thus, before I delve into my examination of how adopted Korean Americans retrieve their preadoption past, I want to address how that past gets erased. The past gets erased via the birth ritual.

The ideology of adoption is informed by the logic of assimilation. In the context of Korean adoption, assimilation is the process by which Korean identity, history, folklore, and culture is erased and supplanted with a predominately white middle-class American identity and way of life. Although multiculturalism and diversity are key frameworks in transracial and transnational adoptions, complete assimilation was the modus operandi of the 1970s and 1980s, when the majority of these Korean American adoptees were adopted. As Katy Robinson bluntly states in her memoir *A Single Square Picture*, "in those days . . . the popular opinion was to make me forget about Korea and assimilate me into the white culture as fast as they could."[11] This process of assimilation is why so many Korean American adoptees describe themselves as Twinkies or bananas: white on the inside, yellow on the outside. Undergoing the process of assimilation is not unique to adopted Koreans. Asian Americans who are not adopted have also described themselves in these terms; however, I suggest that Korean children adopted by predominately white middle-class American families undergo a particular brand of assimilation that is all encompassing. More to the point, the adoption process, which is fundamentally assimilationist, requires the erasure of the child's preadoption way of life in order to successfully assimilate into her or his new adoptive family and begin a new life.

This is precisely why so many Korean American adoptees talk about their adoption as a kind of birth; the day they are adopted is framed as the day they were born.[12] In the literature, life does not begin when they emerge from their biological mother's womb; it begins when they are adopted. Robinson writes: "I became convinced my life simply began the moment I stepped off the airplane on the other side of the world. One day I was Kim Ji-yun growing up in Seoul, Korea; the next day I was Catherine Jeanne Robinson living in Salt Lake City, Utah."[13] Jane Jeong Trenka writes in her memoir *The Language of Blood*, "I am Jane Marie Brauer, created September 26, 1972, when I was carried off an airplane onto American soil."[14] Robinson was seven years old when she was adopted, and Brauer (Trenka) was almost one; yet they both see their life beginning upon arrival at the airport (rather than a hospital labor room) because that is where they received their new names.[15]

According to Bell, the birth ritual involves an extended set of activities including fertility, identifying the sex of the fetus, ensuring the safety of the mother and child, and naming the baby.[16] The last activity best describes the birth ritual of the Korean American adoptee. Naming is a significant part of the birth ritual because it is a crucial part of identity formation. One's identity is usually wrapped up in one's name and assigning a new name leads to a new identity. Because many of the ritual activities associated with biological birth are not applicable to the adoptee, receiving a name and being born become conflated into a single event.

The birth ritual of adoption strips the adoptees of their preadoption past. As a result, adoption becomes as much about gaining a new identity as it is about losing one. And in many cases, this gain and loss is simultaneous. The play "Highway 10," which is embedded in Trenka's memoir, is a prime example of how being assigned a new American identity relies on the erasure of Korean identity, history, folklore, and culture. In "Ideology and Ideological State Apparatuses," Louis Althusser defines interpellation or "hailing" as an operation of subject formation. Interpellation operates as a recruiting tool that transforms individuals into subjects.[17] He goes on to construct a "theoretical theatre" that reveals the process of hailing: a person (usually behind him or her) yells out, "Hey, you there!" Inevitably, an individual turns around knowing that the hail was for him or her, recognizing that "Hey, you!" was directed toward him or her.[18] In recognizing and answering the hail, the subject is formed.[19]

In "Highway 10," Trenka creates a theoretical theater of her own where she reveals the relationship between the ideology of adoption and the subject formation of the adoptee. Sounds of airplanes taking off and landing open the play.[20] After ten minutes, the scene transitions into a rural highway. Sitting in the car are Fred and Margaret (the adoptive parents) and their newly arrived adopted children Mi-Ja and Kyong-Ah—who instantly have been renamed Carol and Jane. Four-and-a-half year old Carol sits alone in the backseat, while Margaret holds Carol's baby sister Jane in the passenger seat. The entire play consists of just three lines: two questions and an assertion.

> Fred: [Looks into the rearview mirror to see Carol.] How you doin' back there?
>
> [Carol continues to scan audience]
>
> Margaret: [Pats baby gently but constantly, like a nervous tic. Turns head to look at Carol but is unable to see her. Speaks over her shoulder.] Are you okay?
>
> Fred: [Louder] Your mother asked you a question.
>
> [Carol does not look at Margaret but searches the faces in the audience, looking for a Korean face, any Korean face. Finding none, she closes her eyes and decides to forget.][21]

In this scene, the Father and Mother interpellate Carol as their adopted child. Even though Carol does not understand English and, therefore, does not comprehend the actual words that are spoken, she does recognize that the words are meant for her. Specifically, she knows intuitively that they are recruiting her to be someone else: not Mi-Ja, a four-and-a-half year old Korean girl but Carol, an American girl whose identity and life are just beginning. Put another way, Fred and Margaret expect Carol, not Mi-Ja, to arrive at the airport; they hail *Carol*, not Mi-Ja.

We know that *she* knows that she is being recruited to transform, not by the words she says (she remains silent for the entire duration of the play), but by the internal decision she makes. Her response: "she closes her eyes and decides to forget."[22] She understands that the words spoken by her adoptive father and mother are not only directed at her but are also soliciting a response that requires conversion. By using reel-to-reel home video footage, Trenka enables the audience to witness Mi-Ja's conversion into Carol. The home video is a visual representation of the psychic workings of adoptee interpellation. After she "decides to forget," which is her response to the hail, a reel-to-reel home movie is projected above and behind the car. It consists of scenes from Mi-Ja's (Carol's) life in Korea, ranging from playing with her sisters and friends to sleeping with her mother to saying goodbye, less than twenty-four hours ago, to her family at Kimpo Airport. Eventually, the memories of her past life in Korea become "blank frames and white noise."[23] The process of assimilation is put on fast-forward as we observe the name, language, family, and history of one Korean child diminish into complete erasure. The ideology of adoption necessitates this erasure in order for her conversion from Korean child to adoptee to take place: "Carol has willed herself to become a girl with no history and is now ready to start her new life."[24] Here, the birth ritual becomes a rite of passage that marks a transition in nationality, making the adoptee's birth a national birth whereby the Korean child becomes American. Working to reclaim this Korean part that has been erased is the motivation behind the adoptees' creative invention of the return ritual.

RITUAL OF (VIRTUAL) RETURN I

The ritual of return involves activities that are done to reconnect with the past in order to recuperate what has been lost during the assimilative adoption process. Returning to the homeland or birthplace (Korea, in this case) takes several forms. First, there is the virtual return. The virtual return takes place in the realm of the imaginary where some vehicle is used to transport the adoptee back to her or his past. Then there is the literal return, where Korean adoptees travel back to Korea, either on their own, or with formal tours like Motherland trips.[25]

The vehicle most commonly used to virtually transport the adoptee back to Korea is the racialized body of the adoptee. In many Korean adoptee narratives, the face that adoptees see in the mirror is discussed in terms of shame and failure. The reflection in the mirror reminds adoptees of their failure at complete assimilation, their failure at becoming white.[26] As a result, the "Korean face," concludes Cathy Ceniza Choy and Gregory Paul Choy, becomes "the synecdoche for the nonwhite body, the foreign nation, the undesirable and unassimilable alien."[27] However, for some adoptees, the reflection in the mirror becomes their only link to their preadoption past. For example, in the poem "In America," Leah Sieck embraces her Korean face because it presents a way to connect with her Korean mother:

> In America / My Korean face / floats in the mirror: / Half-moon eyes, / proud cheekbones, / melon lips, / night black hair / haunt me. If I could break the code, / the secrets of my genes / could take me back / to those first breaths— / Those seven days / when I was my true mother's / daughter / could tell me / if it is her face / I see.[28]

Here, the face in the mirror becomes a vehicle to transport the adoptee, who has no memory of the past, back to Korea. Seeing her reflection in the mirror allows her to create memory, to construct a history that begins in Korea rather than in the United States. The mundane activity of looking in the mirror becomes ritualized because it is framed in a distinctive way. The speaker is not looking into the mirror for vanity's sake; rather, the level of scrutiny and deliberateness in which she gazes at her eyes, lips, hair, and cheekbones informs us that this is no ordinary looking. Her facial features are framed as her genetic code, as her link to a preadoption past where her biological mother is present. Indeed, the face in the mirror becomes a symbolic replication of the missing biological parent. As an inheritor of her mother's genes, the speaker herself becomes a stand-in for her missing mother.

The adoptee's body (face, hands, legs, etc.) is often used as a bridge to the past because sometimes this is all she or he has. Biology and biological ties are given even greater meaning when no other historical document exists (birth certificate, photographs, etc.). By breaking the genetic code, adoptees seem to believe that the secrets of the past will be revealed. This is cinematically portrayed in Me-K Ahn's short experimental film *Undertow*.

Undertow is a cinematic rumination on the condition of exile, of what it feels like to be disconnected from your biological parents, from your birth country or homeland, from your own memories. And these feelings of detachment are visually explored through the disembodied body. The film opens with a voiceover of June (an orphanage director in Korea) speaking on the phone to an adoptee in the United States. As she tries to reassure the adoptee that "no mother gives up a baby or a child because they don't want it," the following text appears on black screen: "Recognition / likeness / familiarity. Most people take these things for granted. They look at themselves and then they look at their parents. They try to find the likeness, the familiarity. They can see where their nose came from; the curl of their hair; the thickness of their waist. They know who conceived them. There is never a question." [29] At this moment, the phone dangles off the hook, signaling that, for the adoptee, there is *always* a question. The emptiness and confusion that comes from simply not knowing these basic pieces of personal history is overdetermined in this film. The film is composed of disjointed shots and scenes that work to recreate the psychological and emotional state of the unnamed main character. Recurring images of a disconnected phone in a telephone booth, of an abandoned building, of a deserted street, along with unfinished conversations, disjointed dialogue, and conflicting narratives all work to create a sense of dislocation and alienation. Indeed, the protagonist herself states, "I have no idea where I am or how I got here." [30]

Adding to the overall tone of disorientation are the recurring images of body parts. Close-up shots of knees, thighs, feet, stomach, waist, shoulders, breasts, hands, and other body parts repeatedly appear in the film with no explanation. Often they appear detached from the rest of the body, further adding to the feeling of disembodiment and disconnection that the film evokes. However, if the body is used to represent alienation, it is this same body that becomes her solution to this predicament: "Sometimes I feel like my life would be different if I just knew what my birth parents looked like," says the adoptee as we see her feet running through the grass. She goes on to explain:

> If I could see where my features came from, if I knew where I came from, maybe I wouldn't feel like my body and mind were detached, like I knew who I really am. I want to be able to see my eyes in my birthmother's eyes, to know where the shape of my legs came from, the softness of my nose, the paleness of my skin.[31]

What seems mundane (in this case, knowing who you physically resemble) is hypervalued because it becomes framed as the link to a buried past, as the key to forming the building blocks of identity. The methodical swinging of the legs, the deliberate stroking of the stomach: these quotidian acts become ritualized activities that help the adoptee to reacquaint herself not only with her mother but also with herself. Ahn, like Sieck, seems to be suggesting that by knowing her biological parents, especially her mother, she will come to know herself.

Furthermore, the nose, the shape of the leg, the curve of the eye, and other parts of the body become a metonym for a past life in Korea; the racialized Asian body is a concrete and literal marker that proves a physical connection to a biological mother and father in Korea. In this instance, the equation of body with country (e.g., Korean body = Korea) that is the hallmark of Asian racialization serves the adoptee well. Because so many adoptees have little or no memory of their lives prior to adoption (because of their young age or because they are repressed), often times the only evidence or trace of their past becomes their own racialized Asian bodies. Scrutinizing the face that reflects back in the mirror or caressing one's hand or leg become ritualized activities that psychically and symbolically transport the adoptee back to Korea and becomes the vehicle in which to contemplate their biological connection to their birth country.

RITUAL OF RETURN II

The second style of return is the literal, physical return to Korea. This type of return ritual is more effective in aiding the adoptee's search for personal history and identity, for a couple of reasons. First, the smells, sights, and sounds of Korea reignite dormant memories, especially in children who were adopted as toddlers or older. There simply is no substitute to being physically present in Korea, which makes this ritual of (literal) return play a significant role in finding the missing pieces to the past. Second, for those adoptees who literally have no recollection, being in Korea aids the work of postmemory, which becomes fundamental when creating memory out of no or "next-to-nothing" memory.[32]

Postmemory, as theorized by Holocaust scholar Marianne Hirsch, is memory that is "mediated not through recollection but through an *imagi-*

native investment and creation."[33] Postmemory invokes the imaginary because it is considered to be the memory of the *second* generation.[34] This distance is what distinguishes it from memory, making postmemory memory once (i.e., one generation) removed. While the memories of Korean adoptees are not second-generational, the distance between their memories and themselves may seem so because of the eradication and forgetting process undergone during assimilation. In addition, their second birth as an adopted American child could be read as becoming second-generation, as it works to further detach adoptees from their pre-adoption past. This distance is why these films are more works of "imaginative investment and creation" rather than literal recollection. Thus, Korean American adoptee films are works of postmemory. By retracing and recreating their past in this way, Korean American adoptee filmmakers become agents of postmemory.

Furthermore, postmemory is memory marked by familial or cultural trauma.[35] To be sure, it is the trauma of loss and separation from their Korean family, folklore, culture, and history that instigates the ritual of return. And almost always this trauma results in dislocation and displacement. Therefore, as Hirsch points out, the diasporic experience, the condition of exile, is a fundamental aspect of postmemory.[36] Like many diasporic communities, Korean American adoptees desire to return back "home," back to the Motherland. And when they return to Korea, one of the first stops is a visit to the orphanage they lived in prior to their adoption.

Visiting the orphanage is a crucial aspect of the return ritual because not only is it the last known location for most adoptees, but it is also the site where key information is reposited which makes it an especially fertile space for imaginative (re)creation. For example, in the documentary film *Passing Through*, Nathan Adolphson (who was adopted as an infant), uses his trip to Korea to recreate history by reenacting certain events that he knows he experienced as a baby. He explains: "Because I don't remember anything about my time in the orphanage, I want to learn everything about these children and their time here."[37] So he volunteers his time, taking care of the children. By studying and recording the daily lives of these children, he is able to reenact his own time spent in an orphanage, creating a postmemory. This becomes the frame in which Adolfson turns mundane activities, such as caressing an infant's cheek, watching children play amongst themselves, and caring for children, into ritualized activities. One boy in particular catches his eye. It is the boy's first day at the orphanage, and he is sitting next to the door surrounded by three other orphans. A close up shot captures the gradual process in which his face contorts itself from a frown into an all-out cry. As he bawls, he covers his face with his hands, wiping away his own tears. Watching this painful scene unfold, Adolfson realizes that "all these children have been through the same thing as this child . . . then it slowly sinks in. I, too, have been through the same thing. In some strange way, it is comforting to know that he'll get through this, just as the other children did. Just as I did."[38] At this moment, a wide-angle shot shows the boy still sitting there alone, as the other children eat their meal. Part of the work that postmemory does is that it attempts to bring back to life memories that have become absent. By reproducing a scene that he most likely went through as an orphan, Adolfson revives a part of his own past, a part of his own history. He is able to make present the absent memory of his time spent at the orphanage through these ritualized activities.

Me-K Ahn also uses the site of the orphanage to reconstruct her past in her first experimental short film *Living in Half Tones*. Third World Newsreel describes *Living in Half Tones* as a "metaphorical reconstruction of the artist's developing identity as an adopted Korean girl in America who returns to Korea for the first time 'to search for bits and pieces of my past.'"[39] Witnessing the sights and sounds of Korea and listening to the orphanage director recall her time spent at the orphanage all work to revive bits and pieces of her past. As the director recalls Ahn's time in the orphanage, Ahn's memory becomes ignited. Flashes of a garden full of purple sage, an *ajuma* (older woman) walking down a dirt country road surrounded by rice fields, and a car speeding down a busy Korean street: these images literally erupt out of nowhere in the film as the director of the orphanage talks to Ahn. They appear with no context; there is no narrative that accompanies their appearance in the film. They are decontextualized and ahistorical. The audience is made to feel like Ahn herself: we have no idea where these images are coming from, when she saw these things, or how old she was when she saw them. The only thing we do know is that they are from Korea and are stored in Ahn's memory. We know that these images are relegated to her memories because they appear blurry at first and are seen in high color. Indeed, Ahn uses color and focus to distinguish memory (high color and unfocused) from reality (black and white, and in focus).

Despite the recovery of these memories, Ahn's film still evokes a deep sense of alienation and disorientation because they remain fragments of repressed memory. Like the disembodied body in *Undertow*, the images of Korea appear without a coherent narrative to link them together, making them disconnected and incoherent. These scenes and images float around in the film, in the same way that they are floating around in Ahn's psyche. These objects and images remain stranded, full of missing links, signaling the project of retrieving memory as irretrievable. This is aptly portrayed in the opening of the film.

In the first thirty seconds, we quickly learn that the past is irretrievable and the quest for "truth" is unattainable. The film begins with a color shot of a little orphan girl with a deep frown on her face and penetrating eyes. The music that accompanies this picture is a haunting, reverberating sound. It's the kind of music that signals something is amiss. As her pictures blurs in and out, we hear the voice of the orphanage director in midsentence: ". . . long time ago. But, ah, you were found, they said, somewhere, you know, in the city . . . hard to remember because it was such a long time ago."[40] Variations of this sentence repeat over and over again, along with the accompanying blurred image of the little girl, as if the filmmaker is trying to highlight the unreliability of memory. The haunting music, the blurred picture, and these words serve as a caveat about the project of recovery.

The longer we listen to the director recall Ahn's time at the orphanage (her narration makes up the entire film script), the more we realize that what is amiss is the director's memory. As the film progresses, we discover that her memory is fuzzy, that her facts are skewed, and that her story is full of holes. For example, the director recounts: "You were found, they said, somewhere, you know, in the city. All I've got on the card is . . . *they*, you know, said that your mother died and your father was, they didn't know where your father was. And I can't, I don't know what to tell you who *they* is. . . . " She then later says, "there was a woman that handled children, you know, that took abandoned children and children that were left some place in the city, so I would imagine that she was the one that uh, you know, brought you." And then again, she later recounts, "The first day, I, they gave you to me, and I held you. You just *clung* to me, and I felt you were very, you know, insecure so your mom could have been gone for awhile and, you know, just raised by a father or a grandmother. But you were very insecure and you screamed a lot."[41] There are several instances where her stories contradict each other. First, she says that *they* (two or more people) brought Ahn to the orphanage. Then she says that the woman who took care of abandoned children in Chejung not only raised her, but also brought her to the orphanage. Then later, she states that she was probably raised by her father (who she categorized as missing earlier in her story) or her grandmother.

Another point of controversy is the card that the director mentions. After the director tells her that she "screamed a lot," Ahn asks, "Do you know how old I was?" The director responds:

> No . . . because, um . . . now you should have told me you were going to do this before [she says in a scolding tone]. I would have brought you your card. I can't think . . . just of the . . . I had to guess at your age because, you know, not getting direct from a family or anything. But as far as I feel now on the ages that I do, it probably, it could be three months, you know, either way. But I have a date on the card in there is when you came, but if I think I remember right, you were here about six months.[42]

Ahn asking how old she was when she came to the orphanage seems like an innocent question; however, the director gets defensive, scolds the twenty-something-year-old Ahn like a child for asking the question and, in the end, evades the question altogether; she only tells Ahn how long she might have stayed in the orphanage. Also, the answer could easily be found on the card that the director keeps mentioning; however, she never provides Ahn with the card. One wonders if the card even exists, or if it does, why the director will not make it available to Ahn.

LIVING IN HALFTONES

Orphanage personnel withholding information from adoptees or not allowing them access to their adoption files is an extremely common experience for returning adoptees. The literature and film of Korean American adoptees are filled with scenarios where files are denied, where questions are evaded, and where orphanage personnel and adoptive agents are uncooperative. It has become the experience for so many adoptees that preparing themselves for this resistance and opposition has become part of their search process.[43] This secrecy presents, perhaps, the greatest obstacle to Korean adoptees who are trying to piece together their past because, for many, these files are their only link to information about their birth parents, their birth date, their birth place, and the circumstances surrounding their placement in the orphanage. Unfortunately, the secrecy and cover-ups that seem so innate in this particular adoption industry hinder any chance of accessing "truth." Consequently, the ritual of return ends up producing more questions rather than less.[44] And this perhaps is the most unexpected part of their search. In searching for bits and pieces of their past, adoptees end up finding more bits and pieces, more pieces to the puzzle, rather than less. Oftentimes, we assume that the discovery of these new pieces will offer cohesion, will work to create a semblance of a whole; however, as most of the film and literature of Korean American adoptees reveal, more is simply more.

Perhaps it is because Korean American adoptees have "memory shot through with holes." "Memory shot through with holes" is, according to French Jewish writer Henri Raczymow, memory with missing links. The experience of familial and communal trauma, of being displaced from one's homeland, causes memory to burst like a balloon, leaving only scraps of memory.[45] The problem of having a memory that is shot through with holes is that discovering bits and pieces of one's past creates more holes not less, more scraps not less. Indeed, by definition, "memory shot through with holes," according to Raczymow, "cannot be filled in or recovered."[46] That is why Ahn's film *Living in Halftones*, as a record of the return ritual, falls short of filling in the gaps of her personal history despite recovering some of the missing pieces of her past. Indeed, the title of her film seems to suggest this.

"Halftone" connotes the state of navigating the middle space, of being in-between.[47] But "halftone" is also a term used to describe a photographic technique that simulates continuous tone imagery using dots. An image that looks to be unified, whole, and complete is, in fact, full of holes, gaps, and breaks when looked at more closely. Ahn appears to be suggesting the same thing about the return ritual and about adoptee identity. On the surface, returning to the Motherland in search of one's roots seems like a journey that will bring about wholeness and a more complete understanding of oneself. Upon closer inspection, however, the ritual of return leads to more holes, more dots, if you will.

Similarly, dominant narratives about adoptee identity create an optical illusion of the well-adjusted, successfully assimilated adoptee; however, the film and literature of Korean American adoptees reveal the fractured identities that come from being expected to completely assimilate and erase their preadoption past. Adoptee identity, like adoptee memory and history, is also fragmented. The spaces between those dots seem to be permanently fixed. As a result, being an adoptee means residing in the spaces between the dots. It means negotiating and navigating one's way through gaps and breaks in history and memory. It means becoming comfortable with the unknown. It means "living in halftones," which has become the adoptee way of life.

CONCLUSION

If the past is irretrievable and memory is irrecoverable, then why invent rituals to connect to the past? Why continue the ritual of return? One reason is because inventing and performing rituals build community. Since the Seoul Olympic Games in 1988, adoptees have been returning to Korea in unprecedented numbers in an attempt to reconnect with their cultural roots and/or to search for the missing pieces to their past.[48] Thousands have returned, and an increasing number of adoptees who return end up staying. Currently, a large community of adoptees live, work, and study in Korea. Originally a group that lacked a unified community, Korean American adoptees have built and are continuing to build community through ritual. Certain activities (e.g., visiting the orphanage) have steadily become fixed elements in the return ritual. Indeed, these activities have quickly become conventional among the Korean American adoptee community through formality, fixity, and repetition, which Bell states are central aspects of ritualization.[49] They have increasingly become more formal and, thus, more ritualized now that private and government organizations sponsor Motherland tours. Motherland tours, according to Kim, "are a means to offering a safe way for adopted Koreans to return to their country of birth, and can also provide an opportunity for adopted Koreans to meet others like themselves from all over the world."[50] The shared experience that these tours provide fosters a sense of communal identity that was absent prior to the invention of the return ritual. Indeed, ritual is integral to the construction of community.[51]

Another reason why Korean American adoptees continue to perform and invent rituals is because ritual is an effective way to connect to their preadoption past. The return ritual enables adoptees to collect memory, but only in fragments. As previously discussed, being at the orphanage allowed Adolfson to recapture a part of his personal history. For Ahn, the orphanage ignited flashes of repressed memory. The ritual of return successfully facilitated the revival and recovery of repressed and absent memories, but because adoptees have "memory shot through with holes," the retrieval of memory through the return ritual left missing links. Postmemory functions to fill in some of the gaps in memory. As works of postmemory, Korean American adoptee literature and film narrate the missing links left by the ritual of return. In so doing, they narrate both individual and collective identity in all their diversity, disorientation, and fragmentation and contribute to the emerging practice of Asian American folklore.

NOTES

1. Catherine Bell, *Ritual: Perspectives and Dimensions* (NY: Oxford UniversityPress, 1997), 81.

2. Catherine Bell, *Ritual Theory, Ritual Practice* (NY: Oxford University Press, 1992), 74.

3. Adam Seligman, Robert Weller, Michael Puett, and Bennett Simon, *Ritual and Its Consequences: An Essay on the Limits of Sincerity* (NY: Oxford University Press, 2008), 5.

4. Ibid., 5.

5. Bell, *Ritual*, 252.

6. Bell, 241.

7. Marianne Hirsch, *Family Frames: Photography, Narrative, and Postmemory* (Cambridge: Harvard University Press, 1997).

8. Eleana Kim, "Korean Adoptee Auto-Ethnography: Refashioning Self, Family and Finding Community," *Visual Anthropology Review* 16.1 (Spring-Summer 2000): 47, 62.

9. Kim, 43. Borrowing from Catherine Russell, Kim describes Korean adoptee films as auto-ethnographies because as autobiographical explorations of identity, family, and history, the films become ethnographic because the filmmaker "understands his or her personal history to be implicated in larger social formations and historical processes" (43).

10. Kim, 62.

11. Katy Robinson, *A Single Square Picture: A Korean Adoptee's Search for Her Roots* (NY: Berkley Books, 2002): 78.

12. Interestingly, naturalization papers often serve as birth certificates for adoptees, further equating birth with adoption. Adoption as the beginning of personal history becomes legally institutionalized through this practice.

13. Robinson, 1.

14. Jane Jeong Trenka, *The Language of Blood: A Memoir* (St. Paul, MN: Borealis, 2003): 14.

15. For more examples, see *Seeds from the a Silent Tree. Seeds: An Anthology by Korean Adoptees*, Eds. Tonya Bishoff and Jo Rankin (San Diego, CA: Pandal Press, 1997). Melis-

sa Lin Hanson writes in her poem "Behind My Eyes," "Two white people decided to adopt / that's where life began" (60). Crystal Lee Hyun Joo Chappell echoes the same sentiment that history or life begins with adoption rather than biological birth when she explains, "In essence, I came to believe that I had been born on the day I was adopted, at age 4" (126). Wayne Alan Berry states, "I had no memory of Korea . . . my birthfamily [*sic*], the food, the culture—it was all erased once I became known as Wayne Alan Berry" (121). This sentiment is not solely a Korean American adoptee phenomenon but one that is felt by Korean adoptees all over the world. Korean-Dutch adoptee filmmaker In-Soo Radake reveals in his documentary film *Made in Korea* several adoptees who say, "I was born twice—once in Seoul and once in Holland."

16. Bell, *Ritual*, 95.

17. Louis Althusser, *Lenin and Philosophy, and Other Essays*, Trans. Ben Brewster (NY: Monthly Review Press, 1972), 174.

18. Althusser, 174-175.

19. Althusser, 175.

20. Trenka, 16.

21. Trenka, 17.

22. Trenka.

23. Trenka.

24. Trenka.

25. Motherland trips are tours provided by the Korean government and/or private organizations that help returning Korean adoptees to reconnect with Korean culture and history. They are also set up to facilitate birth family searches for interested adoptees.

26. For example, Mi Ok Song Bruining, a contributor to *Seeds From a Silent Tree*, explains that despite being raised white, she felt more like an "alien" (66). Her face was the topic of constant torment and abuse from both peers and strangers. Consequently, she avoided looking into mirrors in an attempt to deny her difference, which ended up cultivating her "self-hatred" and "internalized racism" (68). Wayne A. Berry, another contributor to *Seeds*, also talks about how no matter how careful he was to "not display any signs of [his] Asian heritage" in an effort to become white American, he was "always reminded of this when [he] looked into the mirror" (121). His face betrayed him.

27. Catherine Ceniza Choy and Gregory Paul Choy, "Transformative Terrains: Korean Adoptees and the Social Constructions of an American Childhood," in *The American Child: A Cultural Studies Reader*, Eds. Caroline F. Levander and Carol J. Singley (New Brunswick, NJ: Rutgers University Press, 2003), 270.

28. Leah Sieck, "In America," in *Seeds From a Silent Tree*, 94.

29. MeK Ahn, *Undertow* (NY: Third World Newsreel, 1995). VHS.

30. Ahn, *Undertow*.

31. Ahn, *Undertow*.

32. Henri Raczymow, Trans. Alan Astro, "Memory Shot Through With Holes," *Yale French Studies* 85 (1994): 100. Raczymow describes memory as "next-to-nothing," a phrase he borrows from Vladimir Jankélévitch.

33. Hirsch, 23, my emphasis.

34. Hirsch, 22.

35. Hirsch, 127.

36. Hirsch, 243.

37. Nathan Adolfson, *Passing Through* (San Francisco: National Asian American Telecommunications Association, 1998).

38. Adolfson.

39. "Living in Halftones," Third World Newsreel website, http://www.twn.org/catalog/pages/cpage.aspx?rec=984&card=price (accessed 8/15/09).

40. Ahn, *Living in Halftones* (NY: Third World Newsreel, 1994). VHS.

41. Ahn, *Living in Halftones*.

42. Ahn, *Living in Halftones*.

43. Currently, there is a movement for adoptee rights taking place in Seoul, Korea. The Truth and Reconciliation for the Adoption Community of Korea (TRACK) is a "group of internationally adopted Koreans, Korean nationals and diasporic Koreans, and supporters from around the world." Their mission is to advocate for the "full understanding of the practice of adoption, both past and present, [and] to preserve the rights of children and families." In 2011 TRACK was instrumental in helping to pass a new adoption bill that allows adoptees access to their adoption records, as well as preserve the rights of biological parents. For more information, visit TRACK's official website at http://justicespeaking.wordpress.com/.

44. Barbara Yngvesson also dismantles the idea of return as a "form of completion or fulfillment in which one can find oneself" by examining the return trips of Chilean adoptees living in Sweden (9). See Yngvesson, "Going 'Home': Adoption, Loss of Bearings, and the Mythology of Roots," *Social Text* 21.1 (Spring 2003): 7-27.

45. Raczymow, 102, 103.

46. Raczymow, 104.

47. In Eleana Kim's analysis of Ahn's film, she interprets "living in halftones" as "being a hybrid subject, of existing between social categories, and of belonging to two families, across cultural and national borders." See Kim, 62.

48. Eleana Kim, "Wedding Citizenship and Culture: Korean Adoptees and the Global Family of Korea," in *Cultures of Transnational Adoption*, Ed. Toby Alice Volkman (Durham: Duke University Press, 2005), 51.

49. Bell, *Ritual Theory*, 92.

50. Kim, "Wedding Citizenship and Culture," 51. In addition to offering activities that facilitate the search process (such as visiting orphanages, speaking to other adoptees who have searched for birth family members, etc.), Motherland tours can entail the following activities: visiting ancient Korean landmarks; sightseeing; and taking Korean language classes and courses on traditional Korean customs and cuisine (50-51).

51. Bell, *Ritual*, 252.

SEVEN

Filipino Folklore, Space, and Performance

Francis Tanglao-Aguas

LEGEND OF MARCOS AND HIS NINETY MILLION CHILDREN[1]

"The bias in favor of the primate city and the modern elite has left the countryside in the backwaters not only of the economy but the national memory."

"Here I echo Lucien Febvre's energetic plea for a *historie des mentalites*, the reconstitution of the emotional life of man and its manifestations."
—Resil B. Mojares, "Waiting for Mariang Makiling"

Having grown up under martial law in the Philippines during the 1970s, surrounded by rice and corn in San Fernando, Pampanga, Resil B. Mojares' seminal essay about Filipino cultural history was a welcome clarion call by which I was able to graph my own history.[2] The desire to express myself had always been within having been raised by a mother who taught history, albeit using books published under the authorization of Ferdinand Marcos, the tyrant president who extended his reign by declaring martial law. Like most martial law babies, as those of us who were born and raised during that period have come to be nicknamed, I had been raised amid a repressive self-censorship system of the highest caliber that was in full throttle even during sleep.

After I read Mojares' essay, I realized that although I had been only a child, everything I went through under Marco's tyrannical rule bore some significance to a larger community. Further, Mojares liberated me from my internalized Marcosian self-censor, giving me permission to compose my own narrative since no one else would have documented my experience, especially since I was neither one of the "modern elite," nor did I come from the "primate city." In fact, because my siblings and I were raised amidst military rule, I thought nothing of armed soldiers inspecting my book bag at checkpoints on the way to school, or making sure we would always be home before dusk when curfew began. Neither did I hear our parents and elders complain of the hardships and difficulties of living with curtailed freedom.

In hindsight of course, oppressed people do not ponder their oppression everyday nor do they carry a scowl on their face as a badge of honor to mark their sad lot. I raise this to reference some Western visitors to the Philippines who misinterpret the ubiquitous Filipino smile as a symbol of a people's satisfaction or happiness with their state in life. To me, the Filipino capacity to smile amidst suffering is actually an act of revolt against the status quo. With a smile, we declare our strength, preserve our dignity, and propagate our pleasing personality and appearance. Thus we all soldiered on with a smile, thinking nothing was great or extraordinary with our circumstance in all the contexts of these words available. But in the privacy of our homes, unless we thought we were wiretapped, we put aside our smiles that shielded us and let it all hang out as portrayed in this scene based on my earliest memories of martial rule.[3]

PROCOPIO: Your students must think we're poor.

TERESITA: We are poor.

BABY cries.

PROCOPIO: And your co-teachers? Tell the whole world I can't feed you while you're at it.

TERESITA: Grocery store marked up their prices again. It's the inflation. Marcos can't control it. Just last week, I bought twice as much beef for half the price. It's ridiculous.

BABY cries louder.

PROCOPIO: Here's all the money I got! Pay all the bills and whatever goddamned thing you're stressing out about. I work my fucking ass off for this!

BABY cries incredibly loud.

PROCOPIO: Patrick. Patrick. Hush boy, hush.

PROCOPIO: Patrick, what did I tell you? This child! So young, yet so stubborn. If you don't shut up, I'm gonna take you out in the street by the sewer. It's scary out there.

BABY cries and screams for his life.

PROCOPIO: I said shut up!!! Do you wanna be out there on your own? I'm serious, Patrick. It's dark out there. Lots of mangwang-anak out there. Invisible masked men with big guns who'll put you in sacks and sell you in the market. Lots of Patiyanaks out there, dead unborn crybabies like you thrown by their parents in the talahib bushes. Or do you wanna see Tikbalangs, huh Patrick? Big black smelly hairy horses smoking cigars by the mango tree? Shut up. Shut up. Otherwise, a Manananggal will snatch you with her sharp claws and fly you to her family so they can suck your blood and make Patrick blood stew they can eat for dinner. They like babies. Patrick, you hear me boy? No one wants a crybaby but evil spirits.

Raising children and staying happily married are difficult objectives enough for any man and woman; but as shown in this scene, when compounded with systems of oppression, the quest to build a family transforms into something nefarious. After all, Paulo Freire's *Pedagogy of the Oppressed*[4] warrants that oppressed people are bound to learn nothing but oppressing themselves and everyone around them in their quest to be free. To the oppressed, liberation means the capacity to exert willful power over another in the same way that power was enforced on them, which is mostly as violence or as a violation. Thus, as dramatized by the father Procopio who corrupts the narratives of the scarier figures of Philippine Folklore to borderline terrorize his child, our parents became our personalized versions of Ferdinand Marcos. That is, unless they belonged to the few who were able to read and internalize Freire's famed self-liberation manifesto, which was of course banned then in the Philippines.

My siblings and I tolerated the military checkpoints and curfew not only because we were fortunate enough not to be detained for breaking curfew or to be in a bus with a Molotov toting insurgent, but because as children, we based our security on the state of our family. We survived the political system because we did not imbibe it with the meaning that its perpetrators needed in order to oppress us. No matter how Ferdinand and Imelda Marcos asserted their self-proclaimed divine destiny as father and mother of all Filipinos, even going so far as having their likeness painted as Philippine Folklore's Malakas (Strong) and Maganda (Beautiful), no amount of propaganda and psychological warfare could uproot our faith in our family. In effect, domestic conflict like Teresita's and Procopio's did more to erode our sense of security than any massacre or ambush attributed in whispers to the Marcos dictatorship.

Figure 7.1.   A Portrait of Marcos Malakas, by Betsy Westendorp de Brias. "Malakas at Maganda," paintings by Betsy Westendorp de Brias.

Figure 7.2.   A Portrait of Imelda Maganda, by Betsy Westendorp de Brias. "Malakas at Maganda," paintings by Betsy Westendorp de Brias.

Purposely misinterpreting folklore to silence crying children is lazy parenting; but co-opting it to brainwash a people so they equate tyrants as the deities from whom they are descended is perverted despotic ingenuity at its worst. In presenting themselves as Malakas and Maganda, the mythical ancestors of all Filipinos, the Marcoses impaled themselves on Philippine Folklore hoping its powers would penetrate them so they could morph into a tradition and ideology in and of themselves—colonizing the spiritual, emotional, and intellectual processes of the Filipinos in the same way the Spaniards did through the Cross of Catholicism and the Americans through the Celluloid of Hollywood. Much like the foreign invaders, the Marcoses wanted to colonize us body and soul, in our every waking and sleeping hour, perhaps even beyond our death.

THE BANANA SOLDIERS APPARITION

"Dad, there are men in the backyard with guns aimed at our house." I must have been five or six years old when I would awake in the middle of the night screaming at what I could see outside my window. I would scream for dear life, repeating the sight until my parents would come to the room I shared with my siblings.

Sometimes, my older sister Johanna or my younger brother Jerome would wake up. Jerome would squint his eyes, eager to see what I could. "Where are they? I want to see them." I would hush them and then point out exactly where the men hang about in our unlit backyard. "Right there, behind the sour sop tree, perched on the concrete fence. They seem to be waiting for a signal to attack. Or are they just watching us?" We would keep on our own watch until my parents came into the room.

"Go back to sleep, those are just banana leaves flailing in the wind." My father was always adamant there were no such men of danger to us but I was insistent. "Let's turn on all the lights outside so you can see." My father would not budge, even if my mother seconded my motion. "Why would they wait to shoot? There's no one there—just banana leaves." Of course even if he had listened to me and lit up the backyard, the armed men would have left by then, hearing all the commotion and arguing coming from the house. "You're just dreaming is all. Keep quiet and go back to sleep."

Indignant that my testimony was not accepted as truth, the next morning I would walk to the backyard near the fence and outside our house to the vacant lots on both sides to prove my point. We did have some banana trees in the backyard, but not exactly at the spots where I saw the armed men. I would proceed to take my siblings and my mom with me to prove my case even climbing up the fence to try to contort the leaves to show they could not possibly create that detailed of a shadow play.

One weekend, my father brought a man with a long cutlass blade to the house. The man chopped off most of the banana trees in our backyard and in the vacant lots next door. "Now we can all get some sleep," he would exclaim. At that point, I knew better than to retort my defense.

If my father was quick to dismiss my testimony as a dream, my maternal grandmother Apu Deyi[5] seemed to relish each word of my telling. She would ask me to restate every detail of what I had seen, her eyes immersed in my story, her nostrils slightly flaring and her lips holding out a naughty smile—all signs not only of her interest and belief in me but more so her amusement and delight in what I had witnessed. "Could you see their faces?" No, it was too dark. "What kinds of guns did they have?" Rifles. "Which way were they facing?" Our house. "What were they wearing?" Bulky clothes. "Did you hear that? They had long guns and were facing towards the house." Apu would then holler what I had just said to anyone else in hearing distance, whether it was my Aunt who was preparing lunch or my Uncle who was waiting to eat it.

Unbeknownst to me at that time, my family was one of the many families under the surveillance of the Marcos Dictatorship because of my family's political affiliation. My mom's sister and her husband were already incarcerated in the army base in Manila, with their young children. Thus, had my father taken me to a psychologist she might have agreed with my father that my vision could have been a dream indeed but one founded on fears for our safety.

Categorizing what I had seen as a dream was the best recourse my parents had to assuage us of having as near as normal a childhood as we could have given the realities of the Philippines then. They were practicing methods of western psychology and parenting they had learned in universities founded by the former Spanish and American colonizers.

On the other hand, Apu who was born 1907 was practicing the age old oral tradition of storytelling and testimony passed on to her by her own grandmother who had raised her. These two diverse ways of applying meaning to experience would encapsulate my navigation of my contradicting realities. Naturally I gravitated more to Apu and her ways of "knowing and being."

Aware as I was of Apu's unique ways, she did not propagate them to me through indoctrination or rote practice. Rather, like the storytelling and testimony session by which she engaged my encounter with the "banana soldiers," she summoned the practices only when the situation warranted. She never sat me down to introduce a new concept. It was the same with her own stories, which were scarce from her own mouth, even if we asked such as when I asked how my two Aunts had died in their teens. We had been passing by their large portraits every day in the darkly lit hallway of the ancestral house, their seemingly "glow in the dark" eyes fixed on us. Apu said not a single word regarding their passing.

Once, while working on an assignment on the Japanese occupation of the Philippines, I had hoped to retrieve her personal narrative. "If you assume the Japanese to be so cruel and inhumane, wait till you find out what the Americans did," but that was all she would say. Obviously, my great-grandmother, who was alive during the Philippine American War of 1898-1906, had passed on her own narrative to Apu who was obviously not going to pass them on to us. It was as if she was keeping on her role as keeper of the tales, always seeking out our stories for her own safe-keeping.

All semblance of forgiveness I assumed Apu to have bestowed on the Japanese for their occupation vanished the day my Aunt was hosting her Japanese friends. Apu joined the reception, her command of English far better than the guests. It was an awesome sight to see her engage on an international level, she who legend had it did not even make it to fourth grade yet read only English newspapers and watched only American television. But after the Japanese guests left that night, we would never see them again. If ever there were admonishments from Apu for my Aunt never to invite them again, we would never know. It was then I began to depend on the generosity of fabulation to help me make sense of the tectonic shifts and schisms of spaces where I existed — to fill in the blanks my grandmother provided.

My Apu died the year I became an American citizen while studying theater at UCLA. One day, on my way home, I randomly found myself in a lecture at Royce Hall, pulled in by the sound of Kapampangan accented Tagalog emanating from my school's world famous landmark. Going in, I watched mouth agape as a grandmother named Amonita Balahadja publicly recounted her testimony as an enslaved comfort woman raped to satisfy the sexual appetite of the Japanese soldiers occupying the Philippines in World War II. She was from San Fernando, Pampanga my very own hometown.

Apu's silence on her experience during the Japanese occupation and the episode with the Japanese at her house kept haunting me together with Amonita Balahadja's testimony. I wanted to help shed light on their truth the best way I could. So I translated and adapted Balahadja's story, fusing it with my fabulation of Apu's childhood as a tribute to all grandmothers who lived through that ordeal. Here is a condensation of the testimony I created.

> My name is Estrella del Mundo.
> I was born in the Philippines,
> December 8, 1935,
>
> In the River of Rocks where the Americans built
> Roads made of rocks for the planes.
> Planes my Koyang[6] and I liked to watch.

— — —

One day came the Japanese to our house very, very mad.
Say them Tatang[7] is a spy.
Say them Tatang must die.

No more Tatang. No more Koyang.
I earn money, washing clothes for the Americans.
Washing in secret.

One day washing secrets came the Japanese
Came they on horses.
Came they with bigger guns.

Virgin! They yell. Virgin! They laugh.
Me they chase. Me that runs.
Me only washing clothes for the Americans.

Only ten. So they like.
I run. But they caught.
In small room.

Now they rape.
Tonight they rape.
In the morning.
— — —
But one night, Moshi-Moshi tired.
"Estrella, my Japanese penis massage.
And sing. I tired. Sing."

Atin ku pung singsing, metung yang timpukan.
Amana ke iti, kang Indung ibatan.
Sangkang keng sininup, king metung a kaban.
Mewala ya iti, eku kemalayan.

Ing sukal ning lub ku, susukdul keng banwa.
Pikurus kung gamat, babo ning la mesa.
Ninu mang menakit, keng singsing kung mana.
Kalulung pusu ku, manginu ya kaya.[8]

When he sleeps, I run.

LEGEND OF THE INVISIBLE PEOPLE

My mother lived in a modern five-storey house in Angeles City near Clark, the largest American military base outside the United States. Her father was a lawyer who designed the massive house inspired by his visit to Venice in the 1940s. Meanwhile, my father came straight out of a Chekhov play raised in a landed family unable to make the adjustment to the end of agriculture-based aristocracy. Either way, any wealth generated by both families was subject to corruption endemic in the government. By the time we grandchildren entered the scene, all that was left was a bucket full of pride and nary an ounce of wealth to fill it.

The societal gulf between my mother's cosmopolitan family and my father's feudal background was bridged through various forms of folklore practiced by both families. On my mother's side, Apu engaged us children directly, valuing our voices. Meanwhile, my paternal grandparents viewed children as God-given sources of amusement with no perspective. No matter how varied they considered us, both sets of grandparents remained firm that we be banned from playing outdoors between three and five in the afternoon out of respect to the *nuno*. The *nuno*, various venerated forms of invisible ancestral beings, would come out during the hottest time of the day known to be rush hour in daily *nuno* life.

Young as we were, my siblings and I determined early on that our elders were frequent to summon legendary creatures to control us. Obviously, they needed us to take naps so they could rest from our daily ruckus. It was during this quiet that my paternal grandmother made us pajamas from old curtains and bed sheets without fear of a needle puncturing her rambunctious grandchildren. As we got older, she would trust us enough to help her thread the needle, even teaching the lucky among us how to sew.

The patrician set up on my father's side of the family where children were seen and not heard naturally took us children on the path of creating a separate world of our own where we could voice our opinions and interpretations of the world. In our secret world, we could tackle out loud what our elders might have opted to merely whisper about. We could bandy about theories on why dinner always had to be so quiet, with no silverware allowed to make a sound. Was it so the patrolling military would not hear how much food we had, lest they raid us and take it all? Or was it the communist insurgents we were afraid of attracting to our bounty? Whose side were we on? Or were our grandparents just uptight given the military rule? The situation was one rife for conspiracies and collaborations to subvert authority—particularly towards the nap requirement.

I cannot recall exactly if he collaborated with someone or not, but I myself was unaware when my younger brother Jerome managed to escape the eye of our Aunt guarding our nap so he could play in the backyard during the most holy hours of the *nuno*. The manner in which he would be found out cemented the basis of our Grandparents' admonition, convincing us forever of their rationale.

It was a school day and Jerome still had not gotten up to get ready. "What happened to you? Does it hurt?" My mother was in near panic as she stood there looking at Jerome who lay in bed, his face also askance.

One of his legs was suddenly much larger and longer than the other. It was huge, from the thigh right down to his feet as if it belonged to another person altogether. That Jerome was not in pain according to him, gave us permission to joke and laugh at his expense. But my mother was not amused in the least. Immediately, we took him to my Aunt the doctor who lived five houses away.

"What are you doing taking him here? There is nothing I can do to help him." My Aunt shooed us away like the bubonic plague gone knocking at her door. "Go, take him to the Native Healer. Let her do *tawas* on him."

I could not believe my Aunt, the town's most trusted pediatrician, was entrusting my brother's fate to a Native Healer. After all, my father's clan was proud to have various doctors on its ranks—a sign that they were breaking into modernity as opposed to my mother's family, who lived in the city but continued to send us to a Healer when we would get sick.

Taking a patient to the Healer meant asking them to perform the ritual ceremony called *tawas* to diagnose what had caused the ailment. Performing *tawas* looked more like cooking rather than a witches' brew or any other cinematic image evoked by ritual in modern times. The Healer would fill a basin with water, and decide whether to use a candle or an egg, both of which may have been blessed by Catholic rites.

She would then break the egg and pour it on the basin. Had she chosen the candle, the Healer would light it, wait for enough paraffin to melt so she could pour it in the basin. After muttering a prayer, the Healer interprets the figure created by the egg or the paraffin floating on the water.

The Healer told us Jerome had stepped not only on a *nuno* but one who was a prince, as evidenced by the fancy crown formed by the floating egg. Her prescription was for my brother to pour salt on our backyard and to make an offering to gain not only the prince's forgiveness but also his good favor if possible. After all he lived in a realm deeper than the foundation of our house, and for much longer than when our family acquired the land late in the eighteenth century. When Jerome accidentally inflicted pain on the *nuno* prince, the portal between our two worlds opened. His enlarged leg physically embodied both realities coexisting. And because we also shared this space, we all had to help Jerome in the task of nurturing a healthy relationship with the *nuno* prince and his Kingdom.

But what would please a prince enough for him to restore Jerome's leg to its normal size? The Healer was clear: "Think of all a man of power would enjoy, and bring them to the *nuno* in the same hour he played in the backyard. Let him kneel where he played the most so he can lay out his offerings and contrition."

Thus, my mother bought a carton of cigarettes, a bottle of rum, and other consumables men of leisure enjoy. We watched my brother from the stairwell as he walked out into the backyard, limping along with his gigantic leg as he poured salt on the earth. Then after setting out the booty in a spot, he knelt with his back to us.

On sunset, Jerome finally broke from his genuflection and limped back to the house. None of us asked him what he told the prince. The next morning, he was the first to wake up and get ready. His leg was back to its normal size.

Tawas did not always yield such a specific cause of illness. Once, when *tawas* was performed for me on account of a stomachache no medicine could alleviate, *tawas* revealed that my pain was caused by *banis.* The Healer explained something akin to "hexing" or "cursing" in the West.

"But who would do this to me? Does this mean there are witches in town, maybe even in my own house?" The Healer did not make things any simpler. "There may well be witches around you, but even you could *banis* anyone you wished, sometimes even without you knowing you'd done it already." I was getting ready to follow my Western education, which presupposed I had entered into voodoo and witchcraft when the Healer leveled with me.

"It could have been someone you saw before you fell ill who has a secret grudge with you. You could have crossed their path at a time when you were already feeling emotionally or physically vulnerable, like an empty stomach or stress from school that was about to befall you. But if at that moment, you crossed paths with a grudge carrier, by merely seeing each other, *banis* already occurs, multiplying your illness. The severity of the *banis* depends on how deep a person holds their contempt for you."

To be rid of the *banis,* I was to look back at everything I did before I fell ill and recall all of the persons I encountered so that I could assess every person's deepest feelings about me. I was to mark the people whose feelings for me might be less than congenial, go to each person and ask for their healing. "Do not tell them you think they might have *banis* you. Ask them to spit in their hands, and to massage your stomach so you may gain healing."

I told my mother who I thought might wish me ill. But instead of taking me to that person, she asked my siblings to be the first to massage their spit into my stomach. As can be imagined, they delighted in having the chance to rub saliva on me. The entire situation was so hilarious it could have worsened my stomachache. But the laughter ended up drawing the suspect in, protected by the cloak of our convivial humor. Without my playful siblings, it could not have been more inconvenient and awkward with me going from house to house, seeking healing from every neighbor as they used to in the olden times according to my Apu.

Apu and all my grandparents certainly found nothing humorous with my siblings' comportment in breaking the *banis.* To them, no amount of spit slobbered on my stomach could cure me if we disrespected the ritual.

When it was their turn to rub my stomach, I saw the ferocity in their eyes searching for that one ill thought planted within so they could pluck it out and heal me. It was then I realized why our elders made sure to avert their eyes each time they found themselves making eye contact. Much too much could be passed on in so much as a glance.

The Native Healer's *tawas* and *banis* are only two of the many legacies of the *Baylan* or *Babaylan*, priest, chief, and healer of pre-colonial Philippines who more often than not was a woman. The *Baylan*'s main duty to her community had been the preservation of the security and well-being of all its members on all levels, particularly every individual's *loob* or *kalooban*[9] ("inner self or world, the invisible") and the *labas*[10] ("outer self or world, the visible"). Reference to the *loob* means a fusion of body and soul, heart and mind, which when balanced leads to harmony and happiness from within the invisibe *loob* extending out to the *labas* or every visible and physical component of a person and his community, which in turn has its own layers that are invisible *(loob)* and visible *(labas)*.

The prince my brother stepped on existed within our community's *loob* (invisible inner world), his presence materialized in Jerome's enlarged leg (a part of his visible *labas*) so that we in the community visible to ourselves would be aware of our invisible neighbors in the inner world whose well-being intertwined interdependently with ours. In the same way, the *banis* reminds us to be more circumspect and conscientious of how our innermost thoughts and feelings impact everyone and everything in our worlds, visible or invisible, internal or external. Thus, in keeping these traditions, Apu, my grandmother was inculcating in us the capacity to live on a high level of mindfulness that considers the welfare of all in these worlds for our safety and survival, much in the same way the *Baylan* did for our pre-colonial ancestors. Rooted in the knowledge and wisdom of our heritage, with hearts and minds attuned even to the unseen, thus were we equipped to survive and thrive in our migration to the United States where it would be our turn to be invisible to many.

NOTES

1. The National Statistics Office estimates the Philippines' population at 94,349,600 in 2010. The U.S. State Department estimates there are four million Americans of Filipino ancestry living in the United States.
2. Resil B. Mojares, "Waiting for Mariang Makiling" in *Waiting for Mariang Makiling: Essays in Philippine Cultural History* (Ateneo de Manila University Press, Quezon City, 2002), 2.
3. Francis Tanglao-Aguas, "The Sarimanok Travels: The First Play of the Filipino Trilogy of Plays," *Tibuk-Tibok Anthology of Young Filipino Writers* (Tibuk-Tibok Publications, Quezon City, Philippines, 2002).
4. Paulo Freire, *Pedagogy of the Oppressed* (Continuum Press, 1969).
5. Apu: Grandmother.
6. Koyang: Big Brother
7. Tatang: Father

8. She sings the Kapampangan folk song, "Atin Ku Pung Singsing."

9. Enriquez, Virgilio,"Unit 15-Kaugalian, Halagahin, at Pagkatao (Customs, Values & Character)"in *Colonial To Liberation Psychology: The Philippine Experience.* (Quezon City, Philippines: University of the Philippines Press, 1992)

10. These are the primary tenets of Dr. Virgilio Enriquez's Sikolohiyang Pilipino (Filipino Psychology), which centered the Filipino indigenous experience as the basis by which to examine the Filipino psyche, rather than fitting the Filipino experience into Western precepts.

EIGHT

Forging Transnational Folklore

Cambodian American Hip Hop

Cathy J. Schlund-Vials

"My dad would call it [hip hop] jungle music because there was a lot of bass in it. (My parents) said, 'You better go to school, don't go out so much.' Listening to music is okay, but they would hear profanity and say, 'Why are you listening to stuff that has cussing and the N word?' And I would try to explain to them, 'Hey, this is what's happening right now.' My parents (are) more happy with it now 'cause I'm aware of what happened [in Cambodia under Pol Pot] and I'm spreading it in the right way. . . . They're proud that I'm reflecting the culture."
—praCh Ly, "Interview," *Frontline/World*, October 2002.[1]

"Hip-hop has always related to poor people in the struggle...That's why we relate to it. We got a right to say what we say."
—Joe In (AZI Fellas), "Hip-Hop Hopes," *Philadelphia Weekly*, 4 May 2010.[2]

INTRODUCTION

Focused on rap, this chapter commences with a summary of activist rapper KRS-One's song, "9 Elements," which establishes the basic tenets of hip hop. Emphasizing traditions, expressions, and interactions, KRS-One's "9 Elements" assumes folkloric significance. In turn, reading hip hop through folklore makes possible an examination of folklife, which is emblematized by experiences "on the street" and within particular communities. Contextualizing KRS-One's "9 Elements" via S. Craig Watkins' argument about why "hip hop matters," the chapter then shifts to Asian

American folklore and folklife, specifically centering on Cambodian American rapper praCh. Using praCh's three-part hip hop memoir, *Dalama*, this chapter explores how the rapper employs Asian (Cambodian) and American music traditions to convey the traumatic story of Cambodia's killing fields. Between 1975 and 1979, over the course of three years, eight months and twenty days, the communist Khmer Rouge was responsible for the deaths of 1.7 million Cambodians (21–25 percent of the population) due to overwork, disease, starvation, and execution. Combining traditional Khmer music, 1960s Cambodian rock/pop, documentary film, and contemporary U.S. hip hop, praCh strategically uses lyric and sample (e.g., the use of previously released music fragments) to underscore Cambodia's genocidal past, visually depict his parents' stories of survival, and highlight the experiences of contemporary Cambodian Americans in the United States.

HIP HOP FUNDAMENTALS: KRS-ONE'S "9 ELEMENTS"

In the summer of 2003, Koch Records released KRS-One's ninth album, *The Kristyle*, produced by DJ Revolution (a.k.a. Kurt Hoffman), the legendary MC himself (née Lawrence Parker), and DJ Kenny Parker (KRS-One's brother and principal collaborator).[3] With lyrics focused on politics, race, and culture, *The Kristyle* was certainly true to KRS-One form. Known in hip hop circles as an incisive cultural commentator, the ever-provocative MC battled corporations, politicians, and rappers over the course of *The Kristyle*'s twenty tracks.[4] Nevertheless, not everyone bought KRS-One's anti-corporate, progressively political, anti-commercial message. For some, the rapper's activism, forged over the course of a twenty-plus year career, struck a sour chord. For example, *Entertainment Weekly* reviewer Jonah Wiener opined,

> Barking no-logo rants and cred spiels, KRS-One sees mainstream hip-hop being over-taken by bling and fancies himself its conscience. Trouble is, the rapper's become a tiresome caricature soapboxing . . . with as little imagination and as self-indulgently as the cash-'n'-ho's rim twirlers he scorns. He's noble-minded, maybe, but preachy: His ninth album makes you glad purists are on the losing side.[5]

Wiener's criticism of KRS-One grudgingly acknowledges the rapper's supposed noble-mindedness, but is wary and dismissive of KRS-One's alleged penchant for "soapboxing."[6] Taking to task hip hop purists who privilege the message over mad money, the *Entertainment Weekly* reviewer ultimately writes off *The Kristyle* for being selfishly didactic.

Notwithstanding the review's decidedly negative tone, Wiener's critique of KRS-One's album underscores the central stakes that are part and parcel of the hip hop landscape. Accordingly, the *Entertainment Weekly* critic highlights (albeit disparagingly) the critical convergence of politics and poetics in hip hop production. This hip hop marriage of art and activism speaks to a longstanding tradition rooted in orality (via the lyric), aurality (by means of the sample), and struggle (vis-à-vis anti-racist, anti-oppression themes). Correspondingly, S. Craig Watkins notes,

> In addition to being a pop culture force, hip hop's widening sphere of influence has shouldered it with the burden of being a genuine political force. Gone are discussions about *whether* hip hop matters; they have been replaced by the key issues of who and what kinds of values will define *how* hip hop matters. The struggle for hip hop is real, and it is being played out across a remarkably rich and varied terrain: in pop culture, old and new media, colleges and universities, in prisons, through the conduit of community activism, in suburbia, among youth, and through the political minefield of race and gender.[7]

As Watkins makes clear, hip hop *matters* because of its "widening sphere of influence," making its production geographically expansive and demographically diverse. From Philadelphia to Phnom Penh, from Palestine to Paris, hip hop is created, performed, and consumed.

Further, if "the struggle for hip hop is real," then the question is not only where it is produced, but who creates it and how it is used. Indeed, Watkins's interrogation of hip hop is a foundational principal in this essay, which examines how Cambodian Americans use hip hop (specifically rap) to draw attention to larger national and international social justice struggles. Just as important are the means through which hip hop is culturally legible. If hip hop is a genuine political force, then it is an equally potent pop culture force.

Addressing hip hop's blend of language, expression, and performance, the master MC delineates the form's particular styles (or, more accurately, the *elements*). To paraphrase, in a track titled, "9 Elements," KRS-One defines hip hop vis-à-vis genre, language, and education. Backed by a funky 1970s beat, KRS raps about the salient modes and features of hip hop culture: breakdancing, rap, graffiti, DJ'ing, and beatboxing. These artistic elements, which encompass dance, song, art, and sound, are fused with street fashion, local slang, intergenerational knowledge, and community ownership. Following suit, KRS-One breaks down hip hop's local and national dimensions. Most significantly, "9 Elements" makes visible the foundational tenets of hip hop culture. Interdisciplinary (comprised of art, music, dance, and fashion genres) and intergenerational (based on older and younger generations), KRS-One's "9 Elements" accentuate the link between performance, daily practice, and knowledge production.[8]

HIP HOP STORYTELLING: FOLKLORIC EXPRESSIONS IN EVERYDAY LIFE

Equally important, the rapper's "9 Elements" produces a multivalent reading of hip hop through folklore insofar as it emphasizes local cultural modes, community practices, and cultural identities.[9] Accordingly, in "9 Elements," KRS-One focuses on the ways hip hop emblematizes folkloric expressions of everyday life. As Robert Georges and Michael Jones contend, the term "folklore" "denotes expressive forms, processes and behavior (1) that we customarily learn, teach, and utilize or display during face-to-face interactions, and (2) that we judge to be traditional" (1). The two folklorists further define the "traditional" by means of genre ("known precedents") and function ("as evidence of continuities and consistencies through time and space in human knowledge, thought, belief, and feeling").[10] Illustratively, KRS-One argues that hip hop is about street knowledge, common sense, and street entrepreneur realism, which coincide with a set of what Georges and Jones maintain are "expressive forms" and "face-to-face interactions." Though often relegated to the seemingly transient spaces of youth culture, hip hop is temporally past *and* present. It is also geographically here *and* there.

Across the United States and around the globe, DJs, MCs, breakers, beatboxers, and graffiti artists spin, rap, move, and embody hip hop's national, international, and transnational registers. This transcontinental, transnational geography, comprised of traditions from differing regions within the United States, other nations, and alternative countries of origin, is matched by an interconnected sociopolitical history. Hip hop was born in the late 1960s in the South Bronx and was shaped by the civil rights movement. The collective terms of hip hop, evident in KRS-One's use of the pronouns "we," "our," and "elders," calls attention to centuries-old African *griot* storytelling and Puerto Rican/Latino dance traditions.[11] Within the context of nondomestic hip hop, such folkloric traditions, intended to transmit what Georges and Jones observe are elements of "human knowledge, thought, belief, and feeling," draw upon analogous storytelling practices.

HIP HOP ON THE MOVE: IMMIGRATION, MIGRATION, AND CAMBODIAN AMERICAN RAP

Alongside hip hop's ubiquitous presence and international practice, key to the form's ongoing evolution in the United States were mid- to late-twentieth-century immigrant flows, which gave rise to multiple folkloric expressions and revisions. After the passage of the 1965 Immigration Act and the 1980 Refugee Act in particular, Asian, Latin American, and Caribbean immigrants and refugees were granted greater entry into the United States.[12] Therefore, to read hip hop *as* American folklore requires an understanding of migration, immigration, and diasporic movements. If hip hop is considered street communication, then the street is now much wider, marked by different histories and heterogeneous cultural practices.

Moreover, what distinguishes Asians/Asian Americans from other twentieth- and twenty-first-century groups are inextricable linkages to war and relocation (e.g., World War II, the Korean War, the Vietnam War, and the current War on Terror in Pakistan and Afghanistan). As the editors of *Asian American Identities and Practices: Folkloric Expressions in Everyday Life* (Jonathan H. X. Lee and Kathleen Nadeau) maintain contemporary Asian American folkloric expressions are indubitably the "consequence of transplantation, accommodation, transformation, and invention of cultural traditions, material and ideologies, of Asian diaspora communities in America."[13]

Spanning the East and West Coasts, and consumed in the United States and Cambodia, Cambodian American hip hop reflects a global culture and politics. Epitomizing "transplantation, accommodation, and cultural invention," Cambodian American hip hop reveals (via genre and politics) transnational flows of culture and adaptation.[14] As evident in the opening epigraph, Cambodian American rapper praCh's (Prach Ly) hip hop production (what his parents originally denigrated as "jungle music") draws its initial inspiration from African American rap. Nevertheless, praCh alludes to a "cultural accommodation" wherein he uses hip hop to negotiate Cambodian American history and culture.[15] Importantly, praCh's hip hop routes (and *roots*) collide with an unresolved genocidal past that determines the means of folkloric production. Therefore, to engage the *elements* of Cambodian American hip hop, one must revisit the "material and ideological" conditions (*a la* Lee and Nadeau) that foreground, influence, and define it.

RESPINNING HISTORY: U.S. BOMBINGS AND THE KHMER ROUGE

Such conditions mentioned above were initially forged through the rubric of U.S. foreign policy. Between 1969 and 1973, the United States secretly bombed the Cambodian countryside as part of an extended Vietnam War-era policy. This blanket bombing campaign destabilized an already tenuous political situation, fomenting a virulent civil war between the communist Khmer Rouge and the U.S.-backed General Lon Nol regime. On April 17, 1975, two weeks before the fall of Saigon, the Khmer Rouge rolled into the capital of Phnom Penh, signaling the end of the Lon Nol government. Intent on turning the country back to year zero (to a time before alleged Western influence), the Khmer Rouge emptied Cambodia's major cities and forced the population to work in rural labor camps with little food and virtually no medical supplies.

In totalitarian fashion, the regime oversaw periodic political purges, largely prohibited outside access, and dismantled the nation's educational, governmental, and economic infrastructure. Under the Khmer Rouge, Cambodia was thrust into a state of unbridled terror, famine, and uncertainty. Indeed, this period infamously bears the well-known label of the "Killing Fields era," underscoring state-authorized frames of atrocity, impunity, and neglect. Politically, economically, and agriculturally unviable, the Khmer Rouge were eventually deposed after three years, eight months, and twenty days (1975-1979) vis-à-vis a Vietnamese invasion. Undeniably, the regime's human cost was enormous, tragic, and unimaginable. Under Khmer Rouge rule, an estimated 1.7 million Cambodians (approximately 21 to 25 percent of the extant population) perished as a result of disease, famine, execution, and forced labor under the Khmer Rouge.[16] Shortly after the Khmer Rouge dissolution, hundreds of thousands of Cambodians fled into neighboring Thai refugee camps. Many eventually made their way to the United States, France, and Australia.[17] To date, more than 200,000 Cambodians and Cambodian Americans make their homes in the United States.[18]

CAMBODIAN AMERICAN RAP: PRACH'S *DALAMA*

This history of war, genocide, and migration significantly foregrounds praCh's *Dalama* album trilogy, which incontrovertibly reproduces the folkloric contours of the Cambodian American experience via hip hop. Verbally meshing drama with trauma, and aurally reminiscent of Buddhism (e.g., the Dali Lama), the Cambodian rapper's evocative title underscores the album's critical, cultural, and thematic stakes.[19] Taking lyrical cues from parental stories of survival, U.S. foreign policy, and Cambodian domestic policy, *Dalama* marries (in *a propos* hip hop fashion) history, struggle, and witness.

Indeed, suggestive of justice, such lyrical witnessing underscores the rapper's juridical agenda. Redolent of KRS-One's hip hop elements, praCh's commitment to "genocide knowledge" and social justice is evident in his body of work, which consistently and unabashedly battles the Khmer Rouge, U.S. foreign policy, and contemporary Cambodian politics.[20] Corresponding to KRS-One's assertion that hip hop is a viable political movement, praCh's music production company is provocatively titled, "Mujestic: It's Not Just Music, It's a Movement." To be sure, praCh emblematizes community ownership, producing not only his albums, but those of other Southeast Asian American artists (e.g., the female hip hop/ R&B group Universal Speakers and Cambodian American rap crew 2nd Language).

Concomitantly, praCh is, like KRS-One, invested in the message and the wisdom of older generations. This particular message or knowledge principally concerns post–Killing Fields justice. Indeed, when asked by an unnamed *Frontline/World* interviewer, "So what are you channeling when you rap? What is it that's possessing you—anger, rage, an insatiable curiosity?" praCh replies:

> It's just justice. That's how I feel. The people have been murdered, they need justice. You can say bury the past . . . but if you bury something, that means it's dead. And if it's dead, if the spirit don't rest in peace, it's going to come back and haunt you. . . . I don't believe in vengeance, I don't believe in killings, but I do believe in justice.[21]

praCh's response lays bare the global migrations, politics, and poetics at work in Cambodian American hip hop. Identifying those "who have been murdered" and observing that the past does indeed "come back and haunt you," praCh directly confronts genocide trauma. At the same time, praCh affectively configures justice through a clear structure of feeling.

If international justice foregrounds praCh's debut album and its immediate sequel, then it is politically more focused in praCh's *Dalama: Memoirs of an Invisible War* (2010). Thematically, praCh's most recent album marks a slight temporal departure from the previous two *Dalamas*. As praCh asserts, "The last two [albums] were more about the killing fields and my past. This *Dalama* is more about the present and future."[22] Correspondingly, in a track titled, "Hidden Truth, Open Lies," praCh forcefully avers,

> No lies / Two million murdered, it's Genocide! / I know, I know, it's hard to disguise but it's the truth. And if we don't talk about it'll be forgotten / And I'll be damn if I let that happen. / You see its barely even mention, / Barely in school textbooks, / How do you expect the kids to know?[23]

Confronting President Richard Nixon and Secretary of State Henry Kissinger, praCh critiques U.S. involvement via lyric and hip hop rhymes. Correspondingly, praCh connects U.S. foreign policy to the rise of the Khmer Rouge and Cambodia's genocidal aftermath. Emphasizing "truth," praCh draws on the power of communication, stressing that key to remembering is "talk." Given that this is a shared traumatic history, praCh casts the genocide via folkloric terms, which give rise to intergenerational knowledge production (parents and children, teachers and "kids").

What is more, praCh's *Hidden Truth, Open Lies* employs samples from John Pilger's documentary, *Year Zero: The Silent Death of Cambodia* (1979). For those familiar with praCh's previous work, the use of Pilger's work foments an auditory theme between albums. To that end, the film is sampled in both *The End'n is Just the Beginnin'* and *The Lost Chapter*. Consequently, praCh accesses a particular tradition *within* his own oeuvre, centered on an analogous *documentary* hip hop impulse. Concurrently, when juxtaposed with overt critiques of U.S. foreign policy with regard to the bombings of Cambodia, the use of Pilger's film in Hidden Truth, Open Lies reemphasizes a Vietnam War/Cambodian history forgotten and "barely even mentioned." Taken together, praCh employs lyric and sample to foment a multifaceted "knowledge" akin to KRS-One's "9 Elements."

What is more, armed with master Khmer pin peat artists (including Kung Nai, master chapei player known as the "Ray Charles of Cambodia"), samples from sixties Cambodian pop (in particular, Sinn Sisamouth, "The King of Khmer Music," and Ros Sereysothea, "The Golden Voice of Cambodia"), and excerpts from film (e.g., *Year Zero*), praCh forces the listener to *hear* the story of Cambodia's Killing Fields through a varied (and at times traditional) cultural tapestry. Likewise, the use of Cambodian artists makes visible the policing of folklore during the Khmer Rouge era. Within a year zero milieu, folklore posed a memory threat to the Khmer Rouge, a point made tragically clear by the state-authorized execution of an estimated 80-90 percent of traditional Khmer court musicians.[24] Correspondingly, within the context of a Khmer Rouge directive to eliminate all Western influence, Cambodian pop stars who fused traditional Khmer music to sixties R&B and rock (e.g., Ros Sereysothea, Sinn Sisamouth, and Pan Ron) were targeted and killed.

Hence, praCh's use of sixties Cambodian pop continues a more expansive folkloric tradition grounded in Royal Court ballads and pre-Khmer Rouge music flows. For example, in *Dalama: Memoirs of an Invisible War*'s sixteenth track, "praCh's Bopha," the artist raps in Khmer amid a recognizable Cambodian rock backbeat. Replete with direct Cambodian allusions, the track's title refers to an indigenous flower ("bopha"). The sample is taken from Ros Sereysothea's cover of "Bopha Angkor," a haunting 1960s Cambodian pop ballad. Following suit, praCh's use of title, lyric, and song sample allows Cambodia to be reclaimed through native language and traditional Khmer culture.[25] Less intentional, "bopha" is also connected to an apartheid South Africa. Expressly, "bopha" is Zulu for "arrest and detain," and was a rallying cry among anti-apartheid activists. Such culturally-specific readings reinforce the resistive and folkloric politics that infuse praCh's body of hip hop work.

CONCLUSION: RETURNING HOME

If, as Péter Niedermüller asserts, "'Homeland' can be one of the most powerful unifying symbols for mobile and displaced peoples, though the relation to homeland may be very differently constructed in different settings,"[26] then praCh, emblematic of other Cambodian American rappers, imagines and reimagines Cambodia and Cambodian folklore through U.S. hip hop. At the same time, praCh's critiques of U.S. foreign policy make less certain a homeland for Cambodian Americans who, because of war and relocation, are in the United States. In a complicated fashion, praCh not only takes on the U.S. government and the Khmer Rouge in *Dalama: Memoirs of an Invisible War*, but praCh brings this culture war back to his homeland, battling Prime Minister Hun Sen's infamous 1998 directive that his fellow Cambodians "bury the past."[27] Taken together, praCh's transnational folklore project reflects an expansive multinational imaginary that marries social practice to social justice.

In so doing, if KRS-One's "9 Elements" stresses the "local" in hip hop, then praCh emphasizes the "transnational" via the multifaceted cultural performance of history, memory, and struggle. Through different folkloric registers, praCh returns time and again to the politics of hip hop. Negotiating the genocide struggle, praCh incontrovertibly uses hip hop to a social justice-oriented end. Based on intergenerational exchange, focused on tradition and revision, and forged through location and identity, praCh's *Dalama: Memoirs of an Invisible War* is communal in form and juridically-driven in function. Importantly, by demanding justice through transnational folklore practices, Cambodian American hip hop artists like praCh make clear the degree to which hip hop (as S. Craig Watkins maintains) continues to culturally, socially, and politically *matter*.

NOTES

1. This chapter uses two spellings: "hip hop" and "hip-hop." These spellings are determined by those that appear in particular quotes. However, the author of this chapter prefers the nonhyphenated form. See "Cambodia: Pol Pot's Shadow." *Frontline/World*. October 2002. http://www.pbs.org/frontlineworld/stories/cambodia/ly_interview.html.

2. See Miller, G.W. (III). "Hip Hop Hopes: Cambodian rap group AZI Fellas drop a positive beat on their troubled past." *Philadelphia Weekly*. 4 May 2010.

3. *The Kristyle* was originally released in late June 2003 amid controversy. At the time named, *Kristyles*, the album was shorter (totaling seventeen tracks as opposed to a later release of twenty tracks). Moreover, KRS-One alleged that Koch Records had circulated an unfinished product, and urged fans to boycott the album along the lines of fraudulent representation. After court injunction and threats of further litigation, KRS-One and Koch Records settled the dispute, and the revised version was officially released in August that year. Soon after, KRS-One left Koch Records. Given its contentious release, I have elected to use the name KRS-One intended for the album. The following tracks are included in the online version of *The Kristyle* (which includes more than twenty tracks): "Intro"; "Ya Feel That?"; "Somebody"; "Peter the Dreamer"; "Suppose to Be"; "Underground"; "Gunnin' 'em Down"; "Survivin'"; "How Bad Do you Want It"; "Alright with Me"; "Jam Master Jay Tribute"; "That's It"; "Nothing in the World is Impossible"; "Ain't No Stoppin' Us"; "True Story"; "Stop It"; "The Only One"; "It's a Struggle"; "9 Elements"; "Things Will Change"; and "The Movement"' "the Message."

4. A committed social justice activist, KRS-One was one of the founders of the "Stop the Violence Movement" in the late 1980s. Concentrated on gang and drug-

related violence in inner city communities, KRS-One and other hip hop artists (including Public Enemy's Chuck D., Heavy D, and MC Lyte) sought to raise awareness through community action efforts and hip hop summits. Indeed, KRS-One's 1990 album, titled *Edutainment*, makes clear his use of hip hop as a mode of social justice pedagogy.

5. See Weiner, Jonah. "Review: KRS-One's *The Kristyle.*" *Entertainment Weekly.* 27 June 2003. http://www.ew.com/ew/article/0,,459857,00.html.

6. Weiner's use of "soapboxing" reconfigures to sardonic effect the hip hop element of "beatboxing."

7. See Watkins, S. Craig. *Hip Hop Matters: Politics, Pop Culture, and the Struggle for the Soul of a Movement* (Boston, MA: Beacon Press, 2005): 6.

8. KRS-One's "9 Elements" definition expands previous arguments about the basic "elements" of hip hop. As scholars and critics alike have argued, hip hop had four foundational elements (also termed "cultural pillars"): breakdancing, mc-ing, dj-ing, and graffiti.

9. In *From Bomba to Hip Hop: Puerto Rican Culture and Latino Identity* (New York: Columbia UP, 2000), Juan Flores argues that "folklore" is an antiquated, ill-suited frame. According to Flores, "The word *folklore*, the only terminological recourse to differentiate popular cultural expression from the engulfing phenomenon of popular culture qua mass cultural consumption, is so patently outmoded and laden with ideological baggage that its use only sets up the intellectual endeavor for further ridicule" (19). Notwithstanding Flores's warning, this chapter argues for a more updated reading of folklore as focused less on arguments about primordialism and more on issues of cultural exchange. In so doing, this piece—which bridges the terrain between African American and Cambodian American hip hop draws on what editors Jonathan H. X. Lee and Kathleen Nadeau observe is the "consequence of transplantation, accommodation, transformation, and invention of cultural traditions, material and ideological, of Asian diaspora communities in America."

10. See Georges, Robert A. and Jones, Michael Owen. *Folkoristics: An Introduction* (Bloomington, Indiana: Indiana Uuniveristy Press, 1995).

11. See Flores, Juan. *From Bomba to Hp Hop: Puerto Rican and Latino Identity* (New York: Columbia University Press, 2000): 135-137.

12. Prior to the passage of the 1965 Immigration Act (Hart-Cellar Act), each nation was afforded an immigration quota. For the first half of the twentieth century, Asian immigrants were largely prohibited from entering the United States legally. Indeed, the only exclusion act to name a particular ethno-racial group—the 1882 Chinese Exclusion Act—illustrates the racist practices inherent in U.S. immigration policy. The 1965 Immigration Act eschewed nation-state quotas in favor of a hemispheric designation (170,000 were allowed to immigrate from the Eastern Hemisphere, 120,000 were allowed from the Western Hemisphere). Reflective of anti-discriminatory civil rights movement agendas and Cold War politics, the 1965 Act allowed the first *en masse* Asian (and Latin American) migration to the United States. The 1980 Refugee Act in particular enabled Cambodians (and other Southeast Asian groups impacted by the Vietnam War) to enter as a nonquota population.

13. Jonathan H. X. Lee and Katheen Nadeau "Introduction: Asian American Folklore and Folklore." In the *Encyclopedia of Asian American Folklore and Folklife* (Santa Barbara: ABC-CLIO, 2011).

14. See Schlund-Vials, Cathy J. "A Transnational Hip Hop Nation: Cambodian American Rap and Memorialization." Special Issue: "Trauma in the 21st-Century." *Life Writing.* 5:1 (2008 April). Kate Douglas and Gillian Whitlock (Editors): 11-27. (Reprinted in *Trauma Texts*, Kate Douglas and Gillian Whitlock, editors (New York: Routledge, 2009).

15. Schlund-Vials, "A Transnational Hip Hop Nation: Cambodian American Rap and Memorialization."

16. Following the regime's 1979 deposal, more than 150,000 Cambodians refugees came to the United States, gaining access via the 1980 Refugee Act.

17. Not everyone who left Cambodia during this time resettled in other countries. Many were also forced to return to Cambodia.

18. As per the 2000 Census, an estimated 241,025 individuals identified as "Cambodian." See U.S. Census, "Factfinder." http://factfinder.census.gov.

19. See May, Sharon. Interview with praCh. "Art of fact." *Manoa*. 16.1 (2004): 73-82.

20. praCh's work is very much linked to the absence of international justice with regard to the Khmer Rouge era. Despite the passage of more than thirty years since the Khmer Rouge were ousted from power, only five defendants currently stand before U.N./Khmer Rouge War Crimes Tribunal (Extraordinary Chambers in the Courts of Cambodia). The current prime minister, Hun Sen, is a former Khmer Rouge officer who defected during the initial stages of the Vietnamese invasion of Cambodia. To date, Kaing Guev Duch (the lead warden at Tuol Sleng Prison, or S-21) is the only high ranking Khmer Rouge officer to face the tribunal, and his sentencing is scheduled to take place later this year. For the regime's leader, the trial is too late. Pol Pot died in 1998. Similarly, justice was not served for Tam Mok. Known as the "butcher," Mok was in charge of Khmer Rouge military forces. Like "Brother Number One" Pol Pot, Mok died peacefully in his sleep. Of those indicted for crimes against humanity, war crimes, and crimes against the state (including Ieng Sary, Ieng Thirith, Nuon Chea, and Khieu Samphan), only one—Duch—has publicly confessed. Repeatedly, Duch has asked for "forgiveness," though many in Cambodia doubt the former warden's sincerity. See Schlund-Vials, Cathy J. "A Transnational Hip Hop Nation: Cambodian American Rap and Memorialization." Special Issue: "Trauma in the 21st-Century." *Life Writing*. 5:1 (2008 April). Kate Douglas and Gillian Whitlock (Editors): 11-27. (Reprinted in *Trauma Texts*, Kate Douglas and Gillian Whitlock, editors (New York: Routledge, 2009).

21. See "Cambodia: Pol Pot's Shadow." *Frontline/World*. October 2002. http://www.pbs.org/frontlineworld/stories/cambodia/ly_interview.html.

22. See Mellen, Greg. "For Cambodian rapper, 'words are weapons.'" *Press Telegram*. 9 April 2010. http://www.presstelegram.com/news/ci_14853709>.

23. See praCh. *Dalama: Memoirs of an Invisible War*. Long Beach, California: Mujestic Records. 2010.

24. See Meneses, Rashaan. "The Near Extinction of Cambodian Classical Dance." 7 May 2004. http://www.international.ucla.edu/article.asp?parentid=10982.

25. This engagement with Khmer tradition is apparent at the level of artistry. In addition to praCh, the album features compositions by Cambodian American poet U Sam Oeur (who now translates Walt Whitman's work into Khmer), Kung Nai (master *chapei* musician), and artists from Cambodia Living Arts (Sovey, Sinat, and Sophea). These traditional artists are joined by rapper Silong Chhun and members of the aforementioned Universal Speakers.

26. See Niedermüller, Péter. "Ethnicity, Nationality, and the Myth of Cultural Heritage: A European View." *Journal of Folklore Research*. Vol. 36, Nos. 2/3: (Folklore Institute, Indiana University Press, 1999): 248.

27. See Mydans, Seth. "Cambodian Leader Resists Punishing Top Khmer Rouge" (29 December 1998) *New York Times*.

NINE

Japanese American Appropriation of Folkloric Symbols through Origami and Hip Hop

Brett Esaki

INTRODUCTION

In order to comprehend the messages of folklore, it is important to understand how the messages are lived and embodied by those who deliver the folklore. A key element of this living folklore is the appropriation, or incorporation into the body and mind, of symbols. This chapter examines the way that Japanese American artists appropriate folkloric symbols, and draws inspiration from the theory of embodiment developed by performance theorist Phillip Zarrilli. Zarrilli investigates the relationship between different modes of the body's awareness and the creation of art. His theory was designed to develop Western actors' relationship to their bodies, hoping to stretch the craft of acting to embrace more of what some consider an Eastern relationship to bodies. Here, Zarrilli's theory is applied to other crafts, namely origami and hip hop music, and to Japanese American artists. The theory applies well to the artistic process of Japanese American artists, without assuming an East-West dichotomy and asserting that Japanese Americans are bridge figures between the East (Japan) and West (America). Two artists have been chosen to represent Japanese Americans, origami artist Linda Mihara and hip hop musician Mike Shinoda, in order to balance gender and breadth of contemporary Japanese American arts. By looking at these artists with an eye to embodiment, it will be shown that they appropriate folkloric symbols with serenity, where serenity is a sense of wholeness and composure.

Folkloric Immersion

Folklore exists outside of the teller of folklore in the sense that it is accessed from a common reservoir of knowledge and passed on to a listener, yet folklore exists inside the teller in the sense that it must take place through bodily practices. This makes passing on folklore an embodied practice, and the teller into one who embodies folklore. That is, folkloric symbols are incorporated into the artist who tells folklore. In order to better understand artistic embodiment, this chapter draws heavily on performance theorist and actor Phillip Zarrilli's the theory of embodiment. This theory describes how an artist immerses the body and mind (what he calls "bodymind") in an artistic production. Applying it to the production of folkloric art, it follows that an artist is immersed in community knowledge, and through this immersion is expanded to become a communal individual.

Folkloric art reflects this expanded self because it immerses the viewer into the artist's sense of the community's wisdom. Japanese Americans have an artistic tradition of communicating wisdom by immersing the audience into the experiences of an artist: the tradition of *waka* poetry. Ordinary Japanese Americans would compose *waka* poems to describe their present feeling, whether it be entranced in the labor of gardening or entrapped in the winter of a concentration camp. Of course after immersion in these poems, readers may desire to take action to lessen another's labor or to ease winter chills, but this is not the point of these poems, which is to immerse the reader in the poetic moment.

The feeling of the poetic moment can be described as a feeling of serenity, where *serenity* is a sense of wholeness and composure. Serenity is not to be without emotion; rather, it is a momentary sense of who one is and how one feels while passionately viewing what is in front, not falling backward in fear or forward in hate. It is like facing a clear night sky. To some, serenity, even in the face of folkloric horror such as Japanese American internment, would imply a foreign stoicness or romantic naiveté. However, this would be a misunderstanding of the artistic productions. Artists learn to embody the folkloric symbols that they appropriate in order to effectively put the audience into this feeling. By not moving the audience away from this feeling, the artist fully acknowledges the feeling and experience of the folklore, thus acknowledging the community that has been through the actual experience of the folklore and that has been affected by this history. Focusing on the feeling builds a community of empathy; this is neither stoic nor naive. In these ways, Japanese Americans appropriate folkloric symbols with serenity in order to acknowledge the full extent of the emotions of community history.

Linda Mihara, an origami artist, and Mike Shinoda, a hip hop artist, serve as excellent examples of Japanese Americans who create serene art.

This chapter will explore their appropriation of folkloric symbols in the creation of modern-day *waka*.

Phillip Zarrilli's Theory of Embodiment

> Composing *waka*
> About trains, mountains, money
> Breathing in symbols
> In hip hop, origami
> Facing the evening sky[1]

Phillip Zarrilli has been developing a technique to help actors of Western theater work through scripts that are not easily approachable with traditional Western acting methods. Most notably, he is interested in breaking actors away from what he understands as a "Cartesian dualism."[2] Under a Cartesian dualism, there is a split between body and mind. Correspondingly, a Western actor would imagine what a character would do and then move the body to match it. Actress, acting instructor, and Zarrilli's colleague Patricia Boyette explains the typical process of her Western training: "I am also used to working in a very linear, cause and effect, narrative way when going through a piece. Therefore, one moment leads to the next and so on."[3] However, Zarrilli feels that this method is inadequate for some contemporary pieces that do not have a linear plot. Unlearning the mind-body dualism of Western acting methods requires training, and Zarrilli's theory of embodiment is an attempt at grounding such training.

Zarrilli builds upon preeminent drama theorist Konstantin Stanislavski's concept of psychophysical acting. According to Zarrilli, Stanislavski developed his concept of the psychophysical (the mind and body) in part from his encounter with *yoga*. He was particularly influenced by the yogic concept of *prana*, or breath or life force that flows through the mind and body.[4] Zarrilli himself has trained in the Indian martial art *kalarippayattu* and uses this experience to expand on Stanislavski's understanding of *prana* and to develop its application to actor training. This places Zarrilli in a lineage of an encounter of Western dramaturgy with a conception of Eastern consciousness.

He is fully aware of the potential to generalize the East-West dichotomy and of the potential to take the acting exercises he develops as spiritual, and he has rejected these generalizations and presumptions.[5] I would argue that since his audience is primarily actors trained with a distinction between mind and body, iterating the East-West and mind-body dichotomies is a practical tool for training.[6] In this sense, Zarrilli's concept of the bodymind is a practical frame of reference that underlies a kind of artistic experience of the self, irrespective of its "Eastern" or "Western" connotations. There is also a risk that applying Zarrilli's theory to Japanese Americans would reify a presumed foreignness or mystic quality of Japanese Americans, so it must be emphasized that Zarrilli's theory high-lights Japanese Americans' profound experiences of self but not in a way that make the experiences esoteric or incomprehensible.

Whether Zarrilli's theory follows an Orientalist lineage is not the concern of this chapter, but Zarrilli traces his concept of embodiment to theorists Maurice Merleau-Ponty, Yuasa Yasuo, Drew Leder, and to his own training in Indian martial arts.[7] According to his theory, while performing, an actor experiences the art through different parts of the body and through corresponding ways of sensing. There are four "bodies" and corresponding *modes of experience*: surface body with sensorimotor experience, recessive body that senses the visceral, aesthetic inner bodymind that senses the subtle, and the aesthetic outer body that senses the fictive, or what an artistic creation feels and how an audience feels in response to this artistic creation (see table 9.1).

Table 9.1.   Phillip Zarrilli's Four Embodied Modes of Experience.[8]

First body	Second body	Third body	Fourth body
surface body	recessive body	aesthetic inner bodymind	aesthetic outer body (i.e., the character in drama, offered for the gaze of the audience)
Modes of Experience			
sensorimotor	visceral	subtle	fictive

The *sensorimotor* mode is feeling through the five senses and using the senses to balance and react. The *visceral* mode is feeling through internal organs beyond the five surface senses. The visceral mode does not come to consciousness until there is internal pain or dysfunction, though one can become familiar with the viscera by repetitively correcting oneself to avoid such pain (practicing the correct dancing posture, for example). The *subtle* mode is feeling through viscera and ever subtler organs and sense systems. Instead of waiting for the jarring messages of pained viscera as in the visceral mode, one can develop the subtle awareness of internal organs through concentration, exercises, and meditation. These exercises are often developed by artistic traditions and esoteric religions, hence the term "aesthetic inner bodymind." With such subtle feeling, one experiences the connections of organs to proper alignment (visceral mode) and to the function of external senses (sensorimotor mode).

Lastly, the *fictive* mode is feeling through a fictive character's embodied modes of experience. This sense of the character's state is both as character, that is, feeling what a character feels, and as audience, that is, feeling audience members' impressions of the character. This aesthetic sense makes a character outside of the actor since the character lives in the imagination of the audience, yet inside of the actor since the actor feels through the character. An actor with these modes of experience ideally has the modes in balance; accordingly, a character's drinking comes to life as an actor balances the sensorimotor mode of feeling water with her mouth with the fictive mode of feeling the character's quenched thirst.

It follows that a balance of embodied modes of experience must be cultivated in order for an actor to effectively convey a character. This balance fits an artistic tradition, and Zarrilli's theory and method are designed to create a new tradition of acting that allows actors to convey contemporary characters. In addition to tradition, performance is based on context and individual style and choice.[9] For example, one performing a Japanese *noh* dance would have practiced the dance according to a tradition, would be following a script for when and generally how to do the dance, would do particular movements depending on moment and context that also fits the tradition, and the movements would be guided by the individual's choice and style. A master has the tradition, modes of embodiment, and individual style as second nature, so that when performing the actor is immersed in the moment and her bodymind can interact "naturally" with other actors, props, and set.

Zarrilli's conception of embodiment was designed for the art of acting, but it can be used to help understand the arts of origami and hip hop as performed by Japanese Americans. The fourth mode of experience (the fictive) is feeling the experiences of a character and feeling the audience's experiences of a character, which is essentially being consciousness of an artistic creation. An origami sculpture and a hip hop persona are artistic creations, and accordingly an artist may take the fictive mode to sense how a sculpture or persona feels to itself and audience. Balance of the modes, tradition, and individual style are cultivated by actors in order to master their craft, and similarly origami and hip hop artists must practice according to their crafts. By thusly expanding Zarrilli's theory of embodiment it can be applied to Japanese Americans in other arts, bringing to light their connections of body and art and their immersion in the moment that lead to a sense of serenity.

Linda Mihara and Origami

> Composing *waka*
> About trains, mountains, money
> Breathing in symbols
> In hip hop, origami
> Facing the evening sky

Linda Mihara folds paper to create symbols of contemporary Japanese American life.[10] Her artistic tradition can be traced to Japanese origami artist Akira Yoshizawa, who pioneered origami sculptures in the mid-twentieth century that appeared alive, with feeling and personality.[11] Mihara, a third-generation Japanese American, traces her lineage directly to a Japanese American lineage: her family. Her family has run The Paper Tree shop in San Francisco's Japantown for over thirty years, and her grandparents published some of the first origami books in English.[12] In these ways, Mihara's tradition is the bringing of spirited art to Japanese American families. She advances this tradition by exhibiting work internationally, commercially, and for Japanese American ceremonies. For example, she worked on a Mitsubishi commercial that featured origami and was invited to exhibit in Austria and Israel.[13]

She is most well-known for her work with cranes and she traces this work to the *Sembazuru Orikata*, which can be translated as *Ways to Fold One Thousand Cranes*. This book was written by a Japanese Buddhist monk named Rokoan Gido in the late eighteenth century, and it is perhaps the first published work on origami. It contains his meditations on the different possibilities of making multiple cranes from a single, square piece of paper. While one crane can be made by folding one square, four cranes can be made by folding a paper divided into four squares (2 x 2) and nine cranes can be made by folding a paper divided into nine squares (3 x 3). Next to the illustration of each completed sculpture he composed a poem.[14] Thus, Rokoan Gido connected his meditation on the possibilities of a single square to the completed sculptures, and to meditating on the completed sculptures to the process of writing poems; this is the connection of possibility, physical form, and poem.

Mihara became fascinated with this work.[15] She worked through the entire book, and she too meditated on the possibilities of the different folds (though as an artist, not as a Buddhist monk). In particular, she worked on the nine-crane fold made from nine equal squares (3 x 3) where all of the completed cranes faced one direction (figure 9.1). Through it, she realized that the connected cranes formed a sort of surface that could itself be folded to form larger, three-dimensional objects. In this creative process, Mihara balanced her use of hands, paper, focus, and creativity. In addition, Mihara stated that at all times during folding she is thinking of the end product. Therefore, the meditative practice of folding (the subtle mode of experience) places the end product in focus (fictive mode) in order to execute the folds correctly (visceral and sensorimotor modes).

The connected crane pieces that developed from this practice are not only innovative but symbolic of Japanese American folklore. Though the practice has died out in Japan, Japanese Americans continue to fold one thousand cranes for weddings. The crane is a symbol of marital happiness since they mate for life.[16] In addition, a crane is said to live for one

Figure 9.1. Nine connected cranes facing one direction, folded by author.

thousand years, so it symbolizes one thousand years of health and prosperity. For these reasons, one thousand cranes symbolize an infinitely long life, prosperity, and marital happiness. Folding one thousand cranes has also been associated with making a wish, sort of like finding and rubbing Aladdin's lamp or making elaborate preparations for a prayer. In Japan, this wish-symbolism became associated with wishing to heal the sick. After the atomic bombs fell on Japan, it became associated with healing atomic bomb radiation, and subsequently with the wish for world peace.[17] Given the association with illness, contemporary Japanese do not have cranes at weddings, but Japanese Americans follow their prewar lineage by continuing to fold one thousand cranes for weddings. Some Japanese Americans in Hawaii innovated new, more modern ways to display cranes at weddings, such as in the shape of the Japanese family crest. Linda Mihara frequently does such pieces for Japanese American weddings—pieces that express Japanese American traditions in modern, artistic ways. For Mihara, these uses of the crane by Japanese Americans indicate that the crane holds particular significance as a Japanese *American* symbol, representing the connection to both an old Japan and a history of Japanese immigrants struggling to retain culture and solidarity in the United States. Moreover, the new, modern ways to display this symbol make the crane a traditional and modern symbol of Japanese Americans. And, adding this traditional and modern folkloric symbol to ceremonies brings the community together through acknowledging the Japanese American history of struggle and conveying the Japanese American value of family, happiness, and prosperity.

Mihara further modernizes the Japanese American symbol in her three-dimensional connected crane pieces, such as the crane cube (figure 9.2). The crane cube is a cube made of fifty-four connected cranes, folded from one sheet of paper and without glue. In this technically difficult and visionary piece, one sees the uniting of ancient practice, traditional fold-

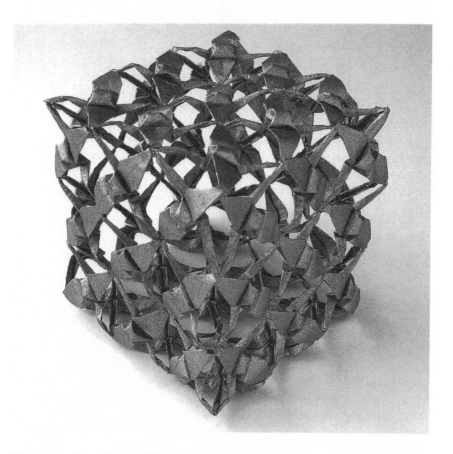

Figure 9.2.   Crane Cube, 2005. Courtesy of Linda Mihara.

ing technique, and modern vision. In fact, though capable of other, more modern folding techniques, Mihara is drawn to the traditional techniques in order to intertwine the ancient, traditional, and modern. The connected cranes, with their crisp lines and form traceable to the eighteenth century, represents all that Mihara seeks to do as an origami artist: "So this technique has been around along for how long, from the 1700s, right? But nobody thought of that before. . . . I was just lucky enough to discover that. And to me, it's a very modern shape . . . it's traditional yet modern, so it's like the perfect definition of what I do."[18] That is, modern configurations of cranes represent Mihara and her place in her family's lineage, because they are symbols of Japanese American origin, tradition, and modern present and they advance her family's lineage by bringing the spirit of life of Japanese Americans to new, modern audiences. This expansive understanding of self that includes family and community and spreading this understanding to others builds a community of empathy. In addition, similar to the purpose of Zarrilli's theory, Mihara engages and masters Japanese American traditions of art to carry out modern pieces with Japanese American folkloric symbols.

Her mastery can be seen in her commercial work. She explained that the rare times when origami felt physically taxing were during extremely time-sensitive commercial work. In these rare contracts, she is required to fold large numbers of pieces and to innovate new sculptures per demand in a matter of hours. Besides these rare, demanding contracts, she said that she can fold for hours on end without tiring or hurting her hands. Instead of being painful, it is the opposite: folding is a way that Mihara relaxes her hands; the practice is sort of yogic, invigorating the body through exercise. Though some projects required several weeks of folding, she has never had repetitive strain injuries. This demonstrates her mastery of the techniques of folding.

One of the sculptures that she designed for a client was folded from a U.S. one-dollar bill (figure 9.3). The bull folded from a dollar originated from a contract for a financial company whose symbol was a bull. The company wanted to incorporate the symbol of money with the symbol of their company, and so contracted Mihara to create the dollar bill bull. While experimenting with folding the bull, she accidentally folded one using the wrong side of the dollar face up. However, this accident placed two swirls of the design near the head, leading her to reconstruct the bull with these swirls as eyes. Then she discovered that the arrows of the eagle's claws looked like straw, so she reconstructed the head to have the arrowheads on the mouth making the bull look like it was chewing straw.

Though the financial company did not use the finalized dollar bill bull, this creative process using dollar bills inspired her to keep working with this medium. She constructed several dollar animals, such as a dragon and a fox, using key features found on bills to bring personality and

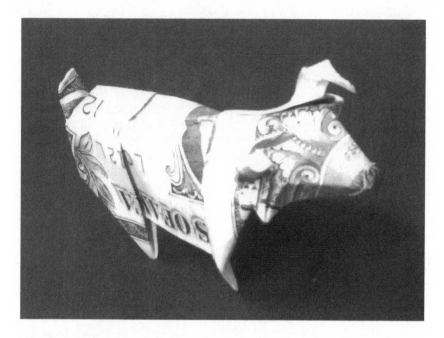

Figure 9.3.   Dollar Bill Bull, 2011. Courtesy of Linda Mihara.

life to the sculptures. In addition, these features increase what Mihara calls the "wow factor," which is the surprise and wonderment that an audience feels upon seeing a fun and creative feature of an origami sculpture. Since the features came from dollar bills, the audience and artist went through a series of discoveries: seeing the feature on the sculpture, connecting it to the sculpture's personality, identifying the feature as coming from a dollar, seeing it on an unfolded dollar, and seeing the feature on the sculpture once more. Since she understands the craft of designing sculptures that inspire these experiences, Mihara considers herself to be an origami designer, as opposed to an origami folder who follows already created origami designs.

Corresponding to this mastery, the power of her designs using the folded American dollar is more about the creative reenvisioning of the mundane than it is about acquisition and wealth. Of course, when one steps outside of the experience of the dollar sculptures, one can see that Mihara is acquiring wealth by making these designs, but the sculptures themselves convey the joy of creative discovery instead of acquisition. She uses dollar folds to bring pleasure into life, a way of bringing joy to one's present possessions as opposed to what one could possibly have in the future. For example, she sometimes will tip restaurant waitstaff with a dollar sculpture. This brings a smile—an increase in value to the tip, if you will—or the "wow factor" to the waitstaff. One time at a restaurant in Denmark, the restaurant owner was overcome with joy when she tipped with a dollar bill bull. It turns out that the restaurant, a symbol of the family who owned it, had a symbol that was a bull. In the dollar bill bull, the restaurant owner may have seen a connection of international friendship through food, a joy at seeing foreign money, and the family tradition of restaurant ownership. That is, through the symbol of the dollar bill bull, the restaurant owner might have seen himself and his restaurant in a new light. This symbolism perhaps was the reason that the executives at the American financial company did not use the dollar bill bull to represent their company: the dollar bill bull embodies a reenvisioning of wealth with joy, a sense of contentment with the money already acquired and the occupations presently undertaken, whereas the financial company would probably prefer a symbol of acquisition and advancement.

In these ways, Linda Mihara's appropriation of folkloric symbols is about illustrating the life that is present. The connected cranes unite the folklore of an ancient Japanese origin with the struggles of a Japanese American past and with the vision of Japanese American present. The dollar bill bull brings wonderment and joy into what has already been acquired, becoming a Japanese American symbol of wealth. Moreover, the appropriation is accomplished by sensing the spirit of the sculpted symbol (fictive mode of experience), taking on a meditative practice of folding (subtle mode), relaxing the body through folding (visceral mode), and deftly folding the paper (sensorimotor mode) making the symbol come alive. Thus, the appropriation of folkloric symbols brings serenity, relaxing the bodymind by focusing on the spirit of symbols, and expanding the understanding of self with symbols of ancient past and tradition configured in ways that symbolize the wealth of the present.

Mike Shinoda and Hip Hop

> Composing *waka*
> About trains, mountains, money
> Breathing in symbols
> In hip hop, origami
> Facing the evening sky

Serenity probably is not the proper way to characterize the majority of hip hop, but the hip hop of Mike Shinoda is serene. Shinoda is a mixed-race Japanese American who became famous as a rapper, singer, guitarist, pianist, writer, and sometimes illustrator for the band Linkin Park.[19] Because of his variety of artistic skills, Shinoda is a prime example of Japanese Americans who have mastered traditions of art. In the hip hop group Fort Minor, Shinoda performed, wrote, mixed, produced, and illustrated the album, *The Rising Tied*.[20] The album is self-reflective in the sense that each song represents an aspect of Shinoda's self. I use the word *represent* because that is the term in hip hop for performing your best to illustrate all that you and your community can do. This includes the performance of self-knowledge and cultural knowledge, such as folklore. Shinoda represents on all of the songs, and three songs illustrate his reflectivity and serenity: "Remember the Name," "Where'd You Go," and "Kenji."

"Remember the Name" may be the most recognizable track on the album, since it has been played often during television broadcasts of the National Basketball Association. The lyrics discuss what Shinoda calls the "science of music," which is essentially the way effort and art are combined to produce a memorable performer.[21] He explains the elements of his musical alchemy: "This is 10 percent luck / 20 percent skill / 15 percent concentrated power of will / 5 percent pleasure / 50 percent pain / And 100 percent reason to remember the name."[22] Combining these elements creates a performer with impact. Note that the elements correspond to the modes of embodiment: pleasure is sensorimotor, pain is visceral, skill and will are subtle, and luck and remembrance are fictive; Shinoda's science of music is his balance of the modes of embodiment.

However, he does not develop his "name," or persona, for fame or fear like many others in hip hop. Take, for example, Jin's song "Learn Chinese": "The barrel of my gun gonna make you speak another language / And amigo I ain't talking about Spanish / Ya'll gon[na] learn Chinese."[23] Jin, a Chinese American rapper, explains that he is to be remembered and feared because of his gun—a double-entendre for the weapon and his penis—which will make those who witness it speak Chinese—a double-entendre for speaking Chinese in fear and in pleasure. In contrast to Jin's persona, Shinoda's is vulnerable: "He [Shinoda] doesn't need his name up in lights / He just wants to be heard . . . He feels so unlike everybody else / Alone."[24] While Jin claims that encountering him will force one to address him properly, Shinoda is reflective and explains that he feels alone and his ultimate goal is to be heard. He explains that "it's not about the salary / It's all about reality," or that he works hard in order to let his reality be known; otherwise, he would continue to feel alone, without a community of empathy.[25]

The path to develop a community of empathy can be seen most clearly in "Kenji," Shinoda's song about the World War II internment of Japanese Americans.[26] The song's title is Shinoda's middle name, so the song is his immersion in the experience of internment. In addition, he stated that Kenji is a common name for Japanese men, so it is a symbol of every Japanese American man. Therefore, the song is the story of every Japanese American man, including himself, in internment.[27] In the tradition of American hip hop, Shinoda samples the testimony of elders in his song.[28] Sampling is a technique in hip hop of taking small portions of different music and other sound recordings and putting them together in a collage. The samples most often create a repetitive musical loop, and some samples root a song in a history or culture with sounds of that history or culture.[29] Shinoda roots "Kenji" in the history of Japanese Americans when he samples interviews of his father and aunt discussing the internment experience. The samples of their interviews make the narrative of the song seem more real, and they serve to split up the narrative into verses. For example, creating a middle of the song, his aunt is sampled saying, "Yeah, soon as war broke out, the F.B.I came and . . . they just come to the house and, you have to come. All the Japanese have to go."[30] The samples—like a mantra—ground the lyrics in reality while framing the rhythm of the piece. Without the samples, there would be no verses, because the lyrics have no natural break. Even with the breaks the lyrics march forward, nearly without places for Shinoda to catch his breath. The structure mimics the experience of internment, where Japanese Americans felt marched to each succeeding location—from home, to assembly center, to concentration camp, then out of camp—with little sense of control or a sense of what was happening.

Although there is the feeling of forced marching, the song does not place blame on anyone for this experience and does not suggest any solutions. Shinoda uses folkloric symbols that evoke the sense of injustice without blame or solutions. Kenji's "whole life [was] packed into two bags / Just two bags" and upon returning from the concentration camp "Japs not welcome anymore" was written on his store. These symbols of internment were not invoked in order to directly condemn government officials or anti-Japanese racists. This is different than other socially-conscious hip hop, which frequently ends with a moral statement or suggests future action. For example, in "Children's Story" Slick Rick describes a teenager who gets involved in mugging, and is shot by police at the end of the story. At the end of the song Rick says, "This ain't funny so don't ya dare laugh / Just another case about the wrong path / [Be] straight and arrow or your soul gets cast."[31] In other words, he tells the cautionary tale to the youth so that they do not get involved with "the wrong path" and eventual death. Moreover, he emphasizes that this is serious, so laughing at the story of death comes with his reprimand. With "Children's Story" in mind, the purpose of "Kenji" is not to suggest a course of action, but to let a reality be known, to let the feeling of injustice be known.

Japanese Americans have a tradition of having words put a reader into the writer's reality: the tradition of *waka* poetry.[32] *Waka* were composed by literate Japanese Americans of all professions, from housewife, to gardener, to scholar. Most were private, diary-like pieces, though many poems were published in Japanese-language newspapers and business association publications. Some were written during internment, such as the poems of newspaper reporter Yasutaro Soga.[33] Soga wrote the following poem while interned:

ikameshiki
nijyu no saku no
kanata niwa
murasaki niou
yama manekiroi

[Here] Forbidding
Double-wired fence,
Outside of this place
A purple-glowing
Mountain invites us.[34]

In this poem, Soga contrasts two symbols of his concentration camp: the space of confinement—defined by the barbed wire fence—with the gorgeous mountain outside of the concentration camp. With this juxtaposition, we get the feeling of injustice from having the fullness of life—represented by the purple-glowing mountain—kept away by the prison fence. Similarly, Shinoda provides the feeling of injustice by putting the audience through a series of encounters with symbols of internment. "So now they're in a town with soldiers surrounding them / Every day every night / looked down at them / From watchtowers up on the wall."[35] Akin to Soga's poem, the confined space, guards' gaze, and watchtowers put the audience in direct contact with the sense of imprisonment. While there is more space to condemn in a hip hop song than in a *waka* poem, Shinoda does not reprimand or condemn and thereby distance the audience from the symbols of injustice.

In addition to communicating the sense of injustice that he has felt, Shinoda is able to communicate the sense of injustice that others have felt, even the injustice that he himself inflicts on others. The song "Where'd You Go" describes the abandonment that one feels when a loved one has gone away for a long time to work. The narrator is Shinoda, so the song is his acknowledgement of the feelings of abandonment that he inflicts on people he loves. A female vocalist (Holly Brook) sings the chorus, so the song can be symbolic of women's feeling of abandonment. With both a man's and a woman's voice declaring feelings of abandonment, the song symbolizes anyone's feeling.[36] The narrator pronounces, "I want you to know that it's a little fucked up / that / I'm stuck here waiting / At times debating telling you that I've had it with you and your career."[37] The narrator is upset at waiting and wishes the long absences to be over, yet the narrator does not condemn the absent person. Even in the song's most declarative moments, there is a softening word, such as "a little" and "I guess." At worst, the narrator says that he or she *might* end the relationship—yet this is an acknowledgement of the feeling of injustice, not that the injustice has a necessary punishment.

Shinoda explained that "'Where'd You Go' makes my wife cry every time she hears it,"[38] presumably because it makes her recall her experience of his absence and because she is touched that he has spent time considering her feelings of abandonment. "Kenji" drew a similar reaction at a family reunion. Shinoda explained, "My uncle, who is a very stoic Japanese guy, cried when he heard the song. He couldn't help it. He said he loved it."[39] To Shinoda, breaking down his stoic uncle meant that his song resonated with the experience of injustice from interment. "That's when I started thinking that I had to put this ['Kenji'] on the album or else I'll end up kicking myself for life."[40] His wife's and uncle's crying demonstrate that Shinoda can connect an audience to the feeling of an experience, that is, can bring a listener into the moment of the song. This demonstrates that Shinoda has control over the fictive mode of embodiment, which is feeling the character's emotions and the audience's experience of the character, because he could understand another's feelings and put himself into the experience of these emotions.

Shinoda demonstrates that he understands the modes of embodiment enough to compose songs that convey the emotions of an experience. The folklore of internment was communicated through a Japanese American tradition of using symbols to bring the reader or listener into the experience of injustice serenely, without condemning or suggesting remedies. Shinoda's portrayal of his hip hop persona is similarly serene. Shinoda communicates the folklore of hip hop success by acknowledging the various aspects of this persona, some that bring pride, others that cause a feeling of injustice. The appropriation of folkloric symbols thus requires deep understanding of presence, both one's present emotions and how to make emotions present within an audience. Accomplishing this requires integrity—in the sense that one must be true to oneself (must "represent" as is said in hip hop)—and dignity—in the sense that one stands open to observation without stepping outside of emotions however unjust it may make one seem. And, with such integrity and dignity of the self, one can use the knowledge of the modes of embodiment to communicate it to others. Shinoda appropriates folkloric symbols to produce art that is serene; they have a wholeness of the present—using symbols of the past to infuse the present with wisdom, and acknowledging various, present aspects of the self (the symbols of a persona) without disavowing the corresponding losses or asking for these losses to be forgotten or forgiven.

Japanese American Serenity

> Composing *waka*
> About trains, mountains, money
> Breathing in symbols
> In hip hop, origami
> Facing the evening sky

While others appropriate a painful past in order to condemn or to advise a remedy, some Japanese Americans—as presently exemplified by Mike Shinoda and Linda Mihara—do so with serenity, standing composed and whole by breathing in the past and facing the dark sky. This serenity does not mean that the painful symbols are forgotten, forgiven, or disavowed; rather, the self is whole only by reincorporating, reenvisioning, and remembering the symbols.[41]

Serenity is delivered through a Japanese American tradition of artistic embodiment, as understood through Phillip Zarrilli's theory of embodiment, that immerses an artist in the moment. For Linda Mihara, the process with origami produced the connected cranes—which are symbols of an ancient practice, Japanese American historic struggles, and modern vision—and the dollar bill bull—which is a symbol of a Japanese American sense of the fullness of current wealth. Through these origami sculptures, the stories and symbols of past and present are brought together leading to a sense of wholeness and serenity. For Mike Shinoda, the process with hip hop produced a song of his great persona—a symbol of Japanese American skill, will, and luck—a song of abandonment—a symbol of the cost of one's greatness to loved ones—and a song of utter injustice that includes symbols of government-sanctioned racism, theft, imprisonment, and fear. Through these songs, Shinoda reexamines and reenvisions himself as great, abandoned, and interned. He lets others know that he has not disavowed them, that he has not forgiven his own transgressions, that he has not forgotten his family's treatment during World War II. Hence, he stands whole by reconstructing the pieces of his self; he stands serene by avowing all of these pieces.

In addition, these pieces of the self, these Japanese American folkloric symbols, are bound together according to Zarrilli's theory of embodiment. By asking how artists practice, observe, and meditate in order to reach an artistic goal, it is uncovered that Japanese Americans appropriate folkloric symbols to create an embodied sense of serenity. This serenity is a sense of the fullness of the present, of individuals connected to a community of empathy, and of a synthesis of ancient Japanese past, of Japanese American struggle, and of modern sensibility.

Here, we compose *waka*.

NOTES

1. A version of this essay has been published in *Amerasia Journal*. The journal version does not contain the section on hip hop, the in-depth discussion of poetry, and the original poems by the author, but it does contain an expanded discussion of origami. Brett Esaki, "Embodied Performance of Folklore in Japanese American Origami," *Amerasia Journal* 39, no. 2 (2013): 71-90.

This poem is by the author. The repetitions of the poem serve as a reiteration for the reader to be in the moment of the poem and to understand the different layers of it. In addition, it serves as a stanza marker (akin to Shinoda's song discussed later) and a break where information is folded into other information (akin to origami folding, also discussed later). In this light, we can view each subheading as a fold in the chapter.

2. Phillip Zarrilli, *Psychophysical Acting: An Intercultural Approach after Stanislavski* (New York: Routledge, 2009), 13, 39; Zarrilli, "Toward a Phenomenological Model of the Actor's Embodied Modes of Experience," *Theatre Journal* 56 (2004): 654-55.

3. Patricia Boyette and Phillip Zarrilli, "Psychophysical Training, Physical Actions, and Performing Beckett: 'Playing Chess on Three Levels Simultaneously,'" *Contemporary Theatre Review* 17, no. 1 (2007): 70-80.

4. Zarrilli, *Psychophysical Acting*, 14.

5. Zarrilli, *Psychophysical Acting*, 213.

6. Some of the actors who undertake psychophysical training may be Orientalists and metaphysicists mining the so-called East as a part of their spiritual or religious practices, but that does not prove that Zarrilli himself is doing anything more than improving acting methods.

7. Phillip Zarrilli traces the development of his theory in *Psychophysical Acting* and "Toward a Phenomenological Model," 653-66. The below exposition is certainly incomplete. Zarrilli's full theory contains a description of the chiasm of the modes of embodiment, which is how the modes are braided together. In this chiasm, there are bodily disappearances and different ways of training the bodymind to become aware of multiple modes at once. The height is when the "body becomes all eyes," or when there is a total awareness of bodymind, fictional character, and the surroundings.

8. Table from Zarrilli, *Psychophysical Acting*, 52. This is a shortened table, and Zarrilli lists many more rows with ways to think of the body that can be used as resources for developing psychophysical acting.

9. Phillip Zarrilli, *When the Body Becomes All Eyes: Paradigms, Discourses and Practices of Power in Kalarippayattu, A South Indian Martial Art* (New York: Oxford University Press, 2000), 5-10.

10. For a sample of Linda Mihara's work, see her website: http://www.origamihara.com (accessed July 29, 2009).

11. David Lister, "The Making of a Paperfolder: Akira Yoshizawa" in *Masters of Origami at Hangar-7: The Art of Paperfolding* (Ostfildern-Ruit, Germany: Hatje Cantz, 2005), 13.

12. The Paper Tree, http://www.paper-tree.com (accessed August 15, 2009). Her grandfather is Tokinobu Mihara, who published in the 1950s.

13. Commercial can be seen on YouTube: "Mitsubishi Endeavor - Origami Commercial," YouTube.com, http://www.youtube.com/watch?v=X507NES2szw (accessed August 20, 2009). Her work in Austria is found in *Masters of Origami*.

14. Original text of *Senbazuru Orikata* found in "Hiden Senbazuru Orikata (The Secret of One Thousand Cranes Origami," Japanese Origami Association Society (JOAS), origami.gr.jp, http://origami.gr.jp/Archives/Model/Senbazuru/index-e.html (accessed August 20, 2009).

15. Wherever there is a discussion of Mihara's opinions and artistic process, these come from Linda Mihara, personal communication, July 30, 2009.

16. Whether cranes and other birds mate for life has been contested, but this is not at issue here. Since this folklore exists for Japanese Americans (as well as the legend that they live for one thousand years), cranes hold this symbolic value.

17. The symbolism of healing atomic bomb radiation can be traced to the story of Sadako Sasaki, a young girl who died on the outskirts of Hiroshima after the atomic bomb. A monument to Sadako is located in the Hiroshima Bomb Memorial, and Japanese children fold one thousand cranes and place them on the monument to pray for world peace.

18. Linda Mihara, personal communication, July 30, 2009.

19. I am pretty sure that Mike Shinoda is a fourth generation Japanese American, since his father was a child during internment. Doing the math, his grandparents had twelve children at the time of internment in 1942, exclusion was in place since 1924, so it is possible that they arrived in the United States in the decade before 1924, making

Shinoda a third generation. However, it would make his father in his forties or older when he fathered Shinoda, so it is also likely that he is fourth generation. General information on Shinoda from Cathy Lim, "Getting Back to His Roots," *Rafu Shimpo,* www.rafu.com, www.rafu.com/mike_shinoda.html (accessed July 17, 2009).

20. Information found on album insert in Fort Minor, *The Rising Tied,* CD (Warner Brothers Records, 2005).

21. Morley Seaver, "Mike Shinoda (Linkin Park, Fort Minor) Interview," antimusic.com, http://www.antimusic.com/morley/05/FortMinor.shtml (accessed July 17, 2009).

22. Fort Minor, "Remember the Name [featuring Styles of Beyond]," *The Rising Tied.* Lyrics are as written in the album insert.

23. Jin, "Learn Chinese," *The Rest is History,* CD (Ruff Ryders, 2004). Lyrics transcribed by author.

24. Fort Minor, "Remember the Name," *The Rising Tied.*

25. Oliver Wang argues that by the mid-1990s Asian Americans in hip hop have often taken an approach that is not explicitly political and anti-racist, but pursue "hip hop as an end unto itself"; "instead, they sought to appeal to an idealized hip hop community in which race and ethnicity are downplayed in favor of more seemingly race-neutral values such as 'talent,' 'skills,' and 'personal expression.' While these values are an important part of hip hop's heritage and belief system, they are also the ones most easily deracinated and therefore an attractive alternative for artists seeking to avoid the authenticity dilemma based on race or ethnicity." With this in mind, Shinoda may be engaging an Asian American hip hop tradition of building a multiracial community by downplaying issues that pertain to race, namely, his universalized examination of self. Yet, "Kenji" is explicitly about race, so Shinoda is innovating a bit here on the Asian American tradition or connecting to race-conscious hip hop. Oliver Wang, "Rapping and Repping Asian: Race, Authenticity, and the Asian American MC" in *Alien Encounters: Popular Culture in Asian America,* ed. Mimi Thi Nguyen and Thuy Linh Nguyen Tu (Durham: Duke University Press, 2007), 45-46.

26. I would like to thank my students for helping me on the analysis of "Kenji." By discussing the song with them, I was able to phrase my perspective better. Fort Minor, "Kenji," *The Rising Tied.*

27. Cathy Lim, "Getting Back to His Roots."

28. Hip hop frequently uses quotations of famous figures, such as Malcolm X, Thomas Todd, and Sun Ra, to bring a sense of gravity and historical continuity to their music. Listen to for example Public Enemy, "Fight the Power," *Fear of a Black Planet,* CD (Def Jam, 1990).

29. For information on electronic sampling, see Joseph Schloss, *Making Beats: the Art of Sample-Based Hip-Hop* (Middletown, CT: Wesleyan University Press, 2004).

30. Fort Minor, "Kenji," *The Rising Tied.* Lyrics are as written in the album insert.

31. Slick Rick, "Children's Story," *The Great Adventures of Slick Rick,* CD (Def Jam, 1995).

32. *Waka* poems are also called *tanka* poems, and have the syllable form 5-7-5-7-7. *Haiku* clubs were also present. For an explanation of several Japanese American poetry styles and excellent samples of *haiku* poetry during internment, see Marvin Opler and F. Obayashi, "Senryu Poetry as Folk and Community Expression," *The Journal of American Folklore* 58, no. 227 (1945): 1-11. *Tanka* and free-form poems were also written during internment. Free-form poems often had condemnations and placed blame, so serenity is not in all of Japanese American poetry. See Peter T. Suzuki, "Wartime *Tanka*: Issei and Kibei Contributions to a Literature East and West," *Literature East and West* 21 (1977): 242-54.

33. For more on Yasutaro Soga, see Yasutaro Soga, *Life Behind Barbed Wire: The World War II Internment Memoirs of a Hawai'I Issei,* trans. Kihei Hirai (Honolulu: University of Hawaii Press, 2008); Jiro Nakano and Kay Nakano, trans. and ed., *Poets Behind Barbed Wire* (Honolulu: Bamboo Ridge Press, 1983).

34. The English is my translation, assisted by the translation in Nakano and Nakano, *Poets Behind Barbed Wire*. The translation in the book is as follows: "Beyond the forbidding fence / Of double barbed wire, / The mountain, aglow in purple, / Sends us its greetings." Nakano and Nakano, *Poets Behind Barbed Wire*, 58.

35. Fort Minor, "Kenji," *The Rising Tied*.

36. I am confident that the song is supposed to symbolize the universality of this feeling because the video of the song highlights both men's and women's experiences of abandonment. See "Fort Minor - Where'd You Go," http://video.google.com/videoplay?docid=1414747251708876747&ei=DreVSoKNLZ_sqAPNmIzIBg&q (accessed August 26, 2009).

37. Fort Minor, "Where'd You Go [featuring Holly Brook and Jonah Matranga]," *The Rising Tied*. Lyrics are as written in the album insert.

38. Morley Seaver, "Mike Shinoda."

39. Todd Inoue, "Summer of '42: Fort Minor's Mike Shinoda Talks about his Family's Internment Camp Story in 'Kenji,'" metroactive, http://www.metroactive.com/papers/metro/02.15.06/shinoda-0607.html (accessed July 18, 2009).

40. Todd Inoue, "Summer of '42."

41. At the center of their work is what I would call a deep silence, a reverence for the folkloric symbols that live in the present through the lives of the present. This silence is productive because it evokes emotion and guides one's own embodiment. For more on the concept of silence, see Brett Esaki, "Desperately Seeking Silence: Youth Culture's Unspoken Need," *Cross Currents* 57, no. 3 (2007): 379-90.

TEN

Igorot American Folk Dance

Performance, Identity, and the Paradox of Decolonization

Mark Sabas Leo and Jonathan H. X. Lee

There were many Igorots in the market place, come down from the mountains to trade with the lowlanders. They walked among the people in their G-Strings with their poisoned arrows and dogs. They had long black hair like mine, but while they knotted theirs and stuck brightly polished sticks through the knots, I tangled my hair like a bird's nest and put a straw hat on it to keep it from falling over my face. The lowland people did not even bother to look at them or at their dogs, when they went around offering their wild honey, rattan, and medicinal herbs. . . . Then they would leave for their tree houses in the mountain villages, dragging their dogs with them and raising the dust as they passed from view.

—Carlos Bulosan[1]

This chapter focuses on how performing Igorot folk dances are essential to two different identities within Filipino America: mainstream pan-Filipino American and indigenous Filipino American. In this chapter, mainstream Filipino American refers to the dominant Tagalog-speaking, Catholic, and hetero-normative Filipino American community.[2] These people originated from various areas of the Philippine mountains, ranging from Manila in Luzon, Cebu City in central Visayas, Ilocos Norte, and Ilocos Sur. Although Filipinos from these areas have their own distinct regional dialects, they are fluent in Tagalog and have been heavily influenced by Spanish and American colonialism. Igorots are from the mountainous region—also known as the Cordilleras. The Igorots are indigenous to the Philippines, and successfully resisted three hundred years of Spanish colonialism.[3] As such, Igorot American identity does not conform to the mainstream historical narrative or identity of the homogenous pan-Filipino America.

Igorot folk dances are employed by both communities to authenticate ethnic and cultural identity. One of the primary sites for Igorot folk dancing is at Pilipino (or Philippine) Cultural Nights (PCN).[4] PCNs are annual cultural shows produced, created, and performed by Filipino American student organizations at university and college campuses throughout the United States. According to Anna Alves, "It serves as a cultural identity entrance point and rite of passage for its participants, becoming folkloric practice of sorts . . . [that results in the] embrace [of] a larger community, *naturalizing* a notion of what it means to be Filipino in the United States. . ."[5] From the perspective of Filipino Americans who self-identify as such, PCN is viewed positively. However, from the vantage point of the Igorot American community, who occupy both the insider and outsider positions within the boundaries of Filipino America, PCN performances of Igorot folk dance are sometimes problematic. By learning and performing Igorot folk dances, Igorot American youth gain knowledge about their distinctive identity that offers a counter narrative to the pan-Filipino American identity and experience. At the same time, the mainstream pan-Filipino American community employs the performances to reinforce multicultural identity, reconnecting with a pre-colonial Philippines as a means to naturalize their identity and sense of self as both Filipino and American.[6] Mehdi Bozorgmehr's notion of "internal ethnicity," which arises from the "existence, formation, or emergence of at least one subgroup within a nationality, along the lines of one or more indicators of ethnicity (e.g., language, regional origin, or religion)" is useful for us to consider in this discussion because "group-level discussions conceal important subgroup differences."[7]

Within the sphere of pan-Filipino America, Igorot identity has largely been invisible. The performance of Igorot folk dance is employed by both dominant (pan-Filipino American) and subordinate (Igorot American) communities to affirm self, ethnic, cultural, and national subjectivities: Filipino American versus Igorot American. Simultaneously, Igorot folk dance is changed: movements are altered, purpose is redefined, and context becomes utilitarian. The transformation in Igorot folk dance is a by-product of not only transplanting and settling Filipino American lifeways, but also the wholesale (mis)appropriation of Igorot folk dance to affirm pan-Filipino American Filipino-ness. Among Igorot Americans, and by extension, Igorot diasporic communities worldwide, learning Igorot folk dances creates self-empowered subjects with agency as well as ethnic and cultural pride. Igorot folk dances and the space in which the Igorot folk dances are performed become sites of resistance and hope. The source of their self-determination is from the esoteric positionality, which is an insider perspective that is unique for those who self-identify—either by blood or culture—with the various Igorot tribes.[8] Pan-Filipino American communities also employ Igorot folk dance as an exercise in decolonization of self and national identity.[9] Although pride and cultural self-esteem is a byproduct of the performances, it is an alternative, exoteric positionality. They are both subjects standing outside the Igorot community, while being simultaneously central in Filipino America.[10] The problem is not with being outside the Igorot American community, but rather with how Igorot is portrayed. The (mis)appropriation of pan-Filipino American Igorot folk dance is problematic, because as non-Igorot, the performance is done out of context and primarily as the object of the pan-Filipino American gaze. More controversial is that it is not inclusive of people from within that community.[11] The lived experiences of pan-Filipino Americans versus Igorot and other indigenous Filipino Americans are different and reveal different processes of ethnic and community formation. The specific experiences of Filipino Americans of Igorot heritage is ignored—directly or indirectly—privileging neat homogeneity of an imagined Filipino American identity and community. The (mis)appropriation of Igorot folk dance by the pan-Filipino American community *a la* Pilipino Culture Night performances at university and college campuses nationwide, gives rise to a paradox of decolonization.

This paradox is the process by which one group colonizes—directly or indirectly—another group in an attempt or act of decolonization. Among Filipino American college students, decolonization from Spanish and American colonialism is achieved through folkloric performances at PCN. However, the decolonization agenda is achieved by PCN through colonizing Filipino natives: liberation and self-empowerment is not completely beneficial for all parties involved, which requires a reflection on the limits and ethics of performing Igorot folk dances. Igorot Americans continue to face prejudice within Filipino American communities because they are conceived as *native*.[12] For instance, on social networks such as Facebook, Igorot Americans post comments or send messages to one another regarding encountering discrimination, experienced either personally or by someone they know. For example, a Filipina nurse tells her fellow coworker of Igorot heritage that one of her Filipino patients had a very noisy visitor during hospital visiting hours. The Filipina nurse began to describe this noisy Filipino guest as looking "like an Igorot." When the nurse of Igorot heritage asked the other nurse to describe what an Igorot looks like, she described the visitor thusly, ". . . you know, she got slit eyes, *mukha niya parang,* Native American Indians, *matapang ang mukha.*"[13] Translated, the nurse is suggesting that Igorot's physical features are similar to Native American Indians, who look "arrogant." The Igorot-heritage nurse revealed she is Igorot, and the other nurse jokingly said, "You do not look like an Igorot." This response illustrates the way Igorot subjectivity is locked in a colonial stereotype: Igorot is embedded in the image of a precolonial savage subject, thus Igorot and Igorot identity does not exist in modernity. The experience of the Igorot nurse is, unfortunately, not uncommon. Hence, examining the paradox and contradiction of decolonization as represented by PCN validates the angst and anxiety that Igorot Americans know, feel, and experience.

THE CREATION OF THE FILIPINO

Like race, nation-state and cultural identities are historically, socially, politically, and economically constructed. The historical development of a homogenous pan-Filipino identity subsumes a multitude of regional ethnic and cultural communities, which includes diverse dialects. The homogenous identity is anchored in one nation-state identity: the Philippines and Filipinos. Initially the origin of the term Filipino referred only to Spaniards born in the Philippines, then slowly began to include native people from the Philippines.[14] They were of the colored cohort of the *Ilustrado*—the enlightened intellectual class that was being educated overseas in Spain. Notable members of this class are José Rizal, Marcelo H. del Pilar, and Antonio Luna, who are considered national heroes of the Philippines because of their participation in the underground revolt against Spain. Luna would later go on to participate in the Philippine War for Independence against the United States. According to Paul Kramer, prior to the Philippine Revolution against Spain, one of the main goals of the *ilustrados* was for "Philippine 'assimilation,' the political normalization of the islands within the Spanish empire through the extension of metropolitan political and legal institutions, including representation in the Cortes."[15] However, these goals were curtailed by Spain on racial grounds, the Philippines were excluded because the island population was undeserving of recognition with their "Catholic *indios* (natives) mired in superstition, its 'savage' *infieles* (infidels, i.e., animists and Muslims) entirely untouched by the saving hand of the church."[16]

Accordingly, the *ilustrados* would begin a campaign of propaganda that would highlight how the people of the Philippines were up to par with the expectations of Spain and, thus, worthy of assimilation. The *ilustrados* limited who they would include in the creation of a new assimilated Filipino subject. This was the beginnings of what Benedict Anderson calls an "imagined community" that is rooted in a colonized Filipino nation-state.[17] Filipino is thus a hybridized entity that mixes Spanish cum colonial, with Filipino *ilustrados*. The colonial process produced a hierarchy of difference that expresses and manifests itself in terms of race, ethnicity, and class.

The imagined "Filipino" was further developed during the Philippine insurrection, also known as the war against the United States. During the forgotten colonial relationship with the United States, the *ilustrados* were seen as the "rich intelligentsia" because they were the children of wealthy landowners who played a big role in the development of Filipino nationalism.[18] As discontent grew toward the American colonizers, Emilio Aguinaldo's rebellion would grow to what would become the Philippine War for Independence that would last from 1899–1902. As David C. Martinez states, "Aguinaldo's pronouncement of intent for his *Republika ng Katagalogan* became the declaration of 'Philippine Independence'; and the history of the Tagalog nation, and apart from being highly romanticized, was passed off as the history of the entire 'Filipino People.'"[19] Martinez suggests that the revolution did not include all inhabitants of the island, but specific people, principally those who spoke Tagalog.[20] A national language thus plays a major role in the creation of the nation-state subject and identity.

The Tagalog speakers of the Philippines nation-state later became the dominant actors in the production of a pan-Filipino American mainstream identity. Its privileged position is attributed to the initial encounter between Spain and the Philippines, when as Martinez points out, the first *datus*, village chieftains who allied with the Spanish colonizers, were Tagalog and Pampanga *datus*, who formed the earliest forms of the landowning *principalia* elite.[21] As Herb Mantawe and Jeb Pesnar, members of the Defenders of the Indigenous Languages of the Archipelago (DILA) argued, "The Philippine government persists in its campaign to eradicate its non-Tagalog population through language conversion. First it went through the motions of developing a national language of Filipino. Armed with provisions in the defect-ridden 1987 constitution that nakedly favor Tagalog, it busily prepares for the final destruction of our non-Tagalog cultures."[22] The creation of the Filipino was a strategic move that was begun by the *ilustrados* during the period of Spanish Colonialism and perpetuated by the succeeding members of the Philippine government. As time progressed, the term became synonymous with the nation-state identity that was being forged, which was mostly of Spanish colonial influence and cultural heritage *a la* Catholicism, and predominately Tagalog speaking. The historical analysis of the term Filipino thus reveals the social, political, and economic privilege that Tagalog-speaking Filipinos possessed, and the ways in which their assimilation into Spanish lifeways and norms benefitted them in the racial hierarchy that oppressed indigenous Filipinos, who fell outside of that sphere of conformity. One target of discrimination were the Igorots, who resided in the mountain regions of Luzon.

CREATING THE IGOROT "OTHER"

As the *ilustrados* sought to gain recognition from their Spanish colonizers, they had to justify why they deserved to occupy positions of privilege. Historian Paul Kramer notes that, "in 1889, one editorialist assured his readers that 'the Filipinos adore Spain.'. . . Our Filipinos . . . already know the most intricate declensions of classical Latin."[23]

As Kramer stated,

> Where the *ilustrado* diasporic experience had led some to challenge notions of *mestizaje*, the propaganda campaign also radically heightened the salience of Hispanic culture that the *ilustrados*—but not all of the islands' inhabitants shared. Where *ilustrado* activities held up their civilization before Spain and Europe more broadly in a quest for recognition and assimilation, Philippine peoples that [*sic*] could not measure up to these standards became increasingly problematic.[24]

Thus, not everyone was included in this imagined concept of what was to become the interlocutor of Filipino national identity. The boundaries of the Filipino would parallel and go as far as Spanish Catholic conquest and conversion, which did not include the animists and the Muslims of the archipelago, who mounted the strongest resistance toward converting to Christianity and were never defeated by the Spanish colonizers. Therefore, the Igorot animists from the mountain regions of Luzon became designated as one of the many groups that found themselves squarely outside the sphere of the conception of Filipino. As such, they were categorized as "other" and unworthy of recognition, not just by the Spanish colonizers, but eventually by their own "colonized" kababayan—Philippine peoples.

Through the circulation of propaganda literature, the definition of who was Filipino and how they should live became accepted as the new social image became self-evident. With this, a new history of the Philippines was recorded. Filomeno Aguilar's work shows how this process unfolded.[25] Aguilar argues that the propagandist writers of the time drew heavily on the theory of "wave migrations" of Ferdinand Blumentritt—a close friend of *ilustrado* Jose Rizal—to justify the hierarchies of difference between the diverse group of peoples who cohabit the Philippines. Based on Rizal's theory, prior to the Spanish colonization of the Philippines there were three waves of migrations, with each group moving further inland due to the succeeding migrations that followed. Blumentritt's theory shows how these different groups were based on a racial evolutionary model. The first wave of people were *Negritos* and were known to be the most "savage," situated in the mountains of the Philippines;[26] the second wave were Malayans that had intermixed with the "savage" *Negritos* and had also made their home in the mountains;[27] and the final wave of migrants to the Philippine islands were also a second wave of Malayans.[28] However, according to Blumentritt, this final wave possessed a "higher civilization and milder morals as compared to the first Malay wave."[29] Aguilar explains that this group, composed of Tagalogs, Pampanguinios, Visayans, Bicolanos, Ilocanos, Pangasinanons, and Cagayanons, conquered the already established groups and drove the remaining groups into the mountains.[30] This narrative reinforces the theory of evolutionary mankind, survival of the fittest, and Social Darwinism, which legitimize inequality and racism. Filipinos who did not conform to this definition stood outside the realm of history and civilization and were regarded as inferior.

However, not all *ilustrado* writers were in agreement with this historical social construction of a Hispanic Catholic core for the newly emerging Filipino community and, by extension, identity. In his writings, Isabelo de los Reyes was one of the few who was willing to include the Igorot animists and Muslims in the imagining of the Filipino nationhood and selfhood. In one of his essays he describes himself as the "[b]rother of the forest dwellers, the Aetas, the Igorots, and the Tinuianes."[31] In another essay, "The Origins of the Races," he argued that different groups were categorized as civilized or savage based on their proximity to areas that were frequented by Spaniards or civilized Ilocanos.[32] However, Kramer argues that most of the *ilustrados* overseas wanted to make sure that these distinct differences were made known to those outside of the Philippines. Many *ilustrados* were displeased to be "misrecognized" for the unconverted "others." The normalization of Filipino as Spanish-like, Catholic, and Tagalog speaking placed the Igorot animists and the Muslims as the barbarous "Other" since they were the descendants of a people considered outsiders and savages. The indigenous Filipinos became the "Filipino man's burden." Those who opposed civilization and Christianity were indeed outside the progress of history. The colonized-self and nation of Filipinos was transplanted in the United States, and transmitted the homogenous imaginary community of Filipino to *Filipino* America.[33]

FILIPINO AMERICANS AND THE PARADOX OF DECOLONIZATION

Filipinos have been migrating to North America as early as the Manila-Acapulco galleon trades from 1565–1815.[34] They also have continued to immigrate to the United States in various ways, as laborers for the sugar plantations in Hawai'i, as laborers for the farms and canneries of the West Coast, and as members of the U.S. military recruited from former U.S. bases in the Philippines.[35] Within this grand narrative of Filipino immigration to the United States, an "invisible" narrative of Igorot immigration also develops, one that includes the Igorots that were on display at the St. Louis World's Fair in 1904[36] and the Alaska Yukon Pacific Exposition 1909.[37] Immigrants from the Philippines gradually adopted and accepted their identity as "Filipino Americans." Moreover, future generations will employ this homogenous pan-Filipino American identity, but for the Igorot Filipino Americans, inclusion into the pan-Filipino identity requires a compromise.

Contemporary Filipino American students learn how to become Filipino Americans through a process that Leny Strobel calls the "born-again Filipinos." The Filipino American community and identity are produced through the "born-again process" that requires the (mis)appropriation of indigenous Philippine culture as a means of affirming a pan-Filipino homogeneity that promotes "diversity" and celebrates various ethnolinguistic and cultural traditions of the Philippines as "Filipino." This obfuscates the heterogenic reality inherent in Filipino America. A counter narrative that focuses on and demands recognition of their particular ethnic and cultural communities and identities is seen in Igorot Americans' attempts to "reclaim" and "decolonize" their subjectivity from the homogenous claws of pan-Filipino American.

The concept of being a "born-again Filipino" is an attempt to "decolonize" Filipino from Western (Spanish and American) influence. It therefore claims the "other," the indigenous—in general, and Igorot, in particular, as part and parcel of a singular Filipino-ness. Strobel describes this process of decolonization," . . . as undoing the effects of colonization on the Filipino psyche by recognizing the master narratives that constructed colonial identity and replacing them with indigenous narratives. The term 'indigenous' is used here to refer to worldviews, values, beliefs, and practices which define Filipino-ness." [38] To be Filipino is simply to be from the Philippines. All people from the Philippines are one and the same. The colonized mentality is taken for granted: Indigenous is over extended. To be a more "authentic" Filipino is to replace the Spanish with the indigenous. This act itself is a colonizing action. As Dylan Rodriguez contends, Strobel's conception of decolonization perpetuates the

> . . . relations of the U.S.-proctored "colonialism" and "empire." The dependence on such opportunistic appropriations of an allegedly traditional or indigenous culture for the purpose of installing a stable, U.S. based cosmopolitanism displaces radical, if uneasy, possibility: the insurgent production of Philippine/U.S. Filipino collective historical memory that articulates from within the constitutive violence and traumatic rupturing of American conquest and colonization, coercive modernist "civilization," and the more fundamental surrender of the 'independent' Philippine nation state form itself. [39]

Along with the production of Filipino, the Spanish cultural influence and mentality is normalized as the *episteme* of Filipino America. [40] The *habitus* is ahistorical and natural: all Filipinos are from the Philippines, speak Tagalog, and are Catholic. [41] Strobel is victim of the colonial apparatus, whereby she reflects what Homi Bhabha describes as "mimicry" and Frantz Fanon describes as the colonized becoming the inverted image of colonizer. [42] Filipino Americans who unquestionably adopt the pan-Filipino American narrative and conception of self and society are, as Bhabha describes, part of the ambivalence of their post–colonial condition. [43]

DECOLONIZING PILIPINO CULTURE NIGHTS?

Pilipino Culture Night (PCN) productions are found on many college campuses around the nation and, in some cases, high schools that have a sizeable Filipino American student population. In his study of PCN in contemporary Filipino America, Theodore Gonzalves argues that these performance productions consist of two genres, one that uses folkloric forms—dance, song, music, and costumes—and the other consisting of theatrical narration—in the form of a play or skit.[44] PCN's mission is twofold: it is meant to preserve what has become the homogenous Filipino heritage, but more importantly to pass this heritage on to the next generation of Filipino Americans despite the truth of cultural, ethnic, religious, and regional differences among Filipinos from within their country of origin. Anna Alves and Xavier Hernandez both touch on these issues in their research on PCN. Both Alves and Hernandez support Strobel's concept of young Filipino American students going through a process of being a "born-again Filipino." According to Alves, "In Pilipino Cultural Night, students express an idea of themselves as an extension of the larger struggle for identity in the Philippines, part of a decolonization process of Pilipinos undertake [*sic*] around the world wherever they have settled or traveled within a global diaspora."[45] Whereas, Hernandez's study of PCN claims that, "The processes that PCN producers, writers, directors, choreographers, and performers navigate to reach some sort of baseline platform amongst these seemingly infinite conversations and embody this ideology through the PCN performance thus illustrates a new culture in and of itself: an expression of how Filipino American youth theorize and physically perform the significance of culture in our past, present, and future lives."[46] Thus, both Alves and Hernandez show that in the development of creating the annual PCN, Filipino American students undergo a process of decolonization and learning of their identity that promotes and perpetuates the "mainstream" Filipino/Filipino American identity. Decolonizing PCN requires a deconstruction of its parts and a critique of its larger intent. "Taking apart the story, revealing underlying texts, and giving voice to things that are often known intuitively does not help people to improve their current conditions,"[47] but does begin the process of decolonizing Igorot Americans from Filipino Americans.

PERFORMING FILIPINO-NESS

The focus here is on PCN's (mis)appropriation of indigenous Filipino folk dances. However, it should be noted that its theatrical narration is just as important in the production of a homogenous pan-Filipino American community and identity as the dances are. As Gonzalves argues, performing Filipino folk dances represents a resistance to the American assimilationist paradigm.[48] Therefore, folk dance performance at PCN is a decolonizing act. It represents what post–colonial scholars describe as a "counter-discursive" activity that is critical of dominant (colonial) discourse.

Organizers of PCNs ignore—wittingly or unwittingly—the problematic issues of authenticity of the dances they perform as a product of colonization. "On the one hand, PCN organizers rely on folk forms invented by Francisca Reyes Aquino to authenticate their understanding of Filipina/o culture. . . . On the other hand, the folk forms also draw from the highly stylized rendition of the Philippine dance theater work popularized since the late 1950s."[49] But the latter, Aquino contends, is "not folkdance" and "therefore does not have a claim on authenticity."[50] According to Alves, students wrestle with this issue every year during the planning stages of the PCN. She notes, "Though I agree with the dangers of its 'essentializing' tendencies, as a consistent PCN producer myself, having participated in five shows as a creator and organizer of content in each, there is something that drew me to that particular arena of production, year in and year out."[51] This "something" that Alves mentions briefly is touched upon again when she argues that,

> The "essential Pilipino" as an ambiguous concept is thus standardized, allowing for individual interpretation of meaning. This ambiguity allows for great maneuvering—what you see is an essentialized package; what you get is distinctive and varied. In other words, the effort to "essentialize" culture in one production during one night is actually an attempt to "socialize" mass numbers of new students into an ideology of "Pilipino is good and valid" in the face of an American society that barely acknowledges their communal existence.[52]

Alves shows a consensus that the end—affirming and creating a baseline Pilipino identity—justifies the means, which (mis)appropriates Igorot folk dances in PCN to essentialize diversity.

PCN performance of Igorot folk dances is, thus, particularly problematic because of its questionable authenticity: the tempo is faster, costume protocols are overlooked, and moreover, the dances are performed out of context and out of sequence. They are learned by counting movements instead of through feeling and intuition.[53] Even more problematic, they are learned from the exoteric positionality. Because PCNs are "theatrical," the contextual authenticity of the dance is not accounted for. This is because the dance is not being performed for its original purpose, but is being performed for theatrical means to inform a Filipino American audience of its identity and subjectivity as Filipinos. What they see, hear, smell, and feel is Filipino-ness. There is a dialectical relationship between the performer and the audience; the performer is creating and projecting an identity to the audience, which in turn, is being consumed by the audience, and simultaneously affirming the performed identity.[54] What happens if the audience does not identify with the pan-Filipino American identity? What happens if they identify with Igorot?[55]

Similar to PCN productions of Filipino culture that affirms a pan-Filipino American identity and conceptualization of Filipino-ness, young Igorot Filipino Americans perform their folk dance traditions as a means to decolonize themselves from multiple colonial complexes: Spanish, pan-Filipino American, and American.[56]

BIBAK, an organization that represents the five major Igorot tribes: Bontoc, Ifugao, Benguet, Apayao, and Kalinga, is found throughout the United States. BIBAK teaches and encourages young Igorot Americans to maintain their folk heritage and lifeways. Igorot youth learn the folk dances from Igorot elders. The direct result of this transmission is the development of Igorot pride and identity that is not subsumed in the pan-Filipino American agenda. For Igorot youth, these dances represent more than just a multicultural event performed once a year. Instead, they reflect a way of life. The dances are performed at community celebrations, during rites of passages (i.e., weddings), and to memorialize stages of Igorot life events (i.e., funerals). For example, the *passing of the gongs* is important for the preservation of Igorot folk dances and folk ways in America. The forces of immigration and modernization have compromised Igorot folkways; Igorot folklore has been lost or modernized to adapt to the new surroundings in America. The BIBAK performance space fuels a consensus and identification with being Igorot and Igorot American. For example, at regional BIBAK gatherings known as *Canyao*, akin to the Native American pow-wow, regional BIBAK chapters meet to network and celebrate with other tribal members.

Igorot folk dances performed at *Canyao* or other Igorot events differ from the performances of those dances at PCNs. Igorot dances performed at PCN are overly choreographed, performed without stylistic flair, and, more importantly, are devoid of feeling. Performed on the basis of musical beats/count, they are rendered emotionless and mechanical. Further, there is a difference in the way the music is played. At PCN performances, dancers beat their gongs differently than in performances in Igorot spaces. PCN gong beating follows the theatrical choreography and movement counts—again, rendering it mechanical. Rather, in Igorot performances, the gong beat dictates the dance steps, allowing for spontaneity of movement, sudden changes in tempo, and depth of emotion since there is no official step count before moving on to a different movement. Igorot American performance of Igorot folk dances at Igorot community and cultural events is organic and inclusive. Audience and performer are not distant or separate; rather the interaction between the two is fluid and merges into one another, resulting in the creation of a shared community. In this way, Igorot American social relationships are forged and affirmed and the Igorot way of life is maintained. For example, during Igorot weddings, it is customary for the bride and groom to perform a rendition of the Igorot family's tribal courtship dance at the reception. Simultaneously, family and friends will perform different celebratory dances from their respective tribes. There is a cacophony of sound and an orderly chaos of movements that comes together organically and emotionally.

PCN's theatrical performance of Igorot folk dance is an unsuspecting act of colonization as it reveals an underlying assumption and colonialist prejudice concerning indigenous people in the guise of multiculturalism and diversity. They perpetuate the Orientalist image of the romantic savagery of the Igorot people as falling outside the sphere of civilization. This is especially evident when PCN performs Igorot war and courtship dances. The performance of these two dances are always depicted as identities of the Filipino precolonial past—what all Filipinos were supposed to be like before the colonization of the country and its introduction to Western modernity. Since Igorot identity is showcased as an identity of the past, it is assumed that Filipinos of Igorot heritage no longer exist, which is quite the contrary. What is more interesting is that the Igorot identity, an identity that is distinct to a specific region in the Philippines, is being absorbed into the pan-Filipino identity in terms of the groups' identity of the past. There is no acknowledgment of Igorot identity in the present. PCN's goal is to decolonize Filipino American subjectivities from Spanish and American colonial *espiteme*. In order to achieve

Figure 10.1.   BIBAK Youth San Diego performing the ballangbang to a crowd at FilAmFest 2013. Courtesy BIBAK Youth San Diego.

decolonized subjectivity, PCN performers and viewers must colonize Igorot folk squarely within the dominate *episteme,* which are based on a set of fundamental assumptions about Filipino and Filipino American identity that are so basic so as to be invisible to the colonial forces operating within it. Invoking Fanon, pan-Filipino American subjectivity as expressed through PCN creates a negative racial construction of a colonized self: the colonized becomes an inverted image of colonizer.[57] This leads to a paradox of decolonization; PCN is a decolonizing act, but it is only possible through colonizing Igorot and other indigenous Filipino and Filipino American folkways and communities. The Igorot and Igorot American communities thus experience double colonialization: one from Western colonial forces, and one internal, from other Filipinos.

When PCN performances showcase precolonial Igorot folk dances to enforce the Filipino American community's homogenous conception of Filipino-ness, it engages in an act of domination. Among Igorot Filipino Americans, reclaiming their folk dances and transmitting them into the future is an act of resistance to the entire discursive field within which PCN operates in a post–colonial world.

Ironically, in an effort to decolonize itself and their community, indigenous Filipino cultures of the Philippines are (mis)appropriated into the homogenous mainstream pan-Filipino American community and, by extension, identity, which is a form of "colonization" because it continues to perpetuate the social hierarchy that originated from the period of Spanish and Christian colonizations. For example, the mainstream Filipino American narrative tells the stories of those immigrants who were defined as Filipino in the Philippines, but the narratives fail to include the narratives of immigrants who were classified as "Other" — those of indigenous heritage. More importantly, it ignores the intra-ethnic discrimination that they encountered, not just from the dominant white society, but from the dominant mainstream pan-Filipino American community. Even today, for instance, the Filipino American community maintains the image and stereotype of Igorot as being "savage" as expressed in Carlos Bulosan's writing. Igorot American youth grow up confronting these stereotypes because they straddle both Filipino and Igorot identities and communities. One of the authors of this chapter, Mark S. Leo, self-identifies as an Igorot Filipino American. He recalls,

> When I was in high school I had taken Tagalog as a foreign language requirement and one of our assignments was to do a "show and tell" public speaking presentation. I had chosen to speak about my Igorot heritage and show a video of a performance that we had at another local high school's PCN. I had presented with a friend of mine who also was in the same BIBAK organization, and during our presentation we encountered laughter and jeering comments. At first I thought it was laughter that came with the lack of maturity that we were all known for in high school, but during our Q&A portion of the presenta-

tion we began to realize it was something else. Many of the comments were about how they heard from their parents and friends that Igorots were dirty savage people from the Philippines who had tails. What made the situation worse, was that our teacher, who was of Filipino descent, intervened the next day and perpetuated the same stereotypes by showing images of Igorots in the past and contrasting them with images of "civilized" Igorots after attending schools that were set up by the United States. What was more infuriating was that our teacher still did not acknowledge that we were of Igorot heritage in the class, since he used examples of "modern" Igorot Filipino images in his lecture to diffuse the tension between my classmates, my friend, and myself.

By analyzing the trends of how PCNs are organized and produced, we can see how the inclusion of Igorot folk performance is problematic. According to Gonzalves, the PCN narrative follows a protagonist that does not know his/her history or culture; as the show progresses the protagonist comes into contact with the culture that is sought in the form of indigenous Igorot folk dance performances, along with many others; the show concludes when the protagonist reaches an epiphany and becomes a "born-again Filipino."[58]

Alves and Hernandez affirm this narrative as the standard storyline in PCN productions. Alves states, "In PCN, it is the same story which repeats itself every year, in different guises. It is basically a story of discovery and initiation. Essentially, that is the case—PCN is a place to begin the 'quest' for a Pilipino identity, Philippine culture, and a Pilipino American community."[59] Hernandez echoes these sentiments in his description of why members of PCN often choose to be the skit coordinator for the annual productions, citing "Informants who described wanting to do PCN for personal reasons framed these motivations around the context of wanting to write a PCN skit which mirrored their own stories of becoming Filipino American."[60] The story line reveals an uneasy problematic objectification of the indigenous, of the Igorot, because it perpetuates the mainstream Filipino American multiculturalist community and identity, but leaves the indigenous "Other" Orientalized in its romanticized savage precolonial conditions. The Igorot and other indigenous Filipino Americans in the audience remain (in)visible as their culture is (mis)appropriated into a mainstream narrative that does not recognize their claim to their heritage. The needs, concerns, and issues of the indigenous members are overlooked, muted, and ignored. Igorot Americans unknowingly become a part of the colonizing project, in which they "self-colonize" their identity, community, and bodies for the greater pan-Filipino American image. This is not just an academic problem, but speaks to the sheer physical survival of Igorot folkways and folklore. Therefore, Igorot and Igorot Americans must heed Maori scholar, Linda Tuhiwai Smith's words: "To acquiesce is to lose ourselves entirely and implicitly agree with all that has been said about us."[61]

CONCLUSION

The colonial history of the Philippines has made a significant impact on the social identity of the Filipino people. The *ilustrados* conception of a Filipino is echoed in the writings of Carlos P. Romulo, where he describes America's influence on the Philippines as vital to the country's ability to be successful and compete politically and economically in the global arena when compared to other developing countries with no American influence.[62] In his book, Romulo reveals his concept of being Filipino by saying,

> Even in the Philippines, to cite one recurrent source of annoyance, stories were frequently sent to America concerning our wild tribes, the Igorots, in which they were represented as Filipinos. *These primitive black people are no more Filipino than the American Indian is representative of the United States citizen.* They hold exactly the same position—they are our aborigines. The fact remains that the *Igorot is not Filipino* and we are not related, and it hurts our feelings to see him pictured in American newspapers under such captions as, "Typical Filipino Tribesman."[63]

Romulo clearly states his contempt for being conflated with the "savage" Igorot people from the Cordilleran region, and shows his annoyance for their representation overseas as a misconception for the historical and national Filipino subject. Romulo goes as far as disowning the Igorots and claims that they are not Filipino or a related people. Romulo's sentiments are not unique or unusual. In fact, Igorot Americans face discrimination and prejudice from Filipino Americans in the workplace and at school. It is thus ironic that the pan-Filipino American community and identity includes all people from the Philippines as one homogenous group of people, when it only represents the voices and concerns of a specific kind of Filipino: Tagalog-speaking, Spanish and American influenced subjects who are predominately Catholic, middle-class, heterosexual, and professionals. There is a schizophrenic relationship between Igorot peoples and their folk customs in the pan-Filipino American goal of achieving homogenous unity because Igorot are simultaneously outside mainstream Filipino America, but utilitarian to its cause apropos PCN.

Igorot folk dance performance is vital to two distinct communities and identities in the United States: the mainstream Filipino American and the Igorot American. The Filipino American community and identity employs Igorot folk dance as way to decolonize and claim an alternative narrative that is outside their colonial heritage, as a way to promote their Filipino-ness, but at the cost of misappropriating Igorot folkways and cultures. On the other hand, performing Igorot folk dance has a completely different meaning for Igorot American youth, one that informs them of their unique identity and imparts a sense of self-empowerment that is especially important. For them, these dance performances repre-

Figure 10.2.   Beyond Performance symposium poster, January 28, 2012. Courtesy BIBAK Youth San Diego.

sent their culture and their way of life; it is something they have grown up with. However, for some Filipino Americans, that performance at PCN is temporary and utilitarian: the performance is just an event that will occur in what is perceived to be a cultural variety show, and is not incorporated into their lives.

As established above, both PCN performers and Igorot American youth engage in decolonizing acts when they perform Igorot folk dances. However, for Igorot American youth, it is double decolonization. Awareness of the multiple forces of colonization on Igorot subjectivities allows Igorot American youth to dismantle the colonial complex that they live in and experience. Through the analysis of PCN, one can also see the perpetuation of the nation-state Filipino identity through Filipino American identity and communities. Although they employ Igorot folk dance to remove it from its closeness to Spain, the nation-state identity remains strong, ever present, and unchanging. As Rodriguez argues,

> The Filipino American figuration is, in this sense, enacted as the *meta-fulfillment* of multiculturalists nation-building telos. Within the problematic of this deformed nationalism, Filipino American common sense not only refrains from sustained critique of the racist and white supremacist institutionalities of the U.S. state "Filipino" and "non-Filipino" localities; it is structurally incapable of it.[64]

The performances found in PCNs help to maintain, directly and indirectly, a nation-state identity that is embedded in a multiculturalist Filipino American community and identity that acts as a level of oppression toward the indigenous people that are showcased to enforce their Filipino-ness. This occurs at the expense of Orientalizing the indigenous Filipinos as people from the precolonial period, as people who have yet to modernize, and as people who remain savagely romantic outside the progress of history. Strobel claims that this process of becoming "born-again Filipinos" is a way of decolonizing ones identity, but at what cost? If decolonization means reclaiming alternative narratives that were once deemed as the "Other" by the mainstream pan-Filipino community, it must be done correctly.

NOTES

1. Carlos Bulosan, *America is in the Heart* (Seattle: University of Washington Press, 1973): 40.
2. For example, Yen Le Espiritu, *Filipino American Lives* (Philadelphia: Temple University Press, 1995); Maria P. P. Root ed., *Filipino Americans: Transformation and Identities* (Thousand Oaks: Sage Publications, 1997); Yen Le Espiritu, *Homebound: Filipino American Lives Across Cultures, Communities, Countries* (Berkeley and Los Angeles: University of California Press, 2003).
3. However, they were not able to resist American colonialism.
4. The word "Pilipino" refers to Filipino Americans, without having to state "American." American is inferred and inherent in Pilipino.

5. Anna Alves, "Pilipino Cultural Night," in *Encyclopedia of Asian American Folklore and Folklife* (Santa Barbara: ABC-CLIO Press, 2011): 396-398. Emphasis added.

6. Both groups rely on body movement and Igorot traditional clothing as expressions of selfhood that is local and transnational.

7. Mehdi Bozorgmehr. "Internal Ethnicity: Iranians in Los Angeles." In *Sociological Perspectives* 40 (3): 388.

Monica Trieu discusses the importance of internal ethnicity with respects to Chinese-Vietnamese American vis-à-vis Vietnamese American ethnic and community formations in *Identity Construction among Chinese-Vietnamese Americans: Being, Becoming, and Belonging* (El Paso: LFB Scholarly Publishing LLC, 2009).

8. Wm Hugh Jansen, "The Esoteric-Exoteric Factor in Folklore," *Fabula: Journal of Folktale Studies,* Vol. 2 (1959): 205–11.

9. This is illustrated by the comments of a non-Filipino American professor who teaches and specializes in Philippines and Filipino American studies. S/he writes, "Based on my observation and work with Filipino students who produce, direct, and perform PCN, also known as Celebration of Filipino Culture Night, they may see the Igorot culture and dance traditions from different 'eyes' that 'see' their manhood in these dances. Part of performing them is to show their cultural pride and manhood, not in an American sense by any means, but as male warriors."

10. Jansen 1959, 205–211.

11. Interestingly, in New Zealand, the Maori Warrior Dance starts off the Rugby Game and is a source of national pride, whereas football teams in the United States coopted Native American symbols disrespectfully and can no longer do that because it was offensive to Native Americans. These are two cases that demonstrate how folk dance can be appropriated: one that respects another's dignity and becomes the pride of the nation versus the other that did not.

12. Mark Leo look at Igorot performance because I come from an Igorot community and know the intricacies of the culture, whereas it would be problematic to speak for other indigenous groups since I would not have the proper point of reference to speak for them.

13. Email correspondence 02/16/10.

14. Reynato Constantino and Letizia Constantino, *Philippines: A Past Revisited: Volume 1 (Pre-Spanish—1941)* (Quezon City: Tala Pub. Services, 1975).

15. Paul Kramer, *The Blood Government: Race, Empire, the United States, and the Philippines* (University of North Carolina Press, 2006): 37.

16. Kramer 2006, 37.

17. Benedict Anderson, *Imagined Communities: Reflections on the Origin and Spread of Nationalism* (New York: Verso, 1983).

18. Stanley Karnow, *In Our Image: America's Empire in the Philippines* (New York: Ballantine Books, 1990): 15.

19. David Martinez, *A Country of Our Own: Partitioning the Philippines* (Los Angeles: Bisaya Books, 2004): vii.

20. Martinez 2004, 210.

21. Martinez 2004, 133.

22. Martinez 2004, 210.

23. Kramer 2006, 66.

24. Kramer 2006, 67.

25. Filomena Aguilar, Tracing Origins: "Illustrado" Nationalism and Racial Science of Migration Waves. *Journal of Asian Studies* 64:3 (2005): 605–637.

26. Aguilar 2005, 612–613.

27. Aguilar 2005, 613–617.

28. Aguilar 2005, 619–620.

29. Aguilar 2005, 617.

30. Aguilar 2005, 617.

31. Kramer 2006, 68.

32. Kramer 2006, 68.

33. Marlon E. Fuentes' *Bontoc Eulogy* illustrates the production of Igorot savagery clearly. Fuentes narrates the story of 1,100 Filipino tribal natives brought to the United States to be a "living exhibit" of Western civilization and historical progress at the 1904 St. Louis World's Fair. The contrast was sharp and disturbing. It reveals the cultural arrogance and glorification of Western progress by focusing on their lack of clothes and seeming undeveloped cultural life ways of the indigenous. See Marlon E. Fuentes, producer, writer, director, and editor. *Bontoc Eulogy*. Independent Television Service, 1997.

34. Ronald Takaki, *A History of Asian American: Strangers from a Different Shore: Updated and Revised* (New York: Back Bay Books, 1998).

35. Takaki, 1998; Espiritu, 1997.

36. Nancy Parezo and Don Dower, *Anthropology Goes to the Fair* (University of Nebraska Press, 2007).

37. (http://www.aype.com).

38. Leny Strobel, Born Again Filipino: Filipino American Identity and Asian Panethnicity. *Ameriasia Jorunal* 22:2 (1996): 38.

39. Dylan Rodriguez, *Suspended Apocalypse: White Supremacy, Genocide, and the Filipino Condition* (Minneapolis: University of Minnesota Press, 2010): 48.

40. Michel Foucault used the term *episteme* in his work *The Order of Things*. *Episteme* is an all-encompassing collection of beliefs and assumptions that result in the organization of scientific worldviews and practices, as well as other forms of discourse.

41. Pierre Bourdieu. *Outline of a Theory of Practice* (Cambridge: Cambridge University Press, 1977).

42. Homi K. Bhabha. *The Location of Culture* (London: Routledge, 1994). Frantz Fanon. *A Dying Colonialism* (New York: Grove Press, 1965); and *Black Skin, White Masks*. Translation by Richard Philcox (New York: Grove Press, 2008).

43. Bhabha 1994, chapter 6.

44. Theo Gonzalves, Dancing Into Oblivion: The Pilipino Cultural Night and the Narration of Contemporary Filipina/o America. *Kritika Kultura 6* (2005): 68–69.

45. Alves, Anna. *In Search of "Meaning": Collective Memory and Identity in Pilipino Cultural Night at UCLA* (University of California, Los Angeles. 1999): 11.

46. Hernandez, Xavier James. *Behind the Curtain: The Culture of Pilipino Cultural Nights*. San Francisco State University (May 2010, 4).

47. Linda Tuhiwai Smith. *Decolonizing methodologies: research and indigenous peoples* (London: Zed Books, 1999): 3.

48. Gonzalves 2005, 72–73.

49. Gonzalves 2005, 72.

50. Gonzalves 2005, 72.

51. Alves 1999, 24.

52. Alves 1999, 56–57.

53. Reyes-Tolentino, Francisca & Ramos, Petrona. *Philippine Folk Dances and Games* (Silver, Burdett & Company: New York): 1935.

54. Catherine Bell, "Performance," in *Critical Terms for Religious Studies*, Mark C. Taylor, editor (Chicago: University of Chicago Press, 1998).

55. Another interesting question not discussed in this paper is: How will the identity of Filipino Americans be perceived by non-Filipinos in the audience?

56. Carl G. Jung's concept of "complex" is employed here. According to Jung, a complex is a core pattern base on perceptions, memories, emotions, and wishes in the personal unconscious organized around a common theme, such as status or power. For Jung, complexes may be conscious, partly conscious, or unconscious. Complexes can be positive or negative, resulting in good or bad consequences. There are many kinds of complex, but at the core of any complex is a universal pattern of experience, or archetype.

See Jung, Carl G. *The Structure and Dynamics of the Psyche*, Collected Works, Volume 8, (Princeton, N.J.: Princeton University Press, 1960, 1969); and Jung, Carl G. *The*

Essential Jung. Edited by Antony Storr (Princeton, NJ: Princeton University Press, 1983).

57. Fanon, 2008.
58. Gonzalvez 2005, 70.
59. Alves 1999, 21–22.
60. Hernandez 2010, 67.
61. Smith, 4.
62. Carlos P. Romulo, *Mother America: A Living Story of Democracy* (New York: Double Day, 1943).
63. Romulo 1943, 59.
64. Rodriguez 2010, 87.

ELEVEN

Guangong

The Chinese God of War and Literature in America: From Celestial Stranger to Common Culture (1850–2011 CE)

Jonathan H. X. Lee

GUANGONG

Since the 1840s, Chinese immigrants brought with them the veneration of Guangong (關公) to America. Today, the legend of Guangong is depicted in new multimedia video games and comics, which allows many American-born, second, and subsequent generation Chinese Americans to know about him. He is popularly venerated in America as a god of literature, wealth, business, and social harmony, although he is historically associated with war throughout China, Taiwan, Hong Kong, and in the Chinese diaspora.

Source of Guangong's Tale

Prior to Guangong's deification, he was an historical figure by the name of Yunchang who lived from 162-220 CE. The legendary account of his life and apotheosis is given in the *Sanguo zhi* (*History of the Three Kingdoms*), and in the novel *Sanguo zhi tongsu yanyi* (*The Romance of the Three Kingdoms*). The novels are about events and heroes at the end of the Han dynasty, when central control was weak and military and civil leaders jockeyed for power. Guangong was born in Shansi province and lived during a period of chaos, of shifting allegiances, and of military unrest when the country was temporarily separated into Three Kingdoms, each headed by a self-styled emperor.

Guangong's Tale

Guangong's story starts in 184 CE, when prefects and governors throughout China called for volunteers to fight against the Yellow Turbans. The Yellow Turbans, believed in the imminent beginning of the new world in 184 CE, and assembled a massive rebellion that engulfed the entire country, except for the southwestern province of Sichuan. They steadfastly believed that the "blue heaven" of the Han dynasty was dead, and that the "yellow heaven" of Great Peace was at hand, thus they shook the Han dynasty to its foundations. Symbolizing this color change, they wore yellow kerchiefs on their heads which resulted in them being called Yellow Turbans. Three men, Guan Yu, Liu Bei, and Zhang Fei, happened to meet and discovered that they were united in a common purpose; consequently they decided to become blood brothers and pledged their loyalties to one another. From the very first moment, Guan Yu commanded respect and was seen to personify integrity even though he was an outlaw. He had killed a local official and the official's uncle on behalf of his neighbor's daughter, who was distressed because she was about to be taken in as their concubine. Guan Yu had to flee after the murder, and his only way out was through the Tongguan mountain pass. Fearing that he would be recognized, he stopped by a mountain stream and washed his face; there he noticed that his face had turned red due to the mineral deposits in the water. From this tale comes Guangong's characteristic iconography of a red face.

When in 189 CE the reigning emperor died without leaving a direct heir, a succession of warlords ascended the throne and proclaimed themselves as emperors. The last of these was Cao Cao, the most efficient and ruthless of them all. In one year he rose from being a minister without a base or an army to being a general of both. Cao Cao succeeded in getting 300,000 Yellow Turbans to surrender to him, after which he organized a disciplined army and became a power to be reckoned with, establishing the Kingdom of Wei in central China.

Since Guan Yu's military prowess had been proven time and again with his sword "Black Dragon" and his horse "Red Hare," his skills were wanted by Cao Cao. Eventually, Cao Cao captured Guan Yu, who agreed to submit on three conditions, the most important of which was that he be able to rejoin Liu Bei if he heard news that his blood brother was still alive. The conditions were accepted, but Cao Cao attempted to compromise Guan Yu in a hundred little ways. He allocated to Guan Yu the same quarters as Liu Bei's wife and concubines who had also been captured, but Guan Yu deflected this trap by standing outside their door the entire night holding a candle. Cao Cao promoted Guan Yu to the rank of General, and presented him with many beautiful serving girls and presents of gold and silk. Cao Cao's efforts to compromise Guan Yu were unavailing. When news of Liu Bei reached Guan Yu, he left everything he had been given by Cao and, taking his sisters-in-laws and his own body of personal guards, forced his way through six mountain passes. Key to Guan Yu's character is that throughout this entire episode with Cao, he showed such a fine appreciation of his duties that even Cao could not feel he had been deserted. In fact, it was Cao who, upon receiving Guan Yu's head, ordered a wooden body to be fashioned to fit the head and full military honors to be accorded him in burial.

Guangong is worshipped not for his might, but because he is the embodiment of "right action," of integrity, bravery, righteousness, and loyalty, all key Confucian traits. Guangong is venerated for certain aspects of wealth, in addition to literature. Guangong is patron of "external harmony," of social stability and peace. He functions as a protector from all forms of evil. Guangong's story is one of the most illustrious examples of an historical man's deification. Guangong's cult was co-opted by the state; he received numerous promotions in rank and title starting in 1102, when the Song emperor Huizong adopted him and promoted him to Duke in the official religion.

In 1128, Emperor Gaozong promoted him to Prince, and in 1594, Ming emperor Shenzong finally granted him title of "*di*," "god" in his eight-character title of *Xietian huguo zhongyi dadi* ("The Loyal and Grand God Who Assists Heaven and Protects the State"). In 1813, Emperor Renzong promoted him to Military Emperor for personally preventing his assassination.

After the Taiping Rebellion had been successfully stamped out in 1864, the Qing dynasty added the title of "*fuzi*" (teacher), thus elevating Guangong to a rank equal to that of Confucius. Guangong's deification began forty years after his death, and reached its culmination nearly fourteen hundred years later. Today, Guangong is dually venerated as a patron of literature, as well as of wealth and business. In addition, his military image is used to promote social stability and cooperation.

Guangong and Chinese Immigration History

The discovery of gold at Sutter's Mill in 1848 was a major catalyst for the migration of adventurous Chinese to California. The Chinese name for America was Gold Mountain, "*Gam Saan*"[1] (金山). Between 1846 and 1848, droughts and floods destroyed much of the stable crops in China. As a result, many people suffered from starvation and poverty. In addition, between 1851 and 1864, millions were killed as the result of the Taiping Rebellion and other peasant revolts. Consequently, the Chinese were pushed to emigrate to *Gam Saan* in search of riches due to poor economic conditions, a collapsing political system, and famine brought on by overpopulation and natural disasters. Most of them came from Guangdong, China, and were able-bodied male laborers. Even before the gold rush, it is estimated that there were already fifty Chinese immigrants living in California.

The Chinese communities in early America established themselves and flourished in towns throughout northern California, Oregon, Nevada, and Idaho. The early Chinese settlers primarily followed the railroad through the Rockies and the Sierras, or became miners in pursuit of precious metals, mainly gold and silver. Other Chinese settlements sprang up in urban coastal areas, and still others arose later in agricultural areas.

Like migrants the world over, early Chinese settlers brought their religious beliefs and practices with them. The principal religions of China are Confucianism, Buddhism, Daoism, and local folk traditions, and most of the Chinese living in the emerging towns in America practiced a combination of all of them. Confucian traditions provided social harmony and ancestral veneration. Buddhism and Daoism provided funerary rituals and a pantheon of celestial helpers (the Buddha, *bodhisattvas*, and the gods and goddesses of the Chinese folk religion, of whom Guangong was one among them). For many years, in nineteenth- and early twentieth-century America, various exclusionary legislations barred Buddhist priests from coming to America to establish temples and serve the immigrant population. Even so, since the Chinese started to immigrate to America in large waves, they were able to establish their communities and build temples that housed their gods and goddesses, one prominent deity being Guangong.

This chapter focuses on the period from 1850 to 2007, the beginning and continual wave of massive Chinese immigration to the United States, both legal and illegal, and the inevitable transplantation of religious worldviews and institutions in their new environment. This chapter seeks to tell the story of Chinese immigration to the United States by looking at various case studies of historic and contemporary Chinese temples dedicated to Guangong. The life of these temples parallels the reception of Chinese peoples into American society. At the same time, these temples reflect the ebb and flow of U.S. immigration laws, which either banned or welcomed Chinese immigrants. Thus, as the life and times of Guangong temples in America are narrated, ask yourselves: What role did Chinese religion play in the transplantation and resettlement of Chinese immigrants on American soil? Why was Guangong a central figure in this religious landscape? Why does Guangong remain important and vital in contemporary immigrant Chinese American communities?

Temple Case Studies 1850-2011

1851 Kong Chow Temple (岡州古廟)

In 1851, 200 Chinese immigrants set up about thirty tents along Clay Street in San Francisco.[2] Chinese laundries and shoe shops could be found along Broadway Street, and the first Chinese temple, the Kong Chow Temple (岡州古廟) was established on Montgomery Street, which housed the red-faced, long bearded, and ancient Guandi (關帝). The temple was demolished and rebuilt in 1853, and rebuilt in 1909 after the fire and earthquake of 1906. The new facility was moved to 520 Pine Street with financial support from Mainland China. It was reported that the Qing dynasty (清朝, 1644-1911) contributed an estimated $93,000 to support the rebuilding project.[3] The new building on Pine Street was a three story brick building that housed a Chinese language school as well as a community meeting hall. In 1867, the Kong Chow Temple and association became a tax-free organization in San Francisco.[4] The Kong Chow Temple managed to keep its doors open to the public until sometime in the 1960s,[5] when it disappeared briefly until it re-opened in 1977 on the fourth floor of the new Kong Chow building, located on the corner of Stockton and Clay Streets in San Francisco's Chinatown.[6] A probable reason why the temple was closed to the public may be due to the virtual halt of any new Chinese immigrants entering the United States after the Chinese Exclusion Law of 1882 was passed. Bill Hing noted that,

> In the 1880s, cities and towns with a Chinatown were scattered throughout the West, though the Chinatown might consist of only a street or a few stores and its inhabitants might number only a few hundred. Eventually, these enclaves disappeared altogether. By 1940 only 28 cities with Chinatowns could be identified; by 1955, only 16.[7]

This directly affected the Kong Chow Temple because its constituents were mostly immigrant-Chinese. Therefore, the temple closed its doors to the public and reopened when Chinese immigration to the United States was re-established with the passage of the 1965 Immigration Law.[8] As Hing stated:

> Since 1965 immigrants have contributed to the rejuvenation of Chinatowns in San Francisco, New York, Los Angeles, and Chicago. One need only walk along Grant Avenue or Stockton Street in San Francisco at noon . . . to feel the vibrant intensity of these resilient enclaves. After World War II these Chinatowns began to shrink and even disappear as the older immigrants died. The first signs of their revival appeared in the early 1960's with the admission of refugees from mainland China. . . . Chinatowns endure because as the second and third generations leave they are replaced by immigrants and because they are sustained by the larger community.[9]

To this day, the Kong Chow Temple's multiple functions are still important aspects of the Chinatown community, as stated in an *Asian Week*
article:

> From its humble beginnings as a house of refuge for those who came to
> America, full of hope and eager to start new lives, [the] Kong Chow
> [Temple/Association] has reached out to many in the community and
> beyond, as a school, a house of worship and as a community gathering
> place, giving all who visit a renewed sense of hope and faith at a time
> when much of both are needed. [10]

In 1969, the *Report of the San Francisco Chinese Community Citizens' Survey
and Fact Finding Committee* documented a heated debate concerning the
Kong Chow Temple's future move to a new location. Some members of
the association wanted the temple to remain on Pine, while others
wanted it to be moved to the corner of Stockton and Clay, which offered
better *fengshui* (風水) possibilities. In addition, the Stockton and Clay location would make it more easily accessible to the general public. At that
time, the committee concluded the relocation to be uncertain, but maintained that the temple was an important symbol of Chinese culture. [11]

    While the temple was located on 520 Pine Street, the soon-to-be First
Lady, Mrs. Bess Truman, visited it in late October 1948 during Harry S.
Truman's presidential campaign for reelection, just a few weeks before
the national election. The press predicted that Thomas Dewey would be
the winner. Bess and Harry Truman made a quick visit to San Francisco's
Chinatown, where the late Albert K. Chow, a staunch supporter of Truman, hosted Bess. Albert suggested to Bess that she visit the Kong Chow
Temple to consult with Guangong, which she did. Bess shook the bamboo talisman sticks (*qiuqian*, 求簽), which predicted Truman's triumph
over Dewey. On the night of the national election, while the major newspapers across the nation claimed an overwhelming victory for Dewey,
Bess and Albert kept their faith. The next day, the fortune reading came
true, so after the election the First Lady requested a copy of the Chinese
fortune. This incident was an historical event that was recorded in several
Chinese language newspapers. In addition, it became a part of the temple's history that they are still very proud of, and share with visitors and
worshippers with a sign detailing the election event at the temple's entrance. [12]

    Besides Guangong, worshippers may venerate the Jade Emperor
(Yuhuang shangdi, 玉皇上帝), Tianhou (天后), Guanyin (觀音), or Beihei-
di (北黑帝), which is indicative of the inclusive nature of Chinese popular
religions.

    Technically, the Kong Chow Temple is the oldest temple in the United
States. But the temple was moved and closed to the public several times
as a consequence of changing immigration policies. Unlike other temples
dedicated to Guangong, the Kong Chow Temple remains an active tem-

ple visited by people of Chinese decent, the majority of them new immigrant Chinese Americans. The following two case studies illustrate and narrate stories of Guangong temples that are no longer active as temples per se, but function as cultural centers and museums.

1867 Temple of Kwan Tai (武帝廟)

The Temple of Kwan Tai is nestled on a small parcel of land facing the Pacific Ocean at 45160 Albion Street in Northern California's historic district of Mendocino is perched on a south-facing hillside above Albion Street. The great-grandfather of Lorraine Hee-Chorley and Loretta Hee McCoard, along with some other Chinese residents, constructed the temple in 1867, after they purchased the property. The temple was built with $12 worth of virgin redwood. On November 4, 1882, a formal opening ceremony was held at the temple that was recorded in an article in *The Beacon*, the local newspaper. Successive members of the Hee family have held and preserved the temple since 1871, when the deed to the property was signed over to Lee Sing John. In 1979, the temple was registered as California Historical Landmark No. 927.[13] In 1995, members of the Hee family deeded the temple property to the newly-established Temple of Kwan Tai, Inc., a nonprofit organization whose mission was to preserve and restore the historic landmark as a celebration of Mendocino's community and diversity. The organization's mission also is to serve and educate local school children and surrounding community members about the history and contributions of the Chinese in America. The organization was established as a nonprofit so public funds could be solicited to help support the restoration project. Before this, ownership of the temple's property had been shared among six members of the Hee family.[14]

The aged temple was in need of stabilization and renovation. The foundation of the entire building had to be resupported. Stabilization work involved raising the building, leveling it on steel support beams, digging new footings, and bringing the structure up to code. The exterior walls were temporarily removed to add additional support and to place insulation between the interior and exterior walls. The exterior of the east wall was replaced because the lumber was not salvageable. Additionally, the interior floor had to be replaced. The exterior walls were newly painted to their original red color with green trim.

A plaque at the bottom of the stairs designates the temple as a California Historic Landmark. On October 13, 2001, the Temple of Kwan Tai was officially rededicated through the efforts of the Hee family, the Temple Trustees, Mendocino youth groups involved with the North Coast Rural Challenge Network, the National Trust for Historic Preservation, and the California Coastal Resources Agency. On October 10, 2002, at the National Preservation Conference in Cleveland, Ohio, the Temple of Kwan Tai was awarded the prestigious National Preservation Honor Award. On receiving the National Preservation Award on October 10, 2002, Lorraine Hee said:

> We have kept a promise for four generations, and it is our ancestors who deserve the praise for their pioneer spirits. The temple has withstood years of turmoil, change and peace. The restoration, rehabilitation ensures that its story will be told for years to come. The Temple of Kwan Tai stands as a reminder to us all that this country was built on diversity and cooperation. [15]

1893 Hanford Taoist Temple

In 1877, the Central Pacific Railroad (known in this region as the Southern Pacific Railroad) constructed a new extension line through the San Joaquin Valley. The first station on the line was named after James M. Hanford, the railroad paymaster. The City of Hanford was formally incorporated as part of Tulare County in 1891 until 1893 when it became part of the newly established King County. When the railroad was complete, many of the Chinese laborers who had settled in the area proceeded to work for the growing farming industries. They started to buy land, construct homes, and build shops; soon there was a viable Chinese community in Hanford. The early Chinese immigrants made a significant contribution to Hanford's agricultural and ranching industries: they were sheepherders, and they worked in the seasonal fruit and vegetable industries of California's San Joaquin Valley. Throughout the 1920s and 1940s, the Chinese community in Hanford was the third largest in California, behind Los Angeles and San Francisco.

Between the 1870s and 1880s, Hanford's Chinatown was colloquially called "Young Chow Alley," after Young Chow, one of the first Chinese pioneers who lived near Hanford. Young Chow was a successful businessman and property owner. Following Young Chow's death, the alley was called "Sue Cheung Kee Alley," after another prominent Chinese businessman and property owner. After Sue Cheung Kee's death, people started to call it "China Alley." [16]

Today, China Alley is situated half a block north of East 7th Street, between Green and White Streets. Historically, it was a flourishing Chinese community and business center. There were boarding houses, restaurants, gambling dens, laundries, Chinese grocery markets, and several traditional Chinese herb stores. Hanford's Chinatown was known for its restaurants and herb stores. A Chinese herb doctor named Dr. L. T. Sue settled in Hanford and established the first herb store called the L. T. Sue Herb Co. In addition to L. T. Sue Herb Co., there were the Y. T. Sue Herb and Choon Soo Herb Co. stores. The L. T. Sue Herb Co. was the first and longest surviving Chinese herb company in Hanford. Dr. Sue was popular with both the Chinese and non-Chinese (e.g., Caucasian) residents.

Oftentimes, non-Chinese residents sought his medical services because Western medicine was not always reliable or available. The L. T. Sue Herb Co. still stands in China Alley, but it is vacant, awaiting future restoration.

China Alley is also home of the Sam Yup Association, an alliance of people from the same district of China. The Sam Yup Association, sometimes called the Canton Company, along with the Sze Yup Association, were the first two Chinese American associations to be established in 1851 in San Francisco. These were two of many ethnic organizations called *huiguan* and *tang*. *Huiguan* were based on primordial sentiments, including home-district associations and clan-surname associations. For those who did not join or were unable to join the *huiguan*, there were *tang*, triads or secret societies, which were based on fraternal principles. The Sam Yup Association is an example of a *huiguan*. The Sam Yup Chinese came from three districts immediately south and west of the city of Guangzhou, located in the Pearl River Delta region of China. They immigrated to both the Island of Hawai'i, as well as to the U.S. mainland. Large portions of the urbanized Sam Yup people became import-export merchants, grocers, butchers, tailors, and were engaged in various entrepreneurial ventures. Hence, it is no surprise that China Alley was a major business center.

Early on, the Joey Sing Tong, an association related to the Sam Yup Association, owned the property for the future site of the Taoist Temple. In 1893, there was a transfer of ownership to the Sam Yup Association, which donated more money for the construction of the Taoist Temple. The temple was to serve as a Chinese school, meeting hall, and association center. The temple was officially dedicated in 1897.

Today, greeting visitors at the top of the staircase upon entering the temple proper, are several wooden plaques engraved with Chinese characters listing the names of the donors who contributed to the construction of the temple association. The Wing family, longtime residents of Hanford, was one of the founding members of the Sam Yup Association, and remain active in it. Members of the Sam Yup Association traveling through Hanford in the early days could stop to rest, shower, eat, meet, and socialize with other Chinese people. Today, the Taoist Temple is listed on the National Register of Historic Places as part of China Alley.

Before the temple was built, the children who lived in China Alley went to school in a basement storeroom of what is now part of the Imperial Dynasty restaurant. In the early 1920s the school was moved to the back room on the second floor of the Taoist Temple. Chinese American children attended regular English school during the day, then after school, during evenings from 4 p.m. to 8 p.m. on weekdays, and all day Saturday, they were required to attend Chinese school. In 1922, a school was built a block away so the local children could attend classes there instead. Even though classes are no longer held at the temple, the wooden tables, stools, and Chinese school supplies are on display for visitors to imagine what it may have been like.

China Alley and the Taoist Temple in particular, are important symbols of Chinese American culture and history. The fact that China Alley continues to be an active business center, tourist attraction, and historic landmark speaks to its importance, not only for Chinese Americans, but for the larger community as well. In 1972, the Taoist Temple Preservation Society was formed to restore and renovate the long inactive temple, community center, and Chinese school. Members of the Sam Yup Association, who wanted to keep the temple's management and ownership within the Chinese community, established the preservation society. By becoming a nonprofit organization, the preservation society was able to seek public funds for restoration. Similar nonprofits were created in order to apply for public funding to restorate Mendocino's Kwan Tai Temple and the Auburn Joss House. The alternative option would have been to relinquish all rights by completely donating the building to the city or state, as was the case with Oroville's Chinese Temple, and the Weaverville Joss House. [17]

Today, the Hanford Taoist Temple is again functional, albeit not in a traditional sense. It is a living museum, a place where local K-12 school children, community college students, and community members may visit to learn about the history of the Chinese in America, in their own backyard. It is a place where visitors can learn about Chinese religion and culture, as well as Chinese contributions to the development of Hanford, California, and to the nation. In addition, the museum continues to allow Chinese American residents and visitors who wish to venerate at the temple, to do so. The Taoist Temple, along with China Alley, continues to mediate and negotiate the new terrain of common culture. Chinese Americans are deeply woven into the large multi-color, multi-textual, multi-cultural tapestry of American life. America is the Chinese railroad worker, the laborer who built the San Joaquin levees, the pioneer gold miners and laundrymen, and the workers who helped construct passes through the Sierra Nevada Mountains.

1982 Teo Chew Association (潮州會館)

The Teo Chew Association is one of several Indo-Chinese associations whose members are Chinese from Vietnam, Cambodia, and Laos, who immigrated to the United States as refugees following the Vietnam War. In 1975, more than 130,000 refugees entered the United States from these countries as communist governments took over. In 1977, the U.S. Congress passed a law allowing Southeast Asians to become permanent residents upon request. Among the Southeast Asian refugees were thousands of Indo-Chinese immigrants. [18]

In the 1990s, the Teo Chew Association appeared in urban Chinatowns across the country in such places as New York City, San Francisco, Seattle, Houston, Austin, Chicago, Honolulu, Boston, Atlanta, and Los Angeles. Most members of the American Teo Chow Association were Indo-Chinese immigrants who can trace their roots to Chaozhou.

The Los Angeles Teo Chew Association was founded in 1982 by Chinese Cambodian immigrants as a social network and community center for fostering solidarity among its members. It provides financial services, assists new immigrants in finding homes, and makes referrals for social and medical services. It is also a place for worshipping the red-faced Guangong, the Chinese god of war, literature, wealth, and social harmony. The temple hall is located in a one-story building that was once a bank. The front room is the main worship hall, while the back portion is a large community hall for banquets and meetings. The Teo Chew Association gives an annual college scholarship to children of members who maintain an overall GPA of 3.5 or better. The Teo Chew Association is now a global association with centers throughout Southeast Asia, Europe, and North and South America. In 2002, during its twentieth anniversary, California governor Gray Davis[19] extended a warm congratulations to the Los Angeles Teo Chew Association for "its commitment to the Asian American community" and for its "investment in the future of our State."[20]

The Teo Chew Association and Los Angeles temple is open every day and welcomes visitors and participants of various backgrounds. Their printed material is usually in Chinese, but sometimes is offered in Vietnamese and English as well. Similar to traditional Chinese temples, the Teo Chew Association does not have a formal membership system because anyone who seeks to worship Guangong is welcome to do so. However, the social, educational, and financial services are provided only to those who are considered official members. On any given day, one may find a dozen or so old-timers whiling their time away in the company of their friends, reading a Chinese newspaper, or sipping a cup of coffee.[21]

CONCLUSION

By selecting the Kong Chow Temple, Mendocino's Temple of Kwan Tai, Hanford's Taoist Temple, and the recently established Teo Chow Association, this chapter has presented a narrative of the life of Guangong's temples in America, one that reflects shifts in policies regarding Chinese immigration. However, Guangong was not only found in temples solely dedicated to him, but also in many other temples, temples that are best describes as "popular Chinese temples," which housed, honored, and venerated Guangong. For example, the Auburn Joss House, established in the 1880s, or the Bok Kai Temple (北溪廟), established sometime in the

Figure 11.1.   Kong Chow Temple, San Francisco, California. Courtesy of Sandra Sengdara Siharath.

early 1850s, or more recently, the Ma-tsu Temple U.S.A. (美國媽祖廟), established by Taiwanese American immigrants in San Francisco's Chinatown in the mid-1980s,[22] all venerate Guangong.

The histories of these Guangong temples reflect the larger life of Chinese religion and religious communities in America, waxing and waning with shifting mainstream attitudes, from exclusion to assimilation, and then to cultural pluralism. It has also correlated with immigration poli-

Figure 11.2.   Mendocino's Temple of Kwan Tai, Mendocino, California. Courtesy of Jonathan H. X. Lee.

cies and the increasing connections forged by transnational networks of religious communities. In the past, the pressure to assimilate affected Chinese American religious life and experience, but the current situation is dramatically different, as witnessed by Teo Chow.[23]

Figure 11.3.   Hanford's Taoist Temple Museum, Hanford, California. Courtesy of Jonathan H. X. Lee.

The Kong Chow Temple, the Kwan Tai Temple, and the Hanford Taoist Temple all exemplify a period of Chinese American religious life and community that reflected exclusion and assimilation. Their historical landmark status demarcates them as pieces of Americana. Although the

Figure 11.4. Teo Chow Association—Los Angeles, California. Courtesy of Jonathan H. X. Lee.

Chinese American communities of Mendocino and Hanford have greatly diminished, the little historic temples have gained increased cultural significance. The Kwan Tai Temple and the Hanford Taoist Temple resemble Confucian temples in cultural China, "Temples of Culture' (*wen miao* 文廟), which preserves Chinese American religious culture and history for everyone within its communities.

Finally, recall the questions invoked in the introduction. What role did Chinese religion play, and continues to play, in the transplantation and resettlement of Chinese immigrants on American soil? Why was Guangong a central figure in this religious landscape? Why does Guangong remain important and vital in contemporary immigrant Chinese American communities? The answers to these questions are multidimensional because they are based on inherent, albeit relative religious inclinations and convictions. Chinese American societies, like their members, form a heterogeneous mosaic, differentiated by linguistic and cultural diversities. Hence, the response to these questions must be considered with reference to individual subjectivities and environmental factors, as well as socio-historical conditions. To some, it was not Guangong who was important to their veneration, but rather Tianhou/Mazu (天后/媽祖), or a host of other deities found in the vast imperial Chinese pantheon.

Life in early America was not simple. Chinese immigrants faced racial discrimination in all aspects of life, which required that they form and establish their own communities and social institutions. Prejudice and discrimination were not just personal and individual, but were institutional, systematic, and legal. Thus, religion offered the early Chinese immigrants release, if not solace. If justice was not available in this world, maybe a meta-justice was possible with the assistance of Guangong. If social harmony was not possible due to constant struggles with non-Chinese peoples and communities, then maybe Guangong was able to provide that harmony, at least within their own community (Chinatown 唐人街) or within themselves. Fundamentally, Guangong offered protection—protection from evil and harm, which the American legal system denied them. Guangong remains, for many Chinese, especially new immigrant Chinese Americans, a provider of harmony and safety, while for many second, third, and even fourth generation Chinese Americans, he is an overall symbol of Chinese culture.[24]

NOTES

1. 廣東說法
2. It is also located in the old Los Angeles Chinatown, near Downtown Los Angeles.
3. Erica Y. Z. Pan, *The Impact of the 1906 Earthquake on San Francisco's Chinatown.* San Francisco: Peter Lang, 1995.

4. "America's Oldest Chinese Organization and Temple." In *Asian Week*, September 2, 1982.

5. Diana Eck, *On Common Ground: World Religions in America*, CD-Rom, New York: Columbia University Press, 1977. The date for the closure of the Kong Chow Temple is an educated guess based on Eck's conclusion that the temple remained open until the 1960s. Mariann Wells, "Chinese Temples in California" Thesis (University of California, Berkeley, 1962) mentioned that it was closed to the public (pp. 19-24).

6. Although this is the latest location for the temple, the interior of the temple is decorated with original woodcarvings and temple ornaments that were salvaged after each move and after the 1906 earthquake and fire.

7. Bill Ong Hing, *Making and Remaking Asian America Through Immigration Policy 1850-1990*, (Stanford: Stanford University Press, 1993), p. 50.

8. The 1965 Immigration Act abolished the 1924 discriminatory national origins provision, which was retained in the Immigration and Nationality Act of 1952, favoring immigrants of Western European origins. The subsequent series of amendments of the 1952 Act in 1990, collectively referred to as the Immigration Act of 1990, provides for an overall increase in worldwide immigration. The 1990 Act increases the allocation for both family related and employment related immigration, and further creates a separate basis by which "diversity immigrants" (nationals of countries previously underrepresented since 1965 due to visa issuance), can enter the United States. Amendments of the 1952 Act that was directed towards the increase of Chinese immigrants entering the United States are as follows: the 1981 amendment creates a separate quota of 20,000 for Taiwan, which Taiwan previously shared with China and Hong Kong. In 1987, the annual quota for Hong Kong was increased from 600 to 5000, then to 10,000 from 1990 to 1993, and subsequently to 20,000. Furthermore, thousands of students were admitted from Taiwan, Hong Kong, the People's Republic of China, and Southeast Asia. In addition, complex ethnic Chinese immigrants entered the United States as refugees from Vietnam, Laos, and Cambodia have been admitted to the U.S. since 1975. See Hing, pp. 81-84.

9. Hing, pp. 84-85.

10. "America's Oldest Organization and Temple," pp. 12-13.

11. *Report of the San Francisco Chinese Community Citizens' Survey and Fact Finding Committee*, pp. 199-200.

12. "America's Oldest Organization and Temple," pp. 12-13. The sign literately reads, "Mrs. Harry S. Truman came to this temple in [October], 1948 for a prediction on the outcome of the election. This fortune came. Therefore, it was put in several Chinese newspapers. Mrs. Truman requested for a copy of this fortune after her departure for Washington D.C."

13. Jonathan H. X. Lee, *The Temple of Kwan Tai: California Historic Landmark No. 927, Celebrating Community and Diversity*. Mendocino, CA: Published by the Temple of Kwan Tai Inc., 2004, pp. 17-21.

14. Jonathan H. X. Lee, "Contemporary Chinese American Religious Life," in *Chinese Religions in Contemporary Societies*, edited by James Miller. Santa Barbara: ABC-CLIO Press, 2006, pp., 240-243.

15. Lee, *The Temple of Kwan Tai*, p. 38.

16. Jonathan H. X. Lee, *Hanford's Taoist Temple and Museum (#12 China Alley): Preserving a Chinese American Treasure*, with a forward by Vivian-Lee Nyitray. Hanford: Published by the Hanford Taoist Temple Preservation Society, pp. 16-20.

17. Douglas and Gina McDonald, *The History of the Weaverville Joss House and the Chinese of Trinity County, California*. Medford: McDonald Publishing, 1986.

18. Lee, "Contemporary Chinese American Religious Life," pp. 254-255.

19. Joseph Graham Davis Jr. (born December 26, 1942), better known as Gray Davis, is an American politician who served as the Chief of Staff to Governor Jerry Brown (1974-1981), a California State Assemblyman (1983-1987), the California State Controller (1987-1995), the Lieutenant Governor of California (1995-1999), and the 37th governor of California from 1999 to 2003. He was reelected to a second term in 2002,

but on October 7, 2003, he became the second governor to be recalled in American history. Davis, a Democrat, was succeeded by Republican Arnold A. Schwarzenegger on November 17, 2003, after a recall election.

20. 《美國南加州潮州會館成立廿周年紀念特輯》, 2002, p. 33.

21. My father is an example of a retired senior who goes there to socialize with his friends.

22. Jonathan H.X. Lee, 「媽祖與台灣新移民的美國化, 《台灣史料研究》, 第25期, 頁114-127.

23. Lee, "Contemporary Chinese American Religious Life," p. 255.

24. I wish to also bring up that Guangong might have been popular to many Chinese Americans in the past, as he is as today, due to his relationship with success in business. Many early Chinese Americans owned and operated small service businesses (for example, restaurants, laundries, merchant stores), as they still do today.

TWELVE

Folklore as a Sacred Heritage

Vietnamese Indigenous Religions in California

Janet Hoskins

INTRODUCTION

On July 20, 2007, California Caodaists consecrated a new cathedral in Garden Grove, California, a 4,000 foot replica of the "Vatican" of Caodaism in Tay Ninh province, Vietnam, but one-third its size. More than 2,000 people attended the ceremony to "lift up the image of the Left Eye of God" and install it on top of a three-tiered pantheon depicting Buddha, Confucius, and Lao Tzu presiding over five levels of spiritual attainment, including the female Boddhisatva Guanyin at the second level, and Jesus Christ on the third level.

This cathedral, planned for over ten years, now serves as a landmark for the colorful, eclectic, and ornate architecture of Vietnam's largest indigenous religion: its gothic towers evoke the austerity of medieval Catholicism, but the bright yellows, reds, and turquoise reflect the shiny palette of Asian religious icons. Pastel dragons coil around pillars covered with lotus flowers, demonic figures associated with good and evil guard the entranceway, and a huge mural depicting the Chinese nationalist Sun Yat-Sen, the Vietnamese poet and prophet Trang Trinh, and the French writer Victor Hugo greet visitors as they enter a space that resonates with the sounds of drums, gongs, and finger cymbals, and that is perfumed by flowers and incense.

When the building permit was finally issued, *Nguoi Viet* (The Vietnamese language newspaper with the largest circulation in the United

States) reported that "when this construction is finished, it will bring to California for the first time a distinctive architecture and pattern of thought found all over southern Vietnam."[1] The successful construction of this cathedral, which adhered to a "divine blueprint" communicated to religious leaders from 1926-1934 in the French colonial city of Saigon, marks a new stage in the public recognition of the indigenous religions of Vietnam. This chapter explores how indigenous religions have brought aspects of Vietnamese culture and folklore to the United States; how they are part of an historical pattern; which practices are shared across religious lines for all Vietnamese; and what the future prospects are for these communities.

WHAT ARE VIETNAM'S INDIGENOUS RELIGIONS?

Most Americans perceive Vietnam as a primarily Buddhist country (current government statistics estimate that there are ten million Buddhists out of seventy-eight million people) with a sizeable Catholic minority (six million). But indigenous religions, a term used to refer to three specific groups, have long been significant, especially in the south. Caodaism, founded in Saigon in 1926, officially has 3.2 million followers and 1,300 temples, Hoa Hao Buddhism, founded in southwestern Vietnam in 1939, has 1.5 million followers,[2] but leaders of these faiths estimate their real numbers at closer to six million and three million people, respectively. Dao Mau (Mother Goddess religion) is considered a "distinct subculture with cultural nuances varying locally," so there is no official documentation of its followers,[3] but recent ethnographic reports indicate it is expanding in both Hanoi and Ho Chi Minh City and it builds on traditional veneration of female divinities and heroes going back many centuries.[4]

Statistics about the religious adherence of Vietnamese Americans indicate that about 40 percent identify themselves as Buddhist or Confucian, and 30 percent as Christian or Catholic.[5] Little is said about the others, who are perhaps presumed to be secular. Although a number of scholars mention Caodaism and Hoa Hao in passing,[6] the only academically detailed and published accounts of American Caodaists are my own.[7] Hoa Hao Buddhists have been studied in Vietnam by Philip Taylor and Pascal Bourdeaux, who also make reference to American congregations and their Internet connections to the homeland.[8] Karin Fjelstad and Nguyen Thi Hien have studied spirit mediums affiliated with the Mother Goddess Religion (Dao Mau), and have coedited a volume and published a co-written ethnography analyzing the transnational connections between spirit medium communities in Vietnam and California.[9] There is obviously much room for more research, a need for an accurate counting of temples, adherents and congregations, and for an ethnographic exploration of the transnational dynamics of indigenous Vietnamese religions migrating to the United States.

Caodaism is a syncretistic religion that seeks to bring the gods of Europe and the gods of Asia together in a conversation that can serve to heal the wounds of colonialism and establish a basis for mutual respect and dialogue. Officially called *Dai Dao Tam Ky Pho Do*, "The Great Way of the Third Age of Redemption," Caodaism combines millenarian teachings with an Asian fusion of Buddhism, Confucianism and Taoism, and Roman Catholicism, an Asia-centric New Age movement that developed in the context of anti-colonial resistance. Established in 1926, its earliest members belonged to the urban educated elite of Saigon. In just a few years, Caodaism grew dramatically to become the largest mass movement in the French colony of Cochinchina, with 20-25 percent of the people of South Vietnam converting to this new faith in the period from 1930-1975.[10] Best known in the United States through Graham Greene's description in his popular 1954 novel *The Quiet American*,[11] Caodaism in Vietnam was the topic of two dissertations in the 1970s,[12] but has not been studied for over thirty years, and there have been no studies of its American congregations.

Hoa Hao is a reformist, millenarian form of Buddhism that was established in 1937; it is now the fourth largest religion in Vietnam after Buddhism, Catholicism, and Caodaism. It has established several temples in California and, like Caodaism, has also developed a series of websites and publishes histories and commentaries in Vietnamese within the United States.

Founded by a young prophet who preached simplicity and egalitarianism, this new religion is, like Islam, opposed to the use of religious icons, and renounces the use of ancestral tablets and images of the Buddha on its altars.[13] It developed in western Vietnam, perhaps influenced by minority communities of Cham Muslims and Khmer Theravada Buddhists. The Mother Goddess Religion of Dao Mau has recently had a resurgence in Vietnam, especially in Hanoi, where a number of recent anthropological studies have been done,[14] but it is generally described as a traditional custom or indigenous practice and so it is difficult to estimate the exact number of followers at the present.

The indigenous religions of Vietnam incorporate many occult aspects unfamiliar to mainstream Americans (spirit mediums, spirit possession, divination, talismanic blessings, etc.). Some ceremonies involve elaborate costumes, pageantry, and music for the Caodai liturgical mass or Mother Goddess performances, while others, such as Hoa Hao chanting of prayers, are conducted without instrumental accompaniments or devotional decorations, aside from the ubiquitous fruit, flowers, and incense. Scriptures are received by spirit messages spoken, sung, or traced by the beak of a phoenix-headed basket.

THE ERASURE OF INDIGENOUS RELIGION IN
U.S. IMMIGRATION STATISTICS

Indigenous religions have been left out of almost all previous studies of Vietnamese immigrants, in part, because the researchers who first surveyed religious preferences of refugees at entry points like Camp Pendleton only provided immigrants with six options for religious affiliation: Christian Protestant, Christian Catholic, Buddhist, Confucian, Hindu, or Muslim, which did not acknowledge the existence of indigenous religious practices, although they were practiced by 15-25 percent of the population of South Vietnam in 1975. It seems likely that followers of these indigenous religions were counted as either Buddhists or Confucians when they were processed for U.S. entry. It is also possible that some of their members were miscounted as Catholics, said to have made up "about half" of the first wave of refugees in several studies, although Catholics represent about 30 percent of the present Vietnamese American community.[15] A substantial dimension of Vietnam's religious diversity has not entered into the statistical data or efforts to quantify them.

Largely missing from accounts of early refugee processing were the pressures placed on non-Christian refugee families to convert to and follow the faith of those Christian churches who sponsored them in the first few years that they lived in the United States. Most of the first wave of refugees were sponsored by faith-based organizations, either the Catholic Relief Fund (which resettled nearly 50 percent of all refugees, and explicitly favored those who identified themselves as Catholic), or a variety of Protestant organizations (notably the Lutheran Immigration and Refugee Service, and the Church World Service).

Family histories revealed numerous cases in which refugees temporarily housed in camps chose to convert, or at least self-identify as Christian in order to secure faster sponsorship and immigration to the United States.These conversions usually lasted as long as the family was being sponsored. After they had immigrated, they reverted back to their indigenous religions or to Buddhism. The novel-memoir *Catfish and Mandala* by Andrew Pham[16] contains an account of his own family's conversion in Louisiana, followed by reversion when the family united with family in San Jose, California.

Committed Caodaists who did not convert to Christianity were told in several instances that "all the other refugee families are now Seventh Day Adventists," or Baptists, etc. There was a clear perception that baptism of the whole family was expected as a gesture of gratitude, and some Caodaists in fact rationalized these baptism ceremonies with the argument that since Jesus was a part of the Caodai pantheon, "giving themselves to Jesus" did not contradict a commitment to Caodai doctrine.

The faith-based organizations that sponsored many Vietnamese refugees have not publicly acknowledged that they pressured refugees to convert, or that they favored Christian refugee families for resettlement and sponsorship, but this was often perceived to be the case by refugee families. The resurgence of indigenous religious in new ethnic enclaves is therefore an especially significant development, as it contradicts early predictions in the immigration literature that conversion to Christianity was simply an aspect of assimilation, and that it was, therefore, also irreversible. This resurgence could also be related to the phenomenon of Vietnamese ethnic resilience as refugees assumed many of the characteristics of a diaspora.

DIASPORA VS. ETHNIC GROUP

Immigration scholars have recognized for some time that for post–1965 Asian immigrants and refugees, religious congregations are the most important community building institutions: they offer resettlement assistance, counseling services, a sense of community, and language courses in English for new immigrants and in Asian languages for the second generation, as well as a cultural context that is familiar, reassuring, and sustaining in the light of the major disruptions created by forced dislocations and differences in language and customs. But recent ethnographic studies have argued that traditional Southeast Asian religions may have failed to translate well in California, as is suggested in the title *Buddha is Hiding* of Ong's 2003 work[17] about Cambodian refugees. Seemingly, more international and inter-ethnic versions of immigrant Asian religions have had somewhat more success, especially those that have developed dynamic, sophisticated websites, used both for online proselytizing and for archiving sacred texts, commentaries, and religious history.

Some immigration theorists have argued that moving to a new country is itself a "theologizing" experience: it forces a radical shift in world view that causes a questioning of earlier religious beliefs while intensifying the need to find solace and continuity in a new and very different context.[18] The theological crisis might be particularly acute for refugees who fled persecution in their home countries versus moving in the hopes of finding better economic opportunities. Forced to leave a land that they remain deeply attached to, many refugees experienced not only the trauma of dislocation, but also separation from family members (often imprisoned in re-education camps) and life-threatening journeys by boat in order to escape. Some refugee populations, especially those with the lowest levels of literacy (Hmong, Cambodians, and Laotians) are identified as "vulnerable" by evangelists, and particularly targeted for conversion by Mormons and Christian fundamentalists. The Vietnamese have been perceived by most scholars as being more resistant, since Vietnamese of all faiths have used churches and temples as sites for maintaining their cultural heritage, language skills, and ties to their homeland. The level of education at the time of emigration is important, since immigrant groups who are able to educate the new generation through books, websites, and multimedia are better able to establish transnational linkages than those who arrive without those skills.

The concept of ethnic resilience when used in sociological studies of Vietnamese Americans usually refers to parameters of socio-economic "success." For example, within ten years of their arrival, most first wave Vietnamese refugees were earning above the national median income.[19] Clustering in ethnic enclaves also made it possible to maintain relatively high levels of bilingualism and even literacy in Vietnamese,[20] which has enabled long distance nationalism[21] and identify to persist—leading to one of the most developed diasporic communities in the United States.

A diaspora, in scholarly terms, is distinct from an ethnic group, because it is grounded in a particular understanding of its social mission as tied to a place of origin. The narrow definition provided by Amesfoot in a discussion of Moluccan refugees in the Netherlands is useful to recall: "A diaspora is a settled community that considers itself to be 'from elsewhere' and whose concern and most important goal is the realization of a political ideal in what is seen as the homeland."[22] The term originated in discussions of Zionism and, as Aihwa Ong has observed, it applies to some other cases in the United States, perhaps especially Cuban refugees,[23] but should not be applied indiscriminately to all overseas communities: "The popular view of diaspora as ethnicity has elided the fact that diaspora is really a political formation seeking its own nation."[24]

The resurgence of Vietnamese indigenous religions has taken place in the context of ethnic enclaves and diasporic politics, but the leaders of these religions stress that their teachings emphasize peace, nonviolence (both Caodaists and Hoa Hao practice graduated forms of vegetarianism), and reconciliation. Perhaps the greatest challenge to these congregations today is how they will reconcile a global faith with the continuing political divisions between their followers in Vietnam and those in overseas communities. I have argued that some Caodai leaders favor a "global religion of unity," modeled on Tibetan Buddhism, which welcomes non-Vietnamese converts and seeks to translate religious scriptures into English, while others emphasize the diasporic ideal of "long distance nationalism," in which followers see themselves as primarily Vietnamese, and elevate their cultural tradition to the level of a religious ideal.[25] Followers of Dao Mau are less explicitly politicized, and do not seek to proselytize to non-Vietnamese, since they see their faith as based primarily on a ritual duty to consult the ancestors of their community. The Hoa Hao Buddhist share aspects of "long distance nationalism," focused especially on their homeland in the western Mekong Delta, but they remain the indigenous religion that is most stringently suppressed and constrained by the communist government.

Caodaists expressed a desire to follow the pathway of Tibetan Buddhists, whose global proselytizing has been linked to a political struggle for greater freedom within their homeland, now in China. This activism highlights another dimension of ethnic resilience in a pluralistic society: connections forged among immigrant communities in California build a grassroots cosmopolitanism that is premised on everyday crossings of minority-minority cultural borders, and specific sets of local-global relationships. (A similar idea has been developed in the notion of the "trans-colony" in post–colonial studies, and arguably all the Southeast Asian homelands whose people immigrated to the United States did so as a result of US military intervention and a somewhat neo-colonial relationship.) Buddhist and Caodaist groups from Vietnam, for instance, are exposed to Theravada Buddhism from Laos, Cambodia, and Thailand, as well as Taiwan-style Mahayana Buddhism at places like Hsi Lai Temple in Hacienda Heights, Los Angeles County (the largest Buddhist temple outside Asia).

An ethnography of religious innovations in California needs to consider individuals who see themselves as exiles, temporary residents of a diasporic community, and others who accept being labeled an American ethnic group. Many religious leaders consider their teachings universal, and that the true community of belief is a nonterritorial one, but they have widely varying positions on whether it makes sense to proselytize to non-Vietnamese. The ethnic and cultural diversity of the increasingly brown population of southern California, with its historically high rates of what has been called miscegenation (i.e., interracial marriage and childbearing) and religiously mixed marriages, has the potential to create a new cross-ethnic and cross-racial flexibility of religious identifications.

The ordination in May 2005 of Linda Blackeny-Hofstetter, an African American woman, as the first non-Vietnamese priest of Caodaism, highlights this potential. After three decades of practicing Taoist meditation and vegetarianism, Blackeny-Hofstetter discovered Caodaism while working in Vietnam as a nurse in an AIDs treatment program, and decided that it was the faith she was seeking since it merged Christian and Asian philosophies in an appealing third world synthesis. She now heads a small chapel in Harlem, New York, which offers solace to all those who have suffered deeply, fusing a new congregation across historically significant racial and ethnic boundaries.

HISTORICAL PATTERNS AND INNOVATION: NEW DEVELOPMENTS IN CALIFORNIA

The idea that the temple defines a community is a familiar one, like a Vietnamese or Taiwanese village, a familiar place where older people can find solace and speak in their own language. In adapting to the American lifestyle, most Caodaists, who were used to a Vietnamese calendar of attending services on the first and 15th of each lunar month, found themselves attending services weekly on Sundays to conform to the American work week. Since the temple became a networking center, its range of social activities expanded to fit a niche defined by other faith-based organizations in California. Church-going has come to be seen as a component of responsible citizenship in many areas, and Caodaists have come to identify their scriptures as Bibles rather than sutras (a term often used to refer to religious teachings in French translations from the colonial period).

Caodaism in Vietnam has a hierarchical organization similar to that of Catholicism. It has a Pope, Cardinals, Archbishops, and a dozen different denominations, but in the United States, early Caodaist congregations were more eclectic and egalitarian than their Vietnamese counterparts. In the 1920s, Caodaists consecrated women as Cardinals, proclaiming equality of the sexes before God, but the most prominent leaders were male. Two women founded the first California temple in San Jose, California, wearing brightly colored ceremonial robes that are usually reserved for men in their homeland. Bold religious innovations continued for several decades, when several volumes of spirit messages directed them to develop a new set of doctrines for the New World. After 1995, when it became possible to travel to Vietnam again, many people returned to go on religious pilgrimages to sacred sites. After a quarter century of separation, there were a number of tensions between American-educated religious followers and those in the homeland. Some American congregations returned to the Vietnamese model, while others moved closer to the individualistic mysticism of Western practitioners of Zen or Tibetan Buddhism. The extent of liturgical innovation in the United States is hard to measure exactly, but it has included the development of a somewhat independent group of spirit mediums and a more egalitarian organizational structure. A similar process can be observed for Dao Mau goddess veneration, since women have emerged as stronger leaders in the diaspora than they have in contemporary Vietnam.

Because Vietnam was closed off by the U.S. trade embargo and by political tensions for almost two decades, the flow of money, material goods, and publications from the homeland to the United States was a period of isolation and because of that, a time of religious innovation when compared to other Asian immigrant religions. When the embargo was dropped, and reforms opened up new pathways for travel, investment, and religious expression, two former enemies became linked in a transnational network that connected religious units at many levels, and was characterized by important flows of diasporic money to rebuild temples in the homeland.

POPULAR RELIGIOUS PRACTICES AND THEIR EFFICACY

Caodaism is a highly institutionalized, hierarchical organization that emphasizes discipline, and respect for senior dignitaries as well as following the many written scriptures that have been compiled, edited, and published for the benefit of its followers.

Hoa Hao Buddhism is more egalitarian and is a lay Buddhist movement without its own clergy, no large impressive pagodas, but a strong emphasis on social service, charity work, and meeting for chanting and praying. It has its own scriptures from the Prophet Huynh Phu So, and these are distributed at each one of its temples, but there have not been recent teachings since his disappearance in 1946.

In the Dao Mau tradition, participants explained their commitment to the practice on the grounds that it worked, that it was efficacious, and that it brought blessings that would help families in times of hardship. The ideals of inner virtue and loyalty were often stressed, although there is also the notion that being part of this practice can result in personal benefits, such as improved health, wealth, and social prestige. Mainly, however, women followers have stressed that Dao Mau spirits came from Vietnamese history, and thus represent the indigenous foundations of Vietnamese culture as a mixture of warlike mandarins, spoiled princes and elegant princesses, ethnic minorities, and finally, impetuous and comical caricatures of the youthful princes.

The focus on ceremonies seems to draw on the diverse cultural sources of Vietnamese identity, and uses these as resources for success in the New World. As an embodied practice, it is idiosyncratic and individualized, wherein each dance is a way of interpreting key aspects of a spirit and communicating those to the audience.

At its foundation, Caodaism is a religion of words, even if the words are accompanied by large-scale rituals in elaborate temples with colorful costumes and music. Spirit mediums in Caodaism primarily dictate verses, either by speaking them in the presence of a scribe, or by tracing them out in cursive letters with the phoenix basket. The importance of written doctrine is much more salient in Caodai publications. Words to the *chau van* songs, which are fairly standardized in Vietnam, function as a kind of scripture since they define the sacred attributes of each spirit and are a required part of each performance.

Spirit seances in Caodaism define a place for Vietnamese people to stand in relation to a cosmopolitan conversation about the relations between the world religions and the specific historical destiny of the Vietnamese today. In contrast, the spirit mediums in Dao Mau seem to be addressing issues in their private lives more often, although they do so by incarnating spirits from the Vietnamese past. Caodai doctrine provides a grand narrative about the process of decolonization and the reasons why Saigon had to fall in 1975 (to permit the globalization of the religion), while the message of Dao Mau spirit mediums seemed to lie not at a discursive level, but as a form of embodiment, enacting certain body postures and gestures that emphasize ties to a cultural repertoire of concepts and possibilities that can be realized in a new setting.

Caodaists explicitly state that their religion is yang (*dương*), although it draws its strength from the world of the spirits who are yin (*âm*). The left eye of God is the sign of a positive, modernist, progressive, and dynamic religion that, in their view, will not be caught in the passive, reclusive, ascetic mode of earlier esoteric traditions. Of course, many people have claimed during the period from 1975 to 1995, it was necessary to "turn back to esoterism" in Vietnam because it was not possible to have the same visible role on the world's stage while the government maintained an anti-religious stance. Although there is a productive and essential tension between the two poles in all teachings, Caodaism is often presented as energizing a dynamic synthesis of what had been an overly quiet, contemplative religious tradition.

Some researchers have argued that Dao Mau identifies itself as a primarily yin practice—in healing yin ailments (*ben hâm*), in honoring female deities, and in engaging with a practice that celebrates female qualities before the power of male spirits are highlighted.[26] The emphasis on compassion and what are often called Buddhist values stresses this as a path of "female spirituality" that seems, however, to also be open to those men who want to call up the female aspects within their own personalities. The Dao Mau ceremonies also emphasize the fact that many healing arts and knowledge about plants and medicines come from ethnic minorities, the "people who live in the mountains and forests."

Caodaists do not really pay much attention to ethnic minorities. Although they are in no way excluded from its theology, the only place they are given is at the lowest level of spiritual attainment, the worship of localized spirits and ancestors (*thần*), and there is little that explicitly addresses ethnic diversity. But there is an ethnic dimension to the arguments that Caodaists present that they encompass all world religions, since Nam Bo/Cochinchina is an area where Muslim/Hindu Cham and Theravada Buddhist Khmer were once strong. Lots of religious imagery is explicitly either Hindu (Brahma, Shiva, and Vishnu sit on top of the roof of the Caodai temple) or Theravada Buddhist (the head spirit medium sits on a throne in front of a seven headed Naga serpent, copied from Khmer images of the giant cobra that sheltered Buddha when he meditated during a storm). The snake is both a symbol of natural powers and the fertility of the land, and also a symbol of earlier peoples who lived in Southern Vietnam and who, in the past two centuries, been largely displaced by the Vietnamese.

Caodaists argue that their faith is the culmination of all the religious diversity that exists in Vietnam, and they see it as synthesizing the essence of each tradition. While they include the worship of ancestors, local spirits, and national heroes like Tran Hung Dao, they do not assume the same importance as literary figures such as the Chinese poet Ly Thai Bach, or the red-faced general Quan Cong from the *Romance of the Three Kingdoms*. There is a liveliness in Dao Mau performances and an emotional intensity that appears to be personally meaningful to their participants. Caodai mystics say that the energy they receive from spirit communications is very intense, and it is sought after as much as the message or teaching itself, but it is a private experience.

The political problems that these three indigenous religions face in the present period of normalization in Vietnam are quite distinct and have an impact on the relationships between diasporic congregations and their homeland. Spirit possession rituals can be seen as efforts to embody and magically access the powers of ethnic predecessors in rites that "both transgress and reconstitute ethnic, gender and ritual boundaries." [27] As contemporary ancestors, they incarnate a hybrid mix of Confucian-Marxist-Daoist approaches that attempt to ritually embody their imagined authentic otherness in festivals that enlist ethnic minorities in the ritual regeneration of the national community, both in Vietnam and overseas. Thus, state policy has changed in a dialogue with popular religious conceptions of minorities, wherein they are now part of a recent shift to find new, spiritualized foundations for national legitimacy.

Because the majority of Vietnamese Americans came to the United States as refugees, attitudes toward their homeland have long been characterized by a certain ambivalence: intense feelings of cultural nationalism and pride in their heritage, combined with distrust of the present Communist government, which, since 1995, has been increasingly open to foreign investment, but not to foreign ideas. One result of this is the use of religious icons and religious congregations to develop an alternative nationalism, etched out in a diasporic space, in which the sacredness of faiths born in Vietnam is presented as transcending the geography of the current state. This phenomenon is realized differently within the different groups that we have studied: for Caodaists, diaspora has been a part of religious doctrine since the birth of their faith during the colonial period in the 1920s, when nationalist leaders were already talking about the loss of the country and the need to reclaim its essence from French overseers; for Dao Mau followers, an entire century of divisive Cold War politics and decolonization was erased in order to evoke the spiritual return to the heroes and heroines of the imperial period; and for Hoa Hao Buddhists, the lineage of teachers from Prophet Huynh Phu So are increasingly placed in the context of global Buddhism, trying to reclaim their place within that wider tradition as a specifically Vietnamese form of Buddhist worship.

PROSPECTS FOR THE FUTURE: HERITAGE POLITICS AND
HOMELAND TIES

The relationship between diasporic congregations and those in the homeland has changed in a significant way over the past decades. From 1975 to
1995, Vietnam was identified as the past, the ancestral source, but a place
that had no future, so it was the aim of refugees and immigrants to forge
a new life in the host country. This did not mean, however, that these
communities were committed to assimilation. On the contrary, their primary commitment seemed to be to recreate the vanished world of the
Republic of South Vietnam in California. This was the ideological impulse behind the creation of one Little Saigon community in Orange
County, and efforts to create a second one in San Jose. The high rate of
nationalization for Vietnamese refugees was tied not to a wish to become
American, but to an intense desire to sponsor other immigrants and family members to come over from Vietnam so that there would be a significant community in California, where religious, cultural, and social institutions could be rebuilt. Since 1995, when it became possible for Vietnamese Americans to return to their homeland to visit, purchase land, retire, or form businesses, this orientation has changed and a more transnational community has been forged, enabled by modern forms of media,
transportation, and entrepreneurial activities. Religious organizations, far
from being bastions of traditionalism, have been at the forefront of these
new developments, with elaborate websites, desktop publications of religious texts, and new opportunities for missionary outreach.

All of the indigenous Vietnamese religions build on a foundation of
ancestor worship that is shared across religious lines, and is even practiced in the homes of devout Catholics. Each family has an ancestral altar,
usually decorated with photographs of dead relatives, and/or ancestral
tablets inscribed with Chinese characters. Offerings of fruit and flowers
are placed on the altar daily in some households, while in others the
ancestral altar is only set up during Tet, the New Year celebration that is
the most important traditional Vietnamese festival. This custom is also
performed in folkloric festivals featuring regional dances and music.
What in Dao Mau is a form of worship is presented as entertainment in
other contexts.

James Clifford has argued that diasporic consciousness oscillates between suffering and survival, so that loss and hope are lived as a defining
tension.[28] Vietnamese Americans commemorate their history as refugees
by placing the yellow flag with red stripes of the Saigon republic on
altars, and flying it in Catholic churches, the Hoa Hao pagodas, and the
eclectic Caodai temples. It is now usually referred to as a "heritage flag"
and represents the community, although it no longer represents a
government. Ritualistic gestures like this one serve to make the diaspora
sacred, infusing folklore with political, spiritual, and, moral significance.

NOTES

1. Research for this article was supported by grants from: The Pew Charitable Trusts to the Center for Religion and Civic Culture at the University of Southern California (2003-2004); the California Council for the Humanities (2007-2008), which funded the production of the documentary *The Left Eye of God: Caodaism Travels from Vietnam to California* (available at http://www.der.org/films/left-eye-of-god.html); and the National Science Foundation grant ##0752511, Ethnic Resilience" and Indigenous Religion: A Transnational Perspective on Vietnamese Immigrant Congregations in California, (2008-2011). *Nguoi Viet (The Vietnamese People)* (City, CA) 15 Nov. 2005. A more complete account of this research is found in Janet Hoskins' *The Divine Eye and the Diaspora: Vietnamese Syncretism Becomes Transpacific Caodaism* (Honolulu: University of Hawaii Press 2015).

2. Statistics retrieved from vietnameseembassy.com www.vietnamembassy.com (16 Aug. 2012).

3. Ngo Duc Tinh, "The Mother Goddess Religion: Its History, Pantheon, and Practices." *Possessed by the Spirits: Mediumship in Contemporary Vietnamese Communities.* Eds. Fjelstad and Nguyen Thi Hien (Ithaca, NY: Cornell Southeast Asia Program, 2006).

4. Karen Fjelstad and and Nguyen Thi Hien, *Possessed by the Spirits: Mediumship in Contemporary Vietnamese Communities* (Ithaca: Cornell University Press, 2006); and Karen Fjelstad and Nguyen Thi Hien, *Spirits without Borders: Vietnamese Spirit Mediums in a Transnational Age* (New York: Palgrave McMillan, 2010).

5. Andrew Lam, "For the Catholic Church, Vietnamese Are the New Irish" *New American Media*, www.newmamericanmedia.org (6 Dec. 2006).

6. For example: Hien Duc Do. *The Vietnamese Americans* (Westport, CT: Greenwood Press, 1999): 8-9.

7. For example: Janet Hoskins, "Preface" *Le Caodaisme: Theories des Trois Trésors et des Cinq Fluides* by Lap Chúc Nguyen Huy and Bui Dac Hum (Redlands: Chan Tam, 2006).

8. Taylor, Philip, "Hoa Hao 'Apocalypse now'? Hoa Hao Buddhism emerging from the shadows of war" *The Australian Journal of Anthropology*, 2001.

9. Karen Fjelstad and Nguyen Thi Hien, *Possessed by the Spirits: Mediumship in Contemporary Vietnamese Communities* (Ithaca: Cornell Univerity Press, 2006).

10. Samuel Popkin, *The Rational Peasant: The Political Economy of Rural Society in Vietnam* (Berkeley: University of California Press, 1979).

11. Graham Greene, *The Quiet American*, (New York: Penguin, 1954).

12. Jayne Werner, "The Cao Dai: The Politics of a Vietnamese Syncretic Religious Movement (PhD thesis, Cornell University, 1976); Victor Oliver *Caodai Spiritism: A Study of Religion in Vietnamese Society* (Leiden: Brill 1976).

13. Taylor, Philip, "Hoa Hao 'Apocalypse now'? Hoa Hao Buddhism emerging from the shadows of war" *The Australian Journal of Anthropology*, 2001.

14. Kristen W. Endres, *Performing the Divine: Mediums, Markets and Modernity in Urban Vietnam* (Copenhagen: NIAS Monographs, 2011).

15. Darrel Montero, *Vietnamese Americans: Patterns of Resettlement and Socioeconomic Adaptation in the United States* (Boulder, CO: Westview Press, 1979).

16. Andrew Pham, *Catfish and Mandala: A Two-Wheeled Voyage through the Landscape and Memory of Vietnam* (New York: Farrar Strauss Giroux, 1999).

17. Ong, Aihwa, *Buddha is Hiding: Refugees, Citizenship, the New America* (Berkeley: University of California Press, 2003).

18. Timothy Smith, "Religion and Ethnicity in America" *The American Historical Review*, Vol. 83, No. 5, (1978): 1155-1185.

19. Freeman, James, *Changing Identities: Vietnamese Americans, 1975-1995* (Boston, MA: Allyn and Bacon, 1995).

20. Min Zhou and Carl L. Bankston III, *Growing Up American: How Vietnamese Children Adapt to Life in the United States* (New York, NY: Russell Sage Foundation: 1998).

21. Benedict Anderson, "Long Distance Nationalism" *The Specter of Comparisons: Nationalism, Southeast Asia and the World* (New York: Verso, 1998): 58-76.

22. Hans von Amesfoot, "The Politics of Diaspora: Moluccan Migrants in the Netherlands" *Journal of Ethic and Migration Studies* Vol. 30 (1) 2004 151-174): 151.

23. Thomas Tweed, *Our Lady of the Exile: Diasporic Religion at a Cuban Catholic Shrine in Miami* (New York: Oxford University Press, 1997).

24. Aihwa Ong 2006 Experiments with Freedom: Milieus of the Human in *American Literary History* March 1, 2006. Oxford: Oxford University Press. Accessed at http://oxfordjournals.org on March 27, 2014.

25. Janet Hoskins, "Caodai Exile and Redemption: A New Vietnamese Religion's Struggle for Identity" in *Religion and Social Justice for Immigrants,* Pierrette Hondagneu-Sotelo, ed. (Rutgers University Press, 2006).

26. Karen Fjelstad and Nguyen Thi Hien, *Possessed by the Spirits: Mediumship in Contemporary Vietnamese Communities* (Ithaca: Cornell University Press, 2006).

27. Oscar Salemink, "Embodying the Nation: Mediumship, Ritual, and the National Imagination" *Journal of Vietnamese Studies* 3:3: 261-290 (2008): 32.

28. James Clifford, "Diasporas," *Cultural Anthropology* 9:3 (August 1994): 328.

THIRTEEN

Of Flying Brooms and Sorcerers

Spell-castings, Love Potions, and Supernatural Plants

Rossina Zamora Liu

> *On Wednesday a client comes to Lady Ha and says she's cursed. She suspects it's her husband. The cramps, she claims, came about after she announced intentions for divorce. "Can you help me," she asks?*
>
> *Lady Ha goes into the back room, crushes dried herbs in a mortar, prays over the powder, and folds it into a paper football. "Take this with your meal," she says. "In a few days, you will expel the curse from your womb."*
>
> *On Friday the woman has a stomachache and goes to the bathroom. When she is done, she looks into the toilet and sees a fish swimming. That weekend, the woman pays Lady Ha another visit. "I want my husband to suffer," she says. "I want him to eat the fish."*

Vietnamese fortune-tellers, the *true* kind, do not require props—no crystal balls, no tarot cards, no charts, no websites, not even a store front. Lady Ha has never had one. People—believers—come to her house on Bird Avenue. They come and they knock and they do not leave until she opens. This is because they know Lady Ha is the real thing. She does not advertise nor does she need to. Clients seek her because they know she relies only on her clairvoyance and sorcery—sorcery "tools" that allow her to cast potent spells, concoct love potions, and command the supernatural. These tools, they hear, are secret artifacts and rituals passed down only to worthy disciples. In the wrong hands, like those of novices and the ungifted, they can do harm, for they are active entities; they are homes to ghosts, ghosts of virgins summoned to perform spells.

My ethnographic research on Vietnamese fortune-telling and sorcery started with the brutal and often thought-to-be ritualistic killing of Lady

Ha in spring 2005. Fascinated and frightened by the rumors of witchery, I opened my ears more widely and began to listen more closely. "She was a witch who died a witch's death," people would say, and although harsh they were, those words, I found them evocative, too. A witch? A modern-day witch? And Vietnamese, too?

During summer 2006, I flew out to Little Saigon in Southern California and started what became a five-year study on Vietnamese American sorcery folk practices, and in the following pages, I present short contemporary tales, which I reconstructed from this research about spell-casting rituals, about love potion concoctions, and about supernatural plants that eat eggs. After each narrative are conversations about the ritual's folk roots and methods of enactment, and the dialectal relationship between the original Vietnamese fortune-telling-sorcery traditions and the translated Vietnamese American adaptations. How has contemporary (and borrowed) culture, for instance, shaped today's fortune-telling-sorcery performances? What defines authentic rituals, particularly when contemporary practitioners become "spiritual capitalists" and sell their psychic and sorcery services to the community? Here, I am referencing those magical spells advertised on glossy brochures and pastel pink flyers, the love potion concoctions that smell a lot like Chanel No. 5, and the mythical, spirit-possessed plant that, depending on its form, could resemble either the thousand-year ginseng root or the ginger tree. Given the contexts of commercialism and the syncretic cultural practices of Little Saigon Vietnamese America, then, I ask: how do practitioners of fortune-telling and sorcery negotiate authenticity? This question has guided my ethnographic research and now guides the stories that stem from that research.

I

I shall begin with a tale of Lady Ha, one that blurs facts and rumors, but that captures the folklore that is of Vietnamese fortune-telling, sorcery, and witchcraft. Hers is a story of fame and notoriety, of a nail technician who became a fortune-teller, a fortune-teller who became a sorcerer, a sorcerer whose spirit, in death, floated above the house the night police discovered her body; the one who guided detectives through their investigations of white paint, bone-filled urns, magical plants, and virgin souls; the one whom people say, could not, would not, and should not be killed. This is her story.

Voodoo but Never Hoodoo (and Certainly Not Witchcraft)

> *The night Lady Ha was found face down in a pool of blood, her hair ripped from scalp, and her hands and head covered in white paint, the phones in Little*

Saigon buzzed with rumors. People speculated, "It's voodoo"—not because she practiced the craft of Haitian voodooists, but because they didn't know any other word for witchcraft; or, maybe they did, but thought voodoo sounded more authentic and carried with it a darker mystique of all things sorcery—Haitian or not.

Tales circulated about the murder, about how Lady Ha had been killed. "A horrid death this one, but appropriate, too," they said. "Hers was one with magic and spells and bua—a true witch's death." Most speculated about the white paint, how it was intentionally poured over the hands and head alone—"perhaps to keep her soul from recognizing her body, perhaps to keep her from reincarnation," some said. "A hybrid-Buddhist take, this one was." Others heard of the multiple stabbings to the neck and face. "Her eyes were gouged, too. And she was scalped; a lotus carved on her forehead—a demonic ritual," they concluded.

The truth was, her eyes were intact and she was never scalped (it was a wig, that flock of hair by the body). The paint, that police later learned was purchased from Walmart, was the only ritualistic artifact in question—though perhaps, one too many it was, because people began to talk, too, of possibilities for why Lady Ha had died the way she had, as if there could ever be a reasonable explanation. "It was because of the bua ngai," they said. "Magic that dark and that powerful is bound to bounce back—fast, strong, deadly."

What they were referring to, of course, was the beloved magical plant that Lady Ha was known to have kept, the one that homed the soul of a virgin, the one that she tended to every evening—fed it, praised it, loved it—the one that her husband sent from Vietnam. "I've blessed it with the boy's being," he had said. And easy it was not, this ritual of which he had spoken. Only the very skilled sorcerers could do it, only those with lineage of the male line—of fathers who were sorcerers and whose fathers' fathers were, too. It was said Lady Ha's husband had dug up the child's grave, crushed the skeletal remains into powder, and summoned the spirit into the plant. The whole ritual took him weeks because each blessing had to be done at the right time, on the right day, with the right amount of chi. Reawakening the dead was a dangerous practice, after all, even if it were the soul of your own child you were summoning—or so it was rumored that this bua ngai, the one Lady Ha owned, was the embodiment of hers and the sorcerer's stillborn child.

In the past, sorcerers who had attempted to capture young spirits often had their hairs turn silver overnight. Others would awaken the next day completely emaciated—skin draped loosely on skeletal bodies. And still, others wouldn't awake at all. But the sorcerer wasn't worried. He knew, if done correctly, the bua ngai would help his wife's spells and curses become especially powerful, and that, in turn, would not only bring in new clients, it would bring back old ones.

Indeed Lady Ha's popularity grew over the years. What were once clients of manicures and pedicures were now seekers of magic and alternative lives. People came from all over California, Texas, New York, Florida, and Washington, D.C. They came and they asked, not for palm readings, not for astrology, not for advice, but for life-changing, fate-altering, spells, spells that ran from $3,000 to $9,000 each: lovers' spells, money spells, welfare spells. People came and people paid, because for them, nothing else had worked to win their lover's *heart, to buy their family home, to regain their health. Nothing. America, as they had discovered, was not the source of possibilities and equality. Lady Ha was. She was the embodiment of people's, of believers' hope—hope for a better, happier, healthier, more prosperous life; hope, that which feeds the most powerful and dangerous confidence of all—faith. Faith, when it is strong, when it is whole, it is blind. Faith, when it is weak, when it is broken, it is destructive— and deadly.*

During the several years that I researched this ritualistic murder, I have also written ten essay renditions on Lady Ha. Of the ten, only three (including this one) have sustained through the process and actually evolved into larger and more meaningful pieces, each sharing the same core—the sorceress, the white paint, the magical plant—but differing in variants that evolved to reflect the cultural and functional contexts in which, and for which, the tale is intended to serve. I comment on my process and decisions only insofar as to suggest the connections they have with the way folktales (including tales of folk practices) are told and retold over time and across cultures. In the case of Lady Ha, depending on whom you ask and to whom you tell her story, hers was either a death of a witch's karma, of a friend's betrayal, or simply of a thief's greed (her home was robbed at the time of the murder).

The story I constructed for, and present in this chapter is the most recent version to date of Lady Ha. It reads less like a traditional storybook tale than it does a recap of one that might have been told through word-of-mouth in the community. In second- and third-hand accounts, the emerged narrative also reveals the instability and shifts behind everevolving rumors surrounding her death, and the sorcery tools and rituals performed. Word choice, tailored by the liking of the storyteller, for example, has affected the way in which the story is interpreted and experienced. Consider the difference between "voodoo" and "witchcraft" and the various images of darkness that each elicits. In my conversations with Vietnamese locals of Little Saigon, many folks said they referenced the term voodoo not only because of vocabulary limitations, but also preference, deeming it synonymous with witchcraft, but wickeder. For them, the word voodoo accentuates the exotic mystique of Lady Ha's magic— an aggressive, unyielding, and unexplainable darkness she was known to cultivate. In fact, on occasions when I had politely suggested use of the word witchcraft, as in, "You mean Lady Ha's witchcraft?" people would shake their heads. "No. Worse. *Voodoo*," they would say. For many, the compound word, witchcraft, bears with it ambiguous and diverse possibilities, one that could mean dark or good powers. People think of green-skinned women with pointy black hats and long, loose-fitting robes—all things related to the *Wizard of Oz* and children's Halloween costumes, all things commercialized and embedded in popular culture. Granted, the same could be said about voodoo because it, too, has been depicted on the silver and high-definition screens via *Serpent and the Rain-*

bow and *Skeleton Key* and more recently, *True Blood*. But the portrayals, for the most part, still play on the stereotypical mystique of the incurable, irreversible "black magic" — with little room for ambiguity or flexibility of interpretation. Moreover, the enactments of the so-called voodoo rituals by Hollywood (i.e., the painted-faced witchdoctor holding instruments that look more like maracas than ancient magical artifacts), in some ways, resemble the performance of Vietnamese sorcery, or at least insofar as how believers would imagine them — through folktales, Vietnamese-dubbed Chinese soap operas, and so on.

Words and vocabulary aside, this most recent tale of Lady Ha also reveals the community's syncretic beliefs — those of religious and folk, of American and Vietnamese, and of younger and older generations. Theories about the white paint found on Lady Ha's hands and head, for instance, suggest a hybrid between opposing practices — Buddhist notions of reincarnation and sorcery rituals of mutilation. Some locals believe the specific locations where the perpetrators poured the paint are related to prohibiting the sorceress from rebirth. According to Buddhist beliefs, if the spirit cannot recognize and reunite with its body, then it will not be able to undergo reincarnation. Still, a few others insist the paint was intended to cover up the rumored scalping and eye-gouging (both of which, as noted, did not occur according to police reports). From the perspective of traditional customs, the color white could also mean death, as in the color of garments worn at Buddhist funerals, or it could mean shame, as in the color of lime powder smeared on faces of adulterous women. From the perspective of contemporary practices, the house paint purchased from Walmart (instead of white lime powder) not only reflects modern time but also the adopted culture, a very American consumer-oriented culture perpetuated, in this case, by a super chain. Such union of belief systems is common in folklore and even more so in Vietnamese American folkway because of the geographical and cultural migration that is true of its history. Given the multicultural variants, what sustains and perpetuates notions of authenticity of rituals, then, are their core of religious and cultural lineages. As such, even if the contemporary adaptation appears to have departed from its roots (via variants), as long as the ritual's ancestry exists (or is communicated), believers are likely to continue their subscriptions.

The magical plant, or *bua ngai*, that Lady Ha was known to keep is an example of where ancestral roots translated to authenticity, and that, in turn, translated to capital gains, the kind that enabled the sorceress to offer $3,000 to $9,000 spells. Moreover, that the blessing of the plant was done by her husband, who was not only a sorcerer-warlock but also a descendent from a long line of other sorcerer-warlocks, certainly added to Lady Ha's credibility. The witchcraft involved in the summoning of the boy's soul into the plant was, in some ways, regarded with more power and authenticity than had it been performed by Lady Ha herself. It

was in the mystique of having the dark magic rooted in Vietnam (and one
that also included a virgin ghost) that appealed to believers.

During my fieldwork in Little Saigon, stories of various fortune-teller-
sorcerers and sorceresses possessing and selling such magical plants
were common, but few, if any, had the kind of family history and reputa-
tion like that of Lady Ha's plant. "American" magic just isn't as powerful
as "Vietnamese" magic, and as such vendors often rely on advertisements of the exotic and supernatural to entice the market, often boasting—*warning*—clients of its exclusive ownership. "To the un-allowed,
death or madness could come," they would say. As outsider to this world
of the *bua ngai*, I wonder about such logic. If the plant were a one-owner
entity, then how is it possible for anyone but the sorcerer who summoned
the spirit, to truly "own" it? I posed this question on many occasions to
clairvoyant-warlocks and witches, themselves, but few answered me directly. In one account, a sorcerer claimed that he only sold "offspring
plants" (or roots) of his main *bua ngai* source. "Clients wouldn't be able to
own mine," he said, "but they could 'adopt' parts that came from it—its
extensions." His assertions would explain, then, why I have heard some
friends of owners say (from their second-hand account), "It looks frightening, almost like a shrunken body floating in water." From these descriptions, the *bua ngai* seems to resemble a charmed root-like organism
rather than an actual sagebrush plant with leaves and flowers as some
claim. Regardless, such rumored qualities of rarity and unverifiable features have perpetuated for the plant its notoriety as a demonic chameleon
of witchery, and one that clients—the ones brave and desperately hopeful
enough—continue to seek.

The following is a profile essay of the magical plant.

Bua Ngai: *The Plant That Eats Eggs*

> *"The plant eats eggs. And sometimes a whole chicken—roasted. When you
> come back to the altar, you'll see only shells and bones."*

> *"It also enjoys good conversation."*

> *"But only thanks and praises. Be sure to bow your head and clasp your
> hands. Like this. Hands swing toward the chest; hands swing away. Three
> times. That's right, like that."*

> *"They say the plant is beautiful."*

> *"Yes, demonically so. It wants to lure you in. Like the Chinese nine-tailed
> huli jing, or fox spirit, who possessed the beautiful Daji and tortured officials
> in the Ming novel,* Fengshen Yanyi. *Like the Japanese kitsune known as*

Lady Kayo who terrorized Prince Hanzoku in The Tales of Genji. *All beautiful. All dangerous."*

"And the leaves have sharp jagged edges. Like fangs."

"But it's not an animal. It's a plant."

"Like a lemon tree?"

"No. A zingiber tree."

"No. A human-body tree."

"In the upper half, there are pointy leaves and pink flowers and red berries. In the lower half, there's a ginseng-like root, though people insist it's not ginseng."

"Caretakers store the roots inside a jar filled with water, sometimes wine — the plant likes to eat and drink. They place the jar on an altar and cover it with a red silk handkerchief because only they, the caretakers, are allowed to see the plant — it's shy."

"And contagious."

"It can harm you."

"Yes. Don't let it see you. You'll go mad."

"Or die."

The Vietnamese word for it is **bua ngai**, *though it originates in Cambodia and Laos where the energies are high and where tribes practice sorcery. The Hmong. The Mien. They grow the bua ngai and ask spirits to inhabit it, to inhabit the root. Children's spirits, the younger the better — preferred are the stillborn or the aborted. Those are the most powerful ones for they are virgins. They are also easiest to control because they are young and malleable.*

Caretakers, especially sorcerers, sometimes boast of owning one. But they say it in a whisper. Like a child, it is very sensitive. Watch what you say, how you say it, when you say it.

Like a child, it requires consistency. Feed it the right food at the right time with the right attention. Like a child, it cannot be disowned. Love it, praise it, keep it.

II

Years ago, maybe at three, I was kidnapped by a woman with uncombed hair—her face blackened with mud, her nose dripped of yellow slime, her hands covered in motor-oil grease. A mad woman, she was, or so they said, for I do not remember this moment or the woman or her face or nose or hands for that matter. I remember only what pumps through my veins at night and causes my heart to beat just a bit faster. I remember the fear. In the dark, I see her, or versions of her. The witch, the one who wandered from three villages away into our neighborhood, a small community outside of Saigon; the witch whom I do not recall but whom I know well in my sleep—a manifestation from that day, from that afternoon when she and I shared the same space, the same body—my legs wrapped around her bony waist, my arms pushing against the black silk pajama sleeves. They said she came to eat me, because my flesh was sweet and tender as all meats of virgin children are. They said she wanted a surplus of young flesh, for consuming such delicacy would keep her strong and full. She would store me under the ground, inside the black dirt where the temperature was cool, where the body stayed fresh for days. They said that had Old Toan not found me in time, had he not questioned the witch, I would've disappeared into her stomach, coiled in her intestines for weeks because the human flesh takes a while to digest. Then they laughed as if to expect me to forget what they had just reminded me of, and I, in turn, smiled because what else was there to do? But inside, underneath my shirt, I sweat.

The thought of possibilities has always frightened me. And still does.

The summer I researched Lady Ha's death, I was consumed by possibilities and I was afraid. I would drive by her house on Bird Avenue, but I would never commit, never got out of the car, never walked up to the house, never knocked at the door. I worried that if I did, Lady Ha's spirit would spot me and mark me as enemy. People say that sometimes in death the soul is stronger, more vengeful, especially that of a witch's, especially that of a witch who had been killed violently. Those are the most dangerous kind. And so for the first month I would visit, instead, other fortune-tellers who also advertised spell-casting and sorcery, and always, I would take my sister, Aurora, who posed as the client. Each visit, the script, without fail, would come in threes: clairvoyant reads client's fortune ("Shall I look at your love life?"), clairvoyant establishes problem ("You'll be destined to endure lost love if you don't rid the curse"), and clairvoyant offers resolution ("I can help with my spell-casting services"). What varied among the vendors, though, were the performances of authenticity, the ways in which they made their cases through setting, through props, and through persona. I remember one in particular.

Her name was also Ha and she had a storefront in Midway City, right outside of Westminster. I was attracted to her, I think, because she shared the same first name as Lady Ha. Supposedly, she was also more famous but less powerful than the one who was killed, although what specifically made her magic weaker and yet her fame greater, was unclear. For these reasons, I knew I had to at least meet her. The following is her story, or maybe it's hers and mine, or likely, it's just mine.

Miss Ha of Midway City: The Lady Who Wasn't a Lady

"Your Visa limit. What is it?"

"Sorry, what again?"

Aurora doesn't understand our clairvoyant's Vietnamese. The woman talks too fast, her accent is too heavy. To the untrained ear it would seem Miss Ha speaks in cursive: no breaks between words, no time to translate each of them into English. It could be intentional or it could be natural. It's hard to say. Despite pictures of friendly smiles on the website, store walls, and business cards, the woman possesses a rugged harshness that sometimes is more reflective of a hustler than a trustworthy counselor. A lot of it has to do with the way she addresses us, her clients. In Vietnamese, there is a polite form of address, and there's a not-so-polite form. Miss Ha speaks a hybrid of both. Depending on her mood, she has referred to us as either sweet children or little fuckers.

"Sorry, what's that again?" Aurora asks.

"Your card, kid. How much credit is on your card?"

"Eight hundred, maybe."

Our clairvoyant sits back, swings her right arm to the back of her chair, and smirks. "Why you so poor?"

"I'm a college student."

"Well, we can't do anything with $800. You know that, right?"

"Want to give me a discount, then?"

I look away and smile. Aurora is a worthy sidekick. Going into this venture, I had asked my sister to let the psychic tell her fortune because I was too afraid to let the woman read mine. The idea of someone else predicting my future and knowing it better than I do feels like a violation. It's like giving someone access to your internal navigation system, a part that by nature's design ought to be untouched. In fact, I don't like the idea of knowing the future at all. I would want to reverse it, to correct it, to control it. And yet, oddly, I am curious about it the way kids are curious about matches. Miss Ha's website boasts of spell-casting training. "Learned from teachers in Cambodia, Laos, Indonesia, and Thailand," it says. These are the places where Vietnamese witchcraft supposedly originated. Who could turn away from that? I'm tempted to see how she works—if she's as good as her website claims, if she's as good as the other Ha in Little Saigon. There are two of them—the one my sister and I are seeing in Midway City, and the one in Westminster, the one with the American names attached. Even more than her clairvoyance, Lady Ha was best known for her spell-casting services. "Ha Jade Smith, when she wasn't killed yet, could cast real spells," people say. "She had special powers." Of course, this is what our current psychic claims on her website, too. "Special powers."

Unlike most Vietnamese clairvoyants who do their readings in their home offices, Miss Ha of Midway City does hers at the shop. At 10 x 10, the room is cluttered with a breakfast table, a few chairs, a reclining loveseat, and a wall-hung television set. For decoration, she has two Persian rugs, a couple of throws with gold and red tassel-fringes, and several photo shots of herself in her finer and sexier youth. I suspect when Miss Ha initially opened for business, she wanted to appeal to both Vietnamese and non-Vietnamese clients because in addition to palm readings, card readings, and spell-casting services, she also subscribes to what I consider to be more stereotypical and contemporary psychic practices and gadgets like tarot cards and crystal balls and mood stones. Despite efforts to keep an open mind, I find it hard to take her seriously. There's just too much going on—in the store and in her.

"So how about it?" Aurora jerks her chin upwards. "A discount, Miss Ha. How about a discount?"

Miss Ha smiles; she is enchanted. "That's a good one, kid. Like I said, your signature and handwriting says you could be very rich and very happy in your love life. Rich men are very attracted to you. But you're also cursed. You have two black moles inside your little birdie." Miss Ha's index finger points to her own crotch. "Birdie." she says. "You need someone to lift off that curse. Know what I mean, kid?"

"Yeah, okay. But..."

"But nothing. Five thousand dollars," Miss Ha says and spreads out all five fingers. After a short pause, she folds down four of them, leaving only the ring finger up, and turns it toward Aurora's face. "See this? CZ. It's fake. Fifty bucks. If I wanted a real one, I would've had to pay $50,000. Get my drift? You want to get rid of these fuckers, don't you?"

Miss Ha is talking about the two old men's spirits following Aurora. "These two guys—probably your dead granddaddies—are lonely and they will block your happiness, including the rich men who love you," Miss Ha says. "The two moles—that's them. You need to get rid of them. Understand?"

"I do. But five grand is a used car."

"Okay, for you, I'll take installments. Pay me monthly."

"That doesn't help. I have only 800 in my account," Aurora says.

"Increase the credit line. Take out another card."

I know people who have used up their life savings and family fortunes trying to redirect their fates. My Grandma Sang, for instance, spent much of her early married life listening to a Buddhist psychic-monk talk about Grandpa Noel's infidelity. She furnished the monk with money, gold, and even diamonds because he said he could keep Grandpa from going astray. Eventually, it didn't really matter that my grandfather was faithful. Grandma Sang was in over her head with spells and superstitions and conspiracy theories. She convinced herself that she needed to stay away from their bedroom. Each night, she'd take out a blanket and pillow from the linen closet and spread it along one side of the main hallway. Curled up in a fetal position, this was where she slept—to keep her husband free from the impurities of sex—for the next fifty years.

This is why fortunetelling is a dangerous and addictive practice, even if you only moderately subscribe to it. This is why my sister is getting her fortunes read and not me. She doesn't subscribe to it, she doesn't believe in it at all, and because of this, she is also untouchable. Isn't that how it works? Predictions are only as true as you believe them to be. Technically, I should be able to tell myself to not believe in clairvoyance and remain safe, except I can't control my predisposition to certain thoughts and beliefs much like I can't control the color of my eyes or the shape of my nose. People are born with these things, just like they are born into their faiths.

"Hey you." Miss Ha snaps her fingers before my face. "Reach under the table. I need to show your sister something."

I push my hands through the Persian print tablecloth until I come to what feels like a box inside a plastic bag.

"What am I looking for? Is it a plastic bag or a box or both?"

"If it's hard, that's the one."

I pull out a Hefty black trash bag, closed with a single knot twisted at the end. If I press my hands on top of it, I can see the contours of a 20 x 20 box. "Is this it?"

"Shake it," Miss Ha says.

I am confused at first. I worry that I might break something inside.

"Shake it, like a Christmas present."

No heavier than puzzle pieces, the box feels hollow as its contents shuffle from one end to the next. "What's in here?" I ask.

"Bua Muoi Ong," she says. "Ten Men's Voodoo. It's the real stuff."

"For what?"

"For your sister. To expel your grandfathers from her birdie." My sister and I look at each other. I smirk. "Not too many people will show you their magic," the clairvoyant continues. "But I don't mind it. I don't hide anything because I have nothing to fear. No one can copy me. I learned from the best." She takes out a stack of tarot cards and starts to shuffle them. "Cut the cards," she tells Aurora. The clairvoyant returns my sister's half to the deck and begins to flip through them—face up on the table. She does not arrange the cards into rows or circles or tiers the way many psychics do. Miss Ha just piles the tarots one on top of the other until she comes to the one with the three swords piercing through a heart. "There!" She points to the card. "Do you believe me now? Three of swords," she says.

"What does that mean?" Aurora says.

"Bad luck in love. Can't you see? The swords are stabbing through the heart—your heart. The sword in the middle belongs to your boyfriend. He'll hurt you. See? He's stabbing through your heart. And the other two criss-crossing on both ends, they are your granddaddies. They don't want you to love anyone but them."

"That sounds perverted," my sister says.

"They're dead. They're men. Dead people don't follow earth rules."

"I noticed you just flipped through the cards randomly," I say. "How did you know to stop at this card?" Miss Ha does not answer my question and instead looks over at my sister.

"If this is going to work, I'll need a handful of pubic hair from you."

"For what?"

"Magic. Spells. To burn with the other stuff in the box—the Ten Men's Voodoo. To rid you of your moles. If you don't believe me, go home and check tonight. Flash a mirror against your birdie, spread it apart and you'll see them."

My sister scrunches her nose and looks at me.

"So kid, what do you want to do?"

"I'll have to think about it," Aurora says.

"Well, don't think too long. I'm closing the shop in three weeks."

"Just temporarily though, right? Like for a vacation?"

"Yeah, whatever. What you need to know my business for?"

"Well, if I'm going to give you money for this spell, I'd like to know you'll be around to complete it."

"Don't worry. I'll finish it. After I burn your hair, the rest would be up to you anyway." Miss Ha looks at the crucifix on Aurora's necklace. "You're Catholic, right? Well, what do you Catholics do? You pray. That's what you have to do after the spells. You pray every day and you ask your God to keep the two moles away. It's all about faith," she says.

How convenient to place it back to the client. What a con, I think, as does Aurora, I'm sure. I can tell by her upside smile and occasional eye-rolling. Still, the back and forth continues for another half hour anyway—Miss Ha hustling Aurora, Aurora hustling Miss Ha. In the end, my sister and I excuse ourselves by promising to return with more money, though the three of us all know that this is a lie, just like the role that Aurora played, the words that Miss Ha spoke, and the spells we said we'd purchase. Such is the nature of the psychic world. There are predictions you need help making, and there are those you just already know.

In the hour that we sat with the clairvoyant, I saw a dynamic business woman, skilled in the arts of marketing and performance. Unlike many other Vietnamese fortune-tellers who use their homes as the place of business, Miss Ha of Midway City, the capitalist that she was, had an actual storefront, and in it were an eclectic collection of stock artifacts, common things you might find at a carnival psychic reading—crystal balls, tarot cards, tasseled-trimmed tapestries, credit card machines—and those you might find at someone's home—altars, figurines of folk deities on altars, incense urns and iron mortars on altars, a wall-mounted television set, and a microwave oven (not on altars). Syncretic was her décor, for Miss Ha aimed to attract more than local Vietnamese clientele. Just outside of Westminster, the store was on the border between Little Saigon and other ethnic communities, situated to target an international market. Reflecting both Western and Eastern notions of fortune-telling, authenticity (depending on which side of the room you looked) existed in the store's surroundings, and as client, you were assumed to recognize the details of "all things psychic" from previous visits to fortune-tellers, from scenes observed on TV shows, from pictures seen in books. Who, after all, does not know of the nomadic, headscarf-wearing clairvoyant? Miss Ha of Midway City, the visionary that she was, was culturally inclusive, serving (and performing) for all.

Smart and cunning, she was also manipulative, persuasive in her pitches. "Want a cubic zirconium or a diamond?" she asked. "The real stuff will cost more." "Only true believers understand the importance of authentic readings and spells. What kind of believer are you?" "Act now or regret later."

Quite the rhetorician Miss Ha of Midway City was, and wickedly charismatic, too. Like many successful vendors I visited that summer, Miss Ha of Midway City, quick-witted and rude at times, was oddly charming and confident, often speaking in assertive tones and declaring requests like, "Pull out the Ten Men's Voodoo from under there. Will ya?" It is her firmness, and sometimes crassness, I suspect, that some clients find honest, reassuring, and perhaps, worthy of patronage. No one wants to spend money on a tentative, uncertain reader after all. Seekers of fortune-telling want confirmation, and ultimately their pursuits are less about the actual reading than they are about the control and power gained from knowing. It is in knowing, and the power of it, that yield reassurance and it is the acquisition of reassurance that breeds security and loyalty; security and loyalty are what bring them back.

Indeed, it is not uncommon for subscribers in the Vietnamese American community to regard their psychics as counselors, advisors, and friends, and often, they come (or call) regularly, seeking advice on love, business, money, and other personal matters. In this way the success of the business, like any small businesses, depends heavily on customer fidelity and rapport between vendor and vendee. Word-of-mouth serves as reviews for prospective clients, and in the age of media, those savvy and prosperous enough also sometimes maintain websites boasting client testimonials, or place advertisements in papers enticing readings and spell-casting services. The next tale begins with such an ad in the local newspaper.

The White Beard Monk

The ad in Viet Weekly *says the man worked miracles, and to prove it, above the text, a portrait unlike any other portrait is a portrait of such a man: white robe, white beard, and white brows—extra long, extra white. He is called the White Beard monk like the sages in the Shaw Brothers kung-fu movies or the statuettes sitting on your grandmother's mantel. For $5.99 (or $3.50 if you bargain), you can get the figurine in a Chinatown gift shop or an Asian grocery store or upstairs at Macy's (though not for $3.50 or $5.99 or any-where close to that for that matter), next to the Ming dynasty vases (made in Taiwan) and the Persian rugs (made in India) and the polka-dotted tea sets (made by Kate Spade—country unknown). The point, though, isn't about the figurine or where it's made or where you get it. The point is the monk, and how he looks like the figurine, or (again) like the sages in the Chinese kung-fu flicks. He's authentic—at least he looks it. That's what matters, and that's what brings the young woman to 15000 Magnolia Boulevard, Apartment A, on this very sunny day.*

Standing before the half-open front door, she tentatively makes her arrival known. "Hello? I have an appointment with Master White Beard."

"Come in. The door is open, can't you see?" says a voice in the back.

Inside, a haze of incense smoke fills the room and the woman rubs her eyes a few times before making way to a desk, a desk among many other large, dark red-colored wood oriental furnishings reminiscent of old Chinatown import-er-exporter stores. The White Beard sees her and directs her to the chair across from his desk, which stands to the immediate right of the door, at a slant.

"What can I do for you?" he asks. His heavy Northern Vietnamese accent forces her ears closer toward him. The woman's family, being from the South, speaks with fewer inflections and prolonged tones. Their speech requires less intention, less force. Not like the White Beard's. Not annoying like his.

"I need to bring my husband back home," she whispers. Her neck slightly tilts downward to a midway bow.

The monk sits back in his chair and examines the woman from head to stomach. "What did you do to scare him off?" he finally asks. "Looks like you must've gotten fat." He jerks his head upward and points his chin toward her belly.

The woman looks down at the pudge. Since the wedding she has outgrown the double zeroes and now wears a two. Not so bad, but Little Saigon can be unforgiving in this way. Nose jobs. Eyelid surgeries. Breast augmentations.

"You're right, Master White Beard," she says. Voice trembling, she forces herself to make the request. "Can you help me win him back?"

"Of course I can help," the monk says. He points his finger directly at her face. "The question is, do you believe?" An odd question, the woman thinks. Why else would she even be there?

Scanning around the room, she notices the almost life-size Monkey King next to a cherry-wood shelf. Back slightly hunched, and left palm in a salute as if blocking from the sun, the Monkey King stands in a lookout pose. In his right hand he holds a golden staff, just like he does in the Vietnamese-dubbed Hong Kong novellas that her mom rents from the video rental at the Mall of Fortune off of Westminster. According to legend, Buddha commissioned the Monkey King to protect a holy monk against demons during their pilgrimage to the west (India). The monk's flesh, rumored to be magically endowed, was the target of all who sought immortality and everlastingness.

On the other side of the apartment are altars with statuettes of folk gods and incense urns. In one corner, on the floor, sits a large bronze-painted Buddha. The woman's grandmother actually owns something similar, except it was half the size and sat at the center of the main family altar. Each night, at around 7:00 p.m. the old matriarch would stand before Buddha and wave a handful of incense sticks up and down before returning to the rocker with her prayer beads, beads that looked very much like a rosary, and once, the young woman even made the mistake of asking if the two were the same. "Nonsense!" her grandmother snapped. "Catholic tools are inferior to those of the one true faith — Buddhism."

"Well, do you believe?" the White Beard repeats.

"Y — yes," the woman replies, not quite sure what he's asking her to believe in.

"Then tell me what you've come for."

In happier days, the woman and her husband were inseparable and friends used to think the two would be together forever. But months ago, while sorting laundry she smelled perfume in his underwear and suspected infidelity.

The woman tells the White Beard this story and as he listens, he cups his right hand around the white mane and runs it down from chin to mid-belly. When done, he goes for the long brows, twirling and twisting the ends until they create a sharp point. "I see," he says. "Perfume. Underwear. Interesting."

"What should I do?" the woman asks.

The White Beard raises his right palm to her face. "Patience," he says. "Men do not like naggers. You talk too much and too soon." He flicks his beard to the side. "I need a picture of you and him," he finally says.

The woman reaches into the handbag and pulls out a photo from her wallet. "Will this do?"

The White Beard does not respond and instead opens his desk drawers and grabs a pair of orange-handle scissors. "Give me the picture," he says. When she does, he examines the glossy paper under the desk lamp, and then without a word he cuts it in half, right between the woman and her husband.

Fingers twitching, the woman can hardly speak. She wants only to grab the two halves out of the monk's hands, but before she can, the White Beard pulls out a red roll of ribbon from the side drawer of his desk and carefully places the print side of the photos against each other and begins wrapping the ribbon around the two halves. "This is so you are both always kissing," he says. "You'll be bound forever." Stepping up from his chair, the monk walks toward one of the cabinets against the wall, and returns with a wooden box that says, "Love" on the lid. "Do you know what's in here?" he asks.

The woman shrugs her shoulders. "Love?"

Inside the box are glass vials, each filled with a twig, a pebble, and small leaves floating in golden liquid. The White Beard takes one out and twists open the lid. "Smell this." He motions the vial across the desk toward her nose.

"Is that Channel No. 5?"

"Smells good, doesn't it? Do you know what it is?"

Again the woman shrugs her shoulders. "Love?"

"That's right," he says. "Love. Love potion. See the floating things? Five Chinese elements—earth, wood, fire, water, and metal. And bua ngai."

"Bua ngai? The voodoo plant? You have one of those?"

"You don't need to know about that," he says. "All you need is this potion. He'll come back. I guarantee it." The White Beard presses his index finger over the opening and tips the vial upside down. Then, he dabs his finger against his lips. "Rub it against your lower lip and speak to your husband in a sweet tone. Everything you say will sound like soft little whispers—because it's magic, this potion."

"How often should I—"

"Every day. Apply it every day and take the plant. Talk to it."

"The plant, too? How much does this all cost?"

"There's no price to love," the White Beard says. "You want them or not?"

"Will I have to feed it every day—the plant? Meat and egg yolk, right?"

The monk leans back in the chair and digs into his nose. "Stop this meat-yolk nonsense. I'll take care of that with the master plant. You just water yours," he says, "and talk to it." He pulls out a white, four-inch loose-leaf notebook from his file cabinet. Like the box, the cover of the notebook also says, "Love." He flips through the plastic page protectors and shows her random pictures of couples and charts of dates and notes. "These are the dates I've performed magic for them," he says. "See, look at this part." He points his finger to the quotations underneath the chart. "These are people's quotes saying they're pleased with my work." The White Beard picks up the halved photo of the woman and her husband, now tied together by a red ribbon, and glues it onto a blank page in the notebook. "There. Forever, you, too, will be in the Book of Love," he says.

The woman smirks, yet oddly, she also feels comforted and reassured. Less impressed with the testimonials and the love potion and the plant, she is intrigued by the idea of being bounded to each other, by witnessing firsthand the sealing of two pieces of a photograph together, of two people once in love. She recalls the wedding day, and her husband's wide smile and constant chuckling as he said his vows. In nervousness as in elation, he tends to laugh, perhaps because he knows just how much everyone loves the dimples that emerge at mid-chin. The woman knew she wanted him for herself the first time she saw those dimples.

"Can you cast spells, too?" the young woman asks.

"What do you think I am? Witchery is of the dark force."

The woman looks down at the floor. "I'm sorry. I just thought because you had the plant—"

"So what that I do? You want witchery, you go down the street to the voodoo lady. Me, I'm a monk—used to be anyway. You see over there on the walls? Buddha. Gods. No devils."

"I'm sorry, I didn't mean to—" Her eyes water and then she outright sobs.

The monk strokes his chin hair again and lets out a sigh of disappointment. "Ai-yah. Stop crying, will you? This is why he left you, I'm sure. You cry over such dumb things. I don't do spells, at least not ones that harm. I call mine: blessings." The White Beard pauses until he sees beam in the young woman's eyes. "I can bless your husband's heart so that he will have love only for you. Whatever he feels toward his mistress right now will disappear. Poof! Understand? Here, read these flyers. They list of my other services — the ones I don't like to advertise."

Heightened with hope, the woman grabs the pastel colored papers and looks through them. Like dinner menus, each sheet displays two columns with the description of the "blessing" outlined on the left column, followed by a series of dotted lines, followed by the price on the right column. The woman notices one blessing in particular, "Blessing of justice," and asks the White Beard about it.

"It's exactly what it sounds," says the monk. "I would need the birth times and dates — yours, your husband's and your husband's mistress. Then I perform the blessing and justice will come to all. Everyone will get what they deserve."

The woman's heart beats faster as she tries to calculate the total cost in her mind. "How much for everything — the plant, the potion, and the blessing?" she asks, all the while eagerly handing over her credit card to him.

"No, no, no, I insist," he says. "Cash only."

"Oh. I'm sorry. I thought — "

"Cash. This is a small venue," he says. "Besides, no one makes donations with credit cards."

Quickly, the woman fumbles through her pocketbook. "How much? I only have — " Her palm, now wet, reaches the green vinyl wallet. It slips a few times out of her fingers as she clears her throat. "I don't carry that much cash usually. Is there any way you could take a check?" Of course he'll say no, but the woman is simply buying time, delaying embarrassment for lack of funds. Prior to visiting the White Beard, her friend had advised her about the cash, about stopping at the bank beforehand, but she didn't think she'd need to. "I doubt this guy will be any good," she remembers saying. "I'm just curious. You know, I want to shop around first." But something about the White Beard, about watching him perform the sealing ritual has given her hope and a feeling of urgency and desperation at once. Despite his oddly grotesque behaviors, the monk, unlike others she's visited, doesn't try to sweet talk to her or sell her some outlandish story about being cursed. She likes this mat-

ter-of-factness about him. He addresses the marital issues with brutal hon-
est—"Get thinner," "Don't nag," "Be demure." His advice makes sense.

"I have this ring here. It's worth at least $5,000. Will this do?" she asks.
"How much did you say, again, do all these services costs?"

The White Beard reaches for the five-diamond-prong band and examines each
stone closely. He pauses for a long while. "This will do." He lets out a long
sigh and continues to look at the precious rocks. "Although, you must know,
the cost is whatever you believe it should be. There is no price to mark one's
faith," he says, cradling the wedding band in his palm.

III

In my past life, I was a little boy immortal who served the Goddess of
Mercy. But I was mischievous, I was told, and as a result, the goddess
sentenced me to one Earth life of suffering. As a child, I heard this story
often, and how the neighborhood monk, very much like the White Beard,
had predicted my arrival. "He said you would drop from the heavens
during harvest, and you did," my grandmother used to say. "The man
was possessed by divine spirits. He saw things others could not." Neighbors would seek him for all sorts of services: counseling, astrological
readings, special herbal concoctions, and lottery numbers. He, being a
spiritually possessed sage, had the ability to interpret dreams and translate them into numeric forms. "If you see a snake in your dream, or hints
of it," he would say, "play the number 32; dragons are 26, but only those
that fly, the lying-down kind, the ones in the water are 10, though those
could also be worms which are 05. Horses are 12, chickens are 28, pigs are
7, oxen are 9, and prostitutes are 21."

In America, being the village sage requires a similar kind of following,
Indeed, people would come to this man for everyday guidance, and
from what I heard it didn't matter whether his advice was sound, or
accurate. As devout believers, the neighbors would simply justify the
inaccuracies, forging parallels wherever available. My grandmother, for
one, never questioned the truthfulness of such accounts and had I asked,
I imagine she would have been confused, if not offended. "Of course
they're true!" she would say, though not before a pronounced eye-roll.

In America, being the village sage requires a similar kind of following,
though to achieve it requires a little more cultural and generational creativity. Contemporary times require contemporary props—things to
which the youthful or rather, the Western-acculturated Vietnamese
American could relate. The White Beard monk understood this, which
was why perhaps he chose a scent like Chanel No. 5 for his magic love
potion. Whether he used the actual perfume, the scent is linked to a long
legacy of French couture, one that elicits notions of elegance and ro-

mance. Even to the unaware, nonperfume wearer the brand (and scents of it) is a cultural icon, ubiquitous in the fashion world as it is in the three-minute film-advertisement depicting the ephemeral love affair of a starlet, portrayed by Nicole Kidman, and a commoner, played by Rodrigo Santoro. Indeed, Chanel No. 5 (or imitations of it) was a smart and appropriate choice for the magic love potion because faith, in many ways, is facilitated by balancing the exotic unknown (e.g., magic), with the familiar.

For the White Beard monk, responding to clients' contemporary cultural expectations also meant facilitating access to services in the form of pastel-colored flyers, ones that translated to "blessing menus," complete with descriptions and price charts. Although Vietnamese America remains an oral culture and word-of-mouth remains a common form of advertisement, the sage understood the importance of written text and the tangibility of paper upon which it is printed. Especially when discussing abstracts such as magical blessings, offering physical documentation for clients to hold in hand helped legitimize the services, making them appear official. The flyers also served as extra advertising props when clients spoke to friends about the White Beard monk and his services. These days, with the community ever so wide and the clientele potentially so demanding, ease of access to services (and information about those services) could make or break business. Faith, at least the modern-day entrepreneurial angle of it, operates on convenience.

It also operates on word choices—"blessings" verses "spells" verses "curses" (and as noted earlier, "voodoo" verses "witchcraft"). Faith performers, like the White Beard monk, understand who their subscribers are and what appeals to them. Although few differences may exist between the terms blessings and curses for the service provider, appropriate wording could affect clients' patronage. Those who deem themselves as peace-loving individuals may shun words that connote harm. Word choices, thus, can manipulate truths—turn a bad curse into a good blessing. Faith is relative, after all; it relies on choice and interpretation.

And then of course, truth, like faith, can mean many different things. To a scientist, the word has neither relevance nor currency. Truth ought to be fixed. To a philosopher, truth is relativity, a flexible and malleable concept shaped by interpretation. Truth ought to be situated. To a folk practitioner, truth is unquestioned because sometimes occurrences are simply unexplainable—or shouldn't be explained at all. Truth ought to be accepted. As a nonfiction writer, I juggle all three at once, but this wasn't always the case, I admit. Going into my research, I obsessed over the word, over an absolute, unwavering meaning of it. Truth, I believed, must be all things authentic, or *real*, including fortune-telling, spell-casting, and sorcery. I searched for *real* psychics with *real* clairvoyance and *real* magical plants because I needed all of them to *fit*. How else could such phenomena exist? How else could it be possible for someone to predict the future, fix the past, and alter fates?

In retrospect, I realize that my queries and expectations lacked dimension for such quest (of truth) is not an "either-or" question. What I came to see is that, authenticity exists in the presence of dichotomies—between religious and folk beliefs, Vietnamese and non-Vietnamese cultures, supernatural and commercial performances. Lady Ha, Miss Ha of Midway City, and the White Beard monk are hybrids of folk roots and translated adaptations in modern-day Vietnamese America. Lady Ha represents the mysterious sorceress with lineage to dark powers. She is the one people went to for curses. Miss Ha of Midway City is the versatile psychic. She is the one people go to for mixed spells—light and dark, good and bad, Western and Eastern. The White Beard monk portrays himself as the good sage who offers blessings. People go to him to be saved as well as to save loved ones.

Regardless, together and individually, the three concoct an alchemy of commercialization and personal, entrepreneurial and spiritual, traditional and contemporary. Different in personas and in ways of enactment, they all understand their roles as clergies and their ability to make real people's faiths—whatever, wherever, and how ever necessary. Shape-shifters, they are. Through them, I came to understand that authenticity is contextual.

And it is performed.

FOURTEEN

Korean Folklore in the Lives of Korean American Christian Women

Christine Hong

INTRODUCTION

I grew up listening to Korean *yeht-nahl yeh-gi* (old stories) abounding with heroines. At bedtime I would pillow my head in my grandmother's lap while she wove magic, spinning tales potent with the electric energy of female spirits and enchanting creatures. New Asian American folkloric traditions continue to emerge today, but they rest on historic traditions embedded in our collective memory. Folklore thrives with immigration. It is often one of the only remnants of an oral and sacred lore passed down through generations. Although children may not remember language, they are apt to remember the stories they heard and lessons learned from them. For me, Korean folklore is a connection to my ethnic heritage, linking me to the immigrant generation and the places they left behind. It connects me to the new world I have inherited through them, the new experiences, religions, and beliefs they embraced in America that often overlap with the traditions and lore left behind in Korea.

Historically, Korean folklore shifted from a tool of feminine agency in the hands of female shamans to an arguable vehicle of female oppression. In the hands of a patriarchal society, folklore relegated the once powerful shaman to a position of shame, while simultaneously instructing the community about gender roles, spirituality, and the principle of filial piety. It continues to function as the latter for Korean American women in the Christian context. Using chain sampling, twelve women who self-identify as Korean American Christians were interviewed via video conferencing and in person using open-ended interviews. Utilizing interview data and a close reading of three major traditions in Korean folklore—the filial woman, spirit, and fox—this chapter reveals tensions and contradictions in the interplay of Korean folklore, Korean patriarchy, social order, and conservative Christian values of gender and gender roles in the contemporary spiritual lives and identities of Korean American Christian women. We see a vexing interconnection between Korean folklore, and Korean American women's agency, that reveals a nuanced understanding between practice and ideology, one that, at times, is contradictory yet reinforcing.

SHAMANISM

We cannot discuss Korean folklore and its implications for Korean American women without introducing its function and importance within indigenous Korean shamanism. Shamanism, whether explicit or implicit, factors in many Korean folktales concerning women. Even when a woman is not a shaman, her abilities and role in a particular narrative indicate otherwise. Mediating between the human and the divine, the shaman's power comes from her gender, sexuality, and ability to communicate with the spirit world. Ultimately, these particular folk traditions taught that women possessed mysterious powers that required control through male dominance, albeit that dominance often meant violence or death. When her spiritual power remained untamed she had the potential to overturn society.

From 57 BC through 668 CE, Korea was divided into three distinct kingdoms: Shilla, Koryo, and Bahkje. As these kingdoms vied for political dominance, religious conflict also brewed. Buddhism, Confucianism, Taoism, and the female-led religion of shamanism were embroiled in a struggle for power.[1] Although contemporary Korea shamanism is perceived as a lower-class religion, prior to the Yi dynasty (1392-1910), shamans were revered and considered key to social balance and prosperity. The *mudang* (female shaman) is the oldest Korean symbol of religion personified. Some scholars believe strains of Korean shamanism date as far back as 6000 and 5000 BCE.[2] Sociologist Jonghyun Lee considers shamanism to have a long history of emancipatory power for Korean women, describing them as individuals capable of entering the sacred world to ". . . bring its wisdom back to the profane world."[3] In the later Koryo dynasty (918-1392 CE), the state sanctioned Buddhism as the official religion, yet shamans still performed religious rituals on behalf of the ruling powers and held court positions as "celestial officials."[4]

This perception of the "good" shaman is lost today. Among the women interviewed for this study, many considered shamans as "not to be trusted," "low class," and "pagan." One woman asserted that ". . . a shaman's work and God's work don't mesh well."[5] Despite their opinionated and negative impressions of shamans, all of the interviewees admitted having little-to-no knowledge of shamanism or its role in Korean society beyond what they had heard in church or learned in conversations with older generations of immigrant women. Why did the interviewees, who possessed only skeletal knowledge of shamans, harbor such strong aversion toward them?

We can strive to understand this by exploring the early fifteenth-century Yi dynasty's official ushering in of Confucianism—a methodological transformation of Korean society, the end explicit of female agency, and the demonization of the shaman and women who resembled her. The *mudang*, once held in great esteem by the king and his kingdom, were cast down to the lowest echelons of society, accused of greed, deception, and licentiousness.[6] The *mudangs'* ability to communicate with spirits, tell fortunes, cure illnesses, and exorcise ghosts and spirits, were devalued.

The lines between the *mudang* and other nontraditional Korean women continued to blur; the shaman became the ultimate symbol of the un-Confucian woman. In the changing religious landscape, through the power of story, she was transformed from a fearsome woman in possession of spiritual and political prowess to a symbol of living shame, a cautionary tale openly shunned in life and lore. The traditionally subtle *yin* (feminine dark essence), was explosive and uncontainable in the shaman. She had strange childlike inhibitions that shocked Confucian ideals and agents: a propensity for hysteria, the mysterious ability to bargain with the dead or predict the future, and she enjoyed *nolda* (play) with unpredictable spiritual forces.[7]

As much as her community despised her, Buddhists, Confucianists, and Christians[8] alike sought the *mudang* when experiencing an abundance of dark energy.[9] If someone in a household experienced sudden sickness, the lady of the house would call for a shaman and host a *Chaesu Kut* (household cleansing). Such events were expensive, but in severe cases it was believed that an evil household spirit, an ancestor, or perhaps a god was unhappy with the actions of the sick person or another household member.[10] To appease the angry spirit the shaman would perform a ritual exorcism by calling on the spirits, bargaining with food, alcohol, money, and "playing" with them using music, dance, song, and folk stories. Shamans also would tell fortunes, divine with spirits, and enjoy the remarkable authority to say anything to anyone—even men—without repercussions.[11] Although often mocked, her spiritual power was still taken seriously; to the community her gifts and powers were useful and real.

Today we see examples of a filial and Confucian shaman in the Korean American church where Korean immigrant woman, many of whom are elderly, fill the ancient role of the shaman's spiritual authority as prayer women and *kwon-sah* (spiritual mother). The *kwon-sah* carries no official decision-making power in the church; she is differentiated from her shaman counterpart in that her title is an honorary reward for years of long service and spiritual faithfulness. She exemplifies the filial woman, without the brash assertive nature of her shaman predecessor. When asked to name and describe which Korean American Christian women were respected in their local churches, all interviewees named women in *kwon-sah* roles. Cynthia,[12] a twenty-year-old woman attending a church in New York stated, "I look up to Lee Kwon-Sah-nim[13] because when she prays, things happen . . . God listens to her prayers."[14]

In my time as a pastor in a Korean immigrant church in New York, I remember a group of *kwon-sahs* who would gather to pray and intercede behind closed doors on behalf of the male pastor as he preached. It was believed that these women had the spirit's attention and could intercede and plead with the divinity for blessing, intervention, and tangible presence. Their spiritual authority was mitigated and perhaps even gained by their subjectivity as women who worked behind the scenes and who, in appropriate Confucian ways, did not openly seek admiration or acknowledgement. Cynthia continued in her description of Lee *kwon-sah*, "She doesn't put herself out there for recognition. . . . I think that's why God listens to her, but also why people respect her and God chose her to serve him."[15]

Like today's contemporary Korean American *kwon-sah*, one cannot simply choose to become a shaman; a spirit does the selecting. Usually after a serious trauma a woman destined to become a shaman would fall under a spirit possession—*Shin-byung* (god-sickness). *Shin-byung* continues to be listed under the DSM-IV[16] as a Korean folk diagnosis for a culture-bound syndrome manifested by severe anxiety and physical afflictions.[17] Korean American and immigrant *kwon-sahs* may not have experienced personal trauma, but much of their spiritual authority and status comes from the community's perception of how well they have borne personal and communal burdens. Janice, a thirty-two-year-old mother of two attending a Korean American congregation in Seattle, Washington, described what she perceived to be the qualifications of *kwon-sah*-hood: "The congregation has to choose you to be a *kwon-sah* after praying about it. Basically, God chooses them through the people they've been serving for years. They [*kwon-sah*] should be prayerful, sacrificial, and have endured faithfully through difficult times in their lives."[18] As a mediator and healer, the *kwon-sah* facilitates the role of the shaman as one who brings the pain and suffering of her people to God. However, she is a shaman who has been tamed, unlike the undomesticated shaman of old. Several of the interviewees hoped to one day become *kwon-sah*. They did not envision themselves as elders, chairs, or decision makers, but as women who worked and prayed behind the scenes. American-born Korean Christian generations have internalized the notion that the desirable aspects of women's spiritual roles in the church are those of servitude and sacrifice. Where did these notions come from? How have they been transmitted? Specific stories and traditions of Korean folklore—the filial woman, spirit, and fox—will be discussed in the following sections.

KOREAN FOLKLORE AND THE KOREAN AMERICAN WOMAN

As children and adolescents Korean American Christian women are taught filial piety and gender roles through both Bible stories and Korean folklore. Thus, it is not surprising that interviewees made strong associations between the themes and morals of biblical stories and Korean folktales. In fact, folk stories about filial women, as well Biblical stories about Mary the mother of Jesus, Queen Esther, Rachel, and Ruth, were the most commonly referenced by interviewees. One interviewee referred to her Biblical heroines as "gentle and humble women."[19] Although feminist theologians[20] would agree that these particular biblical women were anything but meek and mild, we cannot ignore what the interviewees have come to understand about the nature of these women—the women in both genres of stories share characteristics modeling examples of virtuous Confucian filial womanhood.

THE FILIAL WOMAN

The filial woman is a prevalent theme that runs throughout Korean and Korean American folklore. Whether a woman appears in a major or minor role, she plays a primarily filial role. She is the embodiment of the "good" woman, adhering to the Confucian trajectory of service, first to her father, then to her husband, and as a widow, to her son. Stories of filial women are also common in popular Euro-American folklore. Beauty sacrifices herself as the Beast's companion to rescue her careless father. The Little Mermaid would rather be transformed to sea-foam than witness her prince unhappy. These stories carry particular instructive weight and importance when told in a Confucian context, a context where a common and not-at-all subtle idiom is, "man high, woman low." Korea's popular Cinderella story, "*Kkongji* and *Patji*," as well as the well-known "*Shim-Cheong* the Blindman's Daughter," portray the idealized Confucian woman—filial to her last breath and even after her death, afterlife, and rebirth. They expose Korea's patronage of the self-sacrificing woman, a theme that is continually embedded in the identity of both Korean and Korean American women.

The figure of the filial woman is unique because it cross-cuts all class distinctions within Korean folklore as well as all eras. The royal, upper-class woman, the poor, pretty woman, the elderly widow, and the peasant mother all suffer the same fate as self-sacrificing examples of filial piety. These women emerge from ancient myths of origin, as well as from common peasant lore, exemplifying the self-effacing woman of servitude and humility. The popular shamanistic ritual story explaining the origin of the sun and moon exemplifies this. While this myth dates back to the three tribal Koreas and holds key elements of egalitarianism unique to that era, from a Confucian perspective it is ultimately about a filial woman. The god of the celestial heavens creates the moon with a human girl and the sun with her brother. Because of her overwhelming fear of darkness, the girl convinces her brother to switch places. As the sun, she proceeds to shine brighter and brighter over time. Out of modesty, she cannot bear to have men look at her face day after day. Eventually people cannot even look at her without hurting their eyes.[21] Even though she is the sun, the manner by which she attains her position exemplifies the Confucian woman.

Almost all of the interviewees recalled stories venerating filial women, whether as daughters or selfless, suffering mothers. When the filial protagonist dies at the hands of a wicked individual, a deity, community, or family member, she is somehow immortalized. Even though many filial woman stories still retain underlying shamanistic origins and signifiers, the interviewees made startling connections to Christianity. Anna, a thirty-five-year-old woman in Los Angeles, recalled one of her favorite tales, the story of the faithful *Shim-Cheong* who saves her blind father by sacrificing her life. "I love *Shim-Cheong* because she goes above and beyond for her father. This story teaches me what I learn from Jesus every day—to treat others like I would want to be treated."[22] When pressed to explain the story's personal significance to her, Anna replied, "*Shim-Cheong* is like the women I see at my Korean church. They don't give their physical lives, but they sacrifice all the time for everyone else's well-being. She's an example of Christian service."[23]

Ironically, the shaman traditionally reveres *Shim-Cheong* and her predecessor, Princess *Pari*, for their abilities to overcome gender repression by taking on the traditional role of the eldest son in their respective families.[24] However, Christian Korean American women do not consider these folk women as early crusaders against sexism, embracing them instead for carrying out their dutiful roles as filial women. In their minds, *Shim-Cheong* and *Pari* are no longer emancipated subjects, but are examples of idealized Confucian women. These tales resonated with the interviewee's Christian beliefs and morals regarding patriarchal gender roles. Unaware of the overlapping connection with the emancipated shaman, the Christian Korean American women interviewed associated the filial piety of folkloric women with biblical women. Why and how do they internalize the figure of the filial woman?

Folktales with filial women as central figures are often among the first passed from Korean immigrant mothers and grandmothers to their American-born children. But is the storyteller's message the same as the one the listener hears? Is it possible that different forms of oppression are handed down along with the stories we tell? While boys and girls hear the same stories, they may also understand them differently. While boys may hear stories of heroic men, often aided by their clever wives or devoted mothers, girls may hear stories of women, young and old, who sacrifice themselves, enduring insurmountable hardship to purchase a tiny bit of joy for their fathers, husbands, and children.

One of the most heart-wrenching stories I remember from my childhood involved a fisherwoman widow who never had enough to eat or to feed her son. Every night she would bring home a single mackerel for their meal. She always offered the body of the fish to her growing boy, allowing herself only the stringy meat of the fish's head. When her little boy asks about her peculiar eating habits, she tells him the fish's head is the part she enjoys the most. After her son grows up and leaves home, he returns to visit his mother, bringing a gift of several mackerel heads saved from his previous meals.

My mother told me this tale implying that I would never understand all of her secret sacrifices. Today she tells me that as a child I understood the story entirely differently than she had intended. According to my mother, after I first heard the tale, I tearfully refused to eat the last morsel of anything at meals, even refusing to eat until my parents and brother had already eaten. To my mother's surprise, I identified with the woman in the story, not the child. Hearing stories such as these during their formative years, young women are apt to internalize the tale's implications for her gender and place within family and society.

THE SPIRIT

Korean folktales involving spirits primarily revolve around women and their abilities to cross the boundaries between life and death—a key shamanistic skill that is particular to the female gender in Korean folklore. The traditional shaman-like behavior emulated by women from all walks of life implies that all Korean women possess a latent, wild ability to tamper with the boundaries between life and death. This genre of folktales exemplifies the ease with which women waft back and forth between this world and one filled with aberrant and dangerous behavior. Spirit stories warn against the capability of feminine dark magic to destroy and overturn the all-important hierarchy and harmony integral to Korean society. However, order is maintained when this ability is harnessed for the good of others. Spirit stories imply that a Korean woman can only be redeemed of her natural penchant for evil when making the ultimate sacrifice—her life in exchange for the lives of others. Yet even as a spirit she must return and dedicate her spiritual influence to the benefit of her family.

Christian Korean American women see the spirit role of the ancient shaman portrayed in Korean folktales illustrated through the lives of women at their churches. Kay, an eighteen-year-old interviewee who attends a Korean American church in Los Angeles, recalls some of the female spirit stories and reflects on how many filial women in these stories return to their families even after death to bless or care for them. She astutely made the connection between the lessons of filial piety imparted in these tales and the lessons she learned in her local church about female self-sacrifice. She shared with me the memory of her grandmother's funeral: "There were so many people [at the funeral]. She was always the spiritual rock in our family and church. After she died, sometimes people would come up to my parents and tell them that she [grandmother] had appeared to them in a dream. They always took it as a sign or guidance from God."[25] Although the shaman and stories about female spirits are largely shunned in Korean Christian tradition, the spiritual agency and the ability of "special" women to cross the porous boundaries of life and death to safeguard loved ones is nonetheless acknowledged.

The spirit woman can also be a frightening warning for Korean American women to uphold patriarchal and Confucian duties such as marriage and bearing sons. Spirit women in these stories can appear as suffering ghost maidens who died without husband or child. Forsaken maiden spirits have ghostly pale skin, long black hair, and usually dress in white clothes. These women are liminal; their spirits can rest neither with their patrilineal ancestors nor their husbands, thus, they create havoc for the living.[26] Their spirits are steeped in resentment, posing a threat not only to their natal families, but to society. Sylvia, twenty-eight, and unmarried, laments that her mother feels her life is an abject failure. "I'm not married, and I don't have a boyfriend so my mom is *obviously* embarrassed. I feel like it doesn't matter that I make a lot of money or that I bought her a house . . . as long as I don't give her grandchildren I'm not doing right . . ."[27] Patricia, thirty-three, reflects on what older women at church often share with her, "I'm officially a *noh-chun-yuh* (old maid)," she say laughingly, "I get all these well-meaning *kwonsahs* reminding me that marriage is a blessing from God, and that they're praying God helps me meet a good man!"[28] Though Patricia's tone is nonchalant, it is clear she feels a significant amount of pressure and stigma due to her single status in the Korean Christian community. The fact that she calls herself a '*noh-chun-yuh*' at only thirty-three, reveals how deeply she has internalized stigmas against single women. Sylvia and Patricia's stories mirror what Yi dynasty women experienced: self-worth and identities tied solely to matrimony and motherhood.

THE FOX

Folklore not only teaches Christian Korean American women how they should live, but it also teaches them about the pitfalls of straying from normative expectations. Just as filial and spirit women encourage adherence to gendered Confucian-Christian expectations, fox lore, more specifically the word *yuh-woo* (fox) warns women against licentious behavior, a characteristic shared between the fox and the shaman. *Yuh-woo* is a significant word imbued with the entirety of fox lore's meaning.

Most interviewees failed to recall specific examples of fox lore, but they all agreed on the negative connotation of *yuh-woo*. Most interviewees felt the term represented women who were not filial—in Anna's words, a woman who behaves in "un-Korean and un-Christian" ways.[29] One of the most common deviant behaviors of foxes in Korean folklore is their sexually manipulative tendency; reflective of what some in society feared most in shamans. The Korean Christian context emphasizes female sexual purity; therefore, the term *yuh-woo* has undertones of sexual impurity and depravity.

The notion that sexual purity and chaste behavior is tied to divine ordinance is reflected in much of Biblical teaching in the Korean Christian church, perhaps not explicitly, but in a high context manner. When asked what she learned about sex in the church Samantha stated, "Nobody really talks about it, but it's clear we weren't supposed to even entertain the thought of it. In the English Ministry (Second Generation young adult ministry of the Korean American church), people are sexually active, but again, we act like it's not happening, especially between us (women). We're supposed to be pure until marriage."[30] Carol, eighteen, commented that her mother had told her God wanted her to protect herself "down there."[31]

The fox appears in East Asian folk literature as a charmer, a symbol of luck and wisdom, a trickster, and a shape shifter. It is neither good nor evil; its nature changes according to the circumstances and individuals it encounters. However, in Korean folklore the fox is almost always female, sexually deviant, a demon, and a cannibal.[32] Several types of foxes appear in Korean folklore, the most famous being the *kumiho* (nine-tailed fox). The *kumiho* can transform into a beautiful woman or kill a man bare handed and devour his liver (often during a sex act). It is no coincidence that foxes are predominantly female, evil, hyper-sexualized, and magical in Korean lore. The *kumiho* and other foxes *are* the shaman incarnate. Fox stories are examples of Confucian traditions that portray fiendish women as shamans, who, like the fox, hide their magic, tails, and sharp teeth from men until it is too late for their prey to escape. Today, Christian Korean American women hear the term *yuh-woo* and cringe. The negative feelings of Christian Korean women toward the shaman and women like her are echoed in the derogatory connotation behind *yuh-woo*.

Only in exploring the nature of fox lore and its relationship to Korean culture's negative perception of the shaman, can we understand why Christian Korean American women react so strongly against being called *yuh-woo*. Many fox stories depict the fox as a shamelessly sexual cruel killer of men. The fox is a genuine man-eater. Luring men into encounters, she literally and figuratively consumes their flesh in her pursuit to become human. These stories usually end in a man committing sexual violence against her to reveal her true nature, often using the symbolic ripping of the fox-woman's clothing to portray this.[33] In reading these particular stories one is reminded of the sexual humiliation village shamans faced; labeled by men as whores through vicious gossip, they were groped during rituals and violated sexually in an effort to demean and dominate her.[34] The complete opposite of a virtuous woman is one whose sexual virtue is destroyed.

The fox appears in Korean folklore as a thief of man's common sense, integrity, and life force, symbolic of death to moral and social order. In using an animal to depict the shaman and shaman-like woman, she is not only demonized, but is stripped of her humanity. Among the many themes of Korean folk tradition, the fox is the most transparent example of the purposefully blurred lines between woman, shamanistic tradition, and evil. A woman who does not conform to the roles of humility and submission allotted to her by culture and religion, and who has too much authority or power, is considered dangerous and destructive to the community at large. A woman in spiritual authority convolutes the spiritual good in those around her. She is sexually liberated — goes after what she desires. The result of this *yuh-woo*-ness is that ultimately she does not belong. Christian Korean American women understand that in order to belong and be perceived in a positive way, they must put away their inner *yuh-woo* and claim an identity that aligns with the cultural and religious teachings found in filial women and Bible stories.

KOREAN AMERICAN FOLKLORE IN PRACTICE

Growing up, Korean American Christian women hear stories of fox women, spirit women, and filial wives and daughters. Many may not understand this genre of stories from a historical or theological perspective, but the messages are internalized through their cultural and spiritual formation regardless of their bi-cultural positionality. These characterizations of the female support what Christian Korean American women have already perceived and understood as positive and negative aspects of womanhood from a blending of Korean patriarchal culture and Christian practice. These stories, along with the biblical ones that thematically overlap with them, teach women that silent suffering and death for the sake of family or community is a virtue, while agency, creativity, and sexuality for pleasure are deviant and sinful.

Min-hee has attended the same church since infancy. In her long tenure at her local Korean American congregation she does not recall any disparity between the stories she heard at home and those told within church walls. "Growing up my parents pushed me to study so I could be successful, but at home and at church all the stories I heard, and examples I saw conditioned me to yield to other people's successes, especially my father and brothers."[35] Minhee's experience is not extraordinary. Many Christian Korean American women are empowered in society yet find themselves limited to kitchen duty and other menial tasks in their faith communities. While they are raised to succeed in American society, in Korean American society they internalize a sense of womanhood that is repressive and oppressive through the didactic power of story-telling, as well as by the living examples of feminine piety they see in their local congregations. When asked whom she desires to emulate in her spiritual life, Hee-Soo, a Bible study teacher and youth group volunteer, spoke about a *kwon-sah* in her congregation. "She [*kwon-sah*] never seeks recognition and carries her burdens faithfully on her own without being a burden to others. Her faith in God is visible because of the way she supports her husband and the other [male] elders. She reminds me of the women in scriptures."[36] Hee-soo mentioned several filial-woman stories, both from her childhood and the Bible, such as the woman who washed Jesus' feet with her hair. One particular tale that induced her to tears was the *Halmi Koht* (the Grandmother Flower)—a story about a mother so loving she refuses to bother her child by knocking on the door and instead freezes to death in the snow. "Stories like this [*Halmi Koht*] remind me of all the *kwon-sahs* at our church, their pride and joy is serving. . . . I hope I can live up to that one day."[37] Both Min-hee and Hee-Soo's interviews left an indelible impression of the tangled web of biblical stories and Korean folklore in their memories, perspectives, and lives. Their gender and spiritual formation as Korean American Christians was impacted by the stories they heard and the examples they saw in other women.

Not only does folklore have an impact on the women sitting in the pews, but it also has heavy implications for Korean American women in ordained ministry. Ordained women have recultivated the role of the shaman and the woman she personified in Korean folklore into the Christian church. While in traditional culture, women of a certain age and experience attain the title of *kwon-sah* and are sought for special prayers and healing; an archetype of the tamed and acceptable shaman, ordained women are regarded as quite the opposite.

As a Korean American clergywoman, I carry the burden of something ancient and dangerous—the shaman and her counterpart, the fox. It is not surprising that we find so few Korean and Korean American clergywoman in Korean American congregations; we are a paradox. I often hear parishioners young and old pondering aloud about what they should "do" with me. It seems that to officially give a woman agency and voice in faith communities releases something wild and threatening into the open—a Devil in her own right. While my clerical collar identifies me as a filial daughter, in my preaching and authority I embody the power of the fox: uncontrollable, free, and destructive of patriarchy. Female ministers preach from the depth of their painful and joyful experiences rather than dutifully masking these. They wield spiritual and systemic agency that is decidedly imbued with the fullness of dangerous womanhood and is threatening to the traditional masculinity of the pulpit. The Korean American clergywoman, like the shaman of long ago, speaks to the spirits and retells their stories, for they have uniformly called her on behalf of the people. She is, indeed, a paradox, an unexplained phenomenon possessing an unholy nature with holy authority. In the lives of Korean and clerical Korean American women exists the same dualism of good and evil found at the heart of many Korean folklore traditions remembered from childhood. She is both God and Devil, the priestess and the outcast. She holds within her the confusing multiplicity of shaman, spirit, and fox, while being held to the restrictive standard of filial womanhood.

CONCLUSION

I still ask to hear *yet-nahl yeh-gi*. Hearing them I am always reminded of their significance and hidden purpose. They are not simply yarns spun from the boredom of a clever mind. They are literary maps of our thoughts, beliefs, fears, and glimmering reminders of our superstitious past and present. What now seems like simple entertainment was once an important vehicle of religious education ensuring societal order. Korean folklore in its darkest traditions, particularly in spirit and fox lore, existed and continues to exist as a medium to confine women to Confucian hierarchy by vilifying the most prevalent example of the liberated woman— the shaman. If one deconstructs spirit and fox lore, one discovers that the definitions of women and shaman are completely enmeshed and coated with a notion of evil that neither is able to escape unscathed, even today. A myriad of stories regarding filial women—albeit once considered stories of gender liberation by the shaman—now instruct Korean American women on how to navigate Confucian culture and patriarchy. Together with biblical texts in the same vein, they inform Korean American Christian women of the limits to their spiritual agency, relegating them to menial supportive tasks and many times to sacrificial roles in the church. Times have changed; nonetheless these stories linger in our collective memories. We interpret them and live them out in our faith communities and the larger Korean American diaspora. We hear them as girls and let them define us as women, often to our detriment. Folklore does not remain locked in the past; regardless of how we feel about them, our sha-mans and their stories remain active within the walls of our faith commu-nities and in the lives of the women who inhabit them.

NOTES

1. Boudewijn Walraven. *Songs of the Shaman* (London: First UK ed. Rout-ledge,1994), 2–3.
2. Jonghyun Lee. "Shamanism and its Emancipatory Power for Korean Women," *Affilia: Journal of Women & Social Work* 24(No 2)(2009): 186–198.
3. Lee, "Shamanism and its Emancipatory Power for Korean Women," 186–187.
4. Lee, "Shamanism and its Emancipatory Power for Korean Women," 187.
5. Judy, Interview 11/1/11. Her comments illustrate a strong prejudice toward sha-mans even though she knows little about them. It is possible that this perspective is passed down to them through Confucian folklore.
6. Laurel Kendall. *Shamans, Housewives, and Other Restless Spirits: Women in Korean Ritual Life*. Studies of the East Asian Institute. (Honolulu: University of Hawaii Press,1985), 31.
7. Kendall, *Shamans, Housewives, and Other Restless Spirits: Women in Korean Ritual Life*, 24.
8. Christianity was introduced in Korea in 1653 by European missionaries (Jeong Inseop, 25). My great-grandmother told me that as a child she thought these blue-eyed, blond-haired men were "blue-eyed demons."
9. Kendall, *Shamans, Housewives, and Other Restless Spirits: Women in Korean Ritual Life*, 31.
10. Richard W. I. Guisso and Chai-Shin Yu. *Shamanism: The Spirit World of Korea* (Studies in Korean Religions and Culture Vol. 1.) (Berkeley, CA: Asian Humanities Press 1988), 132.
11. Kendall, Laurel. 1985. *Shamans, Housewives, and Other Restless Spirits: Women in Korean Ritual Life*. Studies of the East Asian Institute. Honolulu: University of Hawaii Press, 7.
12. All names have been changed.
13. *-Nim* is a suffix and honorific.
14. Cynthia, Interview 11/04/11.
15. Cynthia, Interview 11/04/11.
16. *Diagnostic and Statistical Manual of Mental Disorders*, 4th Edition
17. Lee, "Shamanism and its Emancipatory Power for Korean Women," 186–198
18. Janice, Interview 11/09/11.
19. Anna, Interview 11/15/11.
20. Some Old and New Testament feminist scholars and theologians who have written on Mary, Ruth, Esther, and Rachel include: Beverly Gaventa, Tammi Schnei-der, Deborah Hearn Gin, Young Lee Hertig, Gale Yee, and Katherine Sakenfeld .
21. Inseop Jeong. *Folk Tales from Korea*. 3rd ed. (Elizabeth, NJ: Hollym International Corp., 1982), 42.
22. Anna, Interview 11/15/11.
23. Anna, Interview 11/15/11.
24. Jung Young Lee, *Korean Shamanistic Rituals* (Berlin: Mouton De Gruyter, 1981), 170.
25. Kay, Interview 11/10/11.
26. Kilsŏng Ch'oe. "Male and Female in Korean Folk Belief," *Asian Folklore Studies* 43 (no. 2 1984): 227–233.
27. Sylvia, Interview 10/25/2011.
28. Patricia, Interview, 10/12/2011.
29. Anna, Interview 11/15/11.

30. Samantha, Interview 11/02/2011.

31. Carol, Interview 10/2/2011.

32. Issendai, "Kumiho: The Korean Fox," *Kitsune, Kumiho, Huli, Jing, Fox: Fox Spirits in Asian and Asian Fox Spirits in the West*, http://academia.issendai.com/fox-korean.html (accessed September 15, 2011).

33. Fenkl, Heinz Insu, "The Tale of the Fox's Den," The Edicott Studio, http://www.endicott-studio.com/rdrm/rrFoxTale2.html (accessed September 15, 2011).

34. Laurel Kendall. "Of Gods and Men: Performance, Possession, and Flirtation in Korean Shaman Ritual," *Cahiers d'Extrême-Asie* 6 (No. 1 1991): 45–63.

35. Minhee, Interview 10/20/11.

36. Hee-Soo, Interview 11/12/11.

37. Hee-Soo, Interview 11/12/11.

FIFTEEN

Late-life, Mortuary, and Memorial Rituals in the Japanese American Community

Ronald Y. Nakasone

In 2006, together with my spouse and daughter, I returned to Hawai'i to celebrate with our extended family, the *beiju* or eighty-eighth birthday of Gladys Hisako Fujioka, my wife's mother. *Beiju* marks a most auspicious milestone in the life of a Japanese elder, especially so when life expectancy was much shorter. This event is part of a series of late-life celebrations, mortuary, and memorial rituals that chart a person's progression through elderhood, transition from a corporal to spiritual being, and maturation into ancestorhood. These rituals, expressions of folkways of the Japanese and Japanese American families and community, are rooted in archaic Japanese beliefs in the continuum of life and death, and the reciprocity between the corporeal and disembodied or spiritual worlds. Sponsored by the immediate and extended family, these rituals instill sentiments of intergenerational responsibilities and family solidarity. Later accretions, Confucian ideas of filiality and Buddhist notions of karma, reinforce and expand these ancient indigenous sentiments; they have been seamlessly incorporated into the ritual cycle.

This chapter reviews the continuing evolution of these traditional rituals that highlight significant milestones in the stages of a person's life-continuum. It begins with a description and the rationale of rituals that draw attention to major landmarks in an individual's progression from a corporeal to spiritual being; continues with a description and discussion of late life celebrations, mortuary, and memorial rituals; and concludes with a few reflections on the transformations of these rituals in the Japanese American experience, their continuing evolution, and prospects for the future. I draw on my training in Buddhist Studies, and experiences as a Pure Land (Jōdo Shin) Buddhist cleric, community leader, and family elder.

The conceptual framework for this review is informed by an observation made by the 1994 Nobel Laureate Ōe Kenzaburō[1] on the cultural independence of the Okinawan people.

> For no matter how Japanized (or "Yamatoized") it may outwardly appear now, Okinawa still maintains its non-Yamato cultural identity; and unlike the insular, unaccommodating, and emperor-focused culture of the rest of Japan, it is blessed with a richness and diversity peculiar to peripheral cultures. Its people possess an openness to the world that comes from knowing the meaning of relative values.[2]

Ōe's comment crystallizes the experience of a people who live on the periphery of the major cultural spheres of East, North, and Southeast Asia. Throughout their history, the Okinawans have been acutely aware of the successive waves of cultural and sociopolitical power that held sway over their lives. Cognizant of the necessity to juggle the proclivities of multiple worlds, Okinawans possess openness to receiving and adapting ideas and customs that are different from their own.[3] The Okinawans greatly benefited from these contacts, but ethnic identify and national survival required that the Okinawans learn, in addition to their own history, language, and culture, the ways of doing and thinking of their more powerful neighbors. Since 1945, they have had to live in the shadow of the U.S. military, whose bases occupy approximately 20 percent of their island home.

Having to live with and negotiate with strangers instilled in the Okinawans an understanding of multiple realities and values. Relative values offers valuable insights for immigrants and immigrant communities who are located on the fringes of their ancestral and cultural origins, and on the periphery of mainstream American society. Like other peripheral people, Japanese Americans continually adjust their traditional ways of thinking and doing to their new home land.

A second insight for understanding the structure and development of late-life, mortuary, and memorial rituals is crystallized in the expression "*jūsōsei*," or "porously-laminated-nature," coined by the Japanese philosopher Watsuji Tetsurō (1888-1960) to explain the spiritual makeup of the Japanese. Additionally, *jūsōsei* describes their spiritual history. Indigenous Shintō beliefs are overlaid by Confucian, Daoist, Chinese and Indian Buddhist, and Neo-Confucian thought and attitudes. In addition, Watsuji maintained that these layers are porous; namely, the Japanese may respond to events from anyone or a combination of these layers.[4] More recently, Christianity, Western attitudes, and modernity[5] can be added to these layers. Within the context of the late-life, mortuary, and

About the Contributors

Jonathan H. X. Lee, PhD, is associate professor of Asian American studies who specializes in Southeast Asian and Sino-Southeast Asian American studies at San Francisco State University. He received his PhD in religious studies from the University of California at Santa Barbara in 2009. He is the Program Co-chair of the Religions of Asia, and Chair of the Asian American religious studies sections for the American Academy of Religion, Western Region (AAR/WR) conference. His work has been published in *Amerasia Journal; Peace Review: A Journal of Social Justice; Nidan: International Journal for the Study of Hinduism; History & Perspectives: Journal of the Chinese Historical Society of America; Empty Vessel: The Journal of the Daoist Arts; Spotlight on Teaching/American Academy of Religion; Asia Pacific: Perspectives; Pacific World: Journal of the Institute of Buddhist Studies;* the *Journal of the International Association of Buddhist Universities;* and other journals and anthologies, both nationally and internationally. He is the editor of *Cambodian American Experiences: Histories, Communities, Cultures, and Identities* (2010); and co-editor with Kathleen M. Nadeau of the *Encyclopedia of Asian American Folklore and Folklife* (2011). He has published widely on Chinese, Cambodian, Vietnamese, Chinese-Southeast Asian, and Asian American histories, folklore, cultures, and religions.

Kathleen Nadeau, PhD, is professor of anthropology at California State University, San Bernardino. She is author of *Liberation Theology in the Philippines: Faith in a Revolution; The History of the Philippines;* and, coeditor with Jonathan H. X. Lee of the *Encyclopedia of Asian American Folklore and Folklife.*

Lorraine Dong received her PhD from the Department of Asian Languages and Literature at the University of Washington. She is currently professor and chair of the Asian American Studies Department at San Francisco State University. Her teaching, writing, and research interest ranges from literature to popular culture, expressed in print and other venues such as films and exhibitions. Her recent foci are in Asian American children's literature and the evolution of Mulan from the sixth to twenty-first century.

Brett Esaki received his PhD in religious studies from the University of California, Santa Barbara, in 2012, and holds a master's degree in religious studies from the University of South Carolina, Columbia. His research areas include the religions and arts of ethnic minorities (particularly Asian Americans and African Americans), the intersection of race and sexuality, American history (late nineteenth century to the present), and popular culture. His dissertation is an exploration of the concept of silence as it is expressed in Japanese American arts and spirituality, and it illustrates how silence in Japanese American history and in ethnographic case studies has been both a tactic of resistance and an expansive experience. Overall, his work examines the complex negotiations of marginalized peoples in the United States to maintain their full sense of humanity.

Janet Hoskins is professor of anthropology at the University of Southern California, and author of *The Play of Time: Kodi Perspectives on Calendars, History and Exchange* (winner of the 1996 Benda Prize for Southeast Asian Studies), *Biographical Objects: How Things Tell the Story of People's Lives*, and *Headhunting and the Social Imagination in Southeast Asia*, as well as editor of *Anthropology as a Search for the Subject: The Space Between One Self and Another*, and *Fragments from Forests and Libraries*.

Winston Kyan received his PhD in Art History from the University of Chicago in 2006. He currently teaches at the University of Utah, where he offers courses on the art and visual culture of Asia and the Asian diaspora.

Mark S. Leo is a community activist-scholar who holds an MA degree in Asian American studies from San Francisco State University. His primary research focus is on indigenous Filipino American cultures and communities, in particular among Igorot Americans. He has presented his work at the Association for Asian American Studies, International Conference on Southeast Asia , and at the Igorot International Consultation. He is also an active member of BIBAK, serving in various leadership positions since 1989.

Rossina Zamora Liu, MFA, is a graduate of the Nonfiction Writing Program at the University of Iowa. Her writing and research interests center on folklore and education, including Vietnamese American sorcery and witchcraft, supernatural phenomenon, folk narratives, local literacies, and community writing programs. She has published in both literary and scholarly venues on topics such as family curses, witchery, trauma narrative construction, creative nonfiction writing pedagogy, cultural and literacy identities, writing across disciplines, and Vietnamese American fortune-telling practices. She is currently a doctoral candidate in the Language, Literacy, and Culture Program at the University of Iowa, College of Education.

Ronald Y. Nakasone is a member of the Core Doctoral Faculty at the Graduate Theological Union (GTU) in Berkeley, California, and a faculty member at the Stanford University Geriatric Education Center. He has published more than 100 academic books and articles on Buddhist doctrine, ethics, and aesthetics, aging and spirituality, and Okinawan Studies. Students and colleagues contributed essays to *Memory and Imagination, Essays and Explorations in Buddhist Thought and Culture*, a festschrift that commemorates his completion of one life cycle (sixty years) according to the Chinese zodiac. He received the Sarlo Excellence in Teaching Award from the Graduate Theological Union in 2011.

Vivian-Lee Nyitray received her PhD in Chinese religions at Stanford University. She is the founding Dean and chief academic officer, responsible for introducing liberal arts and sciences curriculum and pedagogy (small classes, interactive teaching, stimulating creativity, encouraging student responsibility for learning) at two sister colleges: the Yuanjing Academy of Yitong College, College of Mobile Posts and Telecommunications in Chongqing, and the Taigu Academy of the College of Information at Shanxi Agricultural University.

SooJin Pate received her PhD in American studies at the University of Minnesota, with a minor in African American and African studies. She specializes in Asian American studies, African American studies, cultural studies, and multi-ethnic literatures. She is currently a visiting assistant professor at Macalester College, where she teaches courses on critical race theory, immigration, and post–colonial approaches to the study of U.S. history and culture. She is also a contributing scholar for Absent Narratives, a project spearheaded by the Minnesota Humanities Center. Her book *Genealogies of Korean Adoption* is forthcoming.

Cathy J. Schlund-Vials is associate professor of English and Asian American studies at the University of Connecticut. She is also the Director for the Asian American Studies Institute. She has authored two monographs: *Modeling Citizenship: Naturalization in Jewish and Asian American Writing* and *War, Genocide, and Justice: Cambodian American Memory Work*. In addition to two edited collections, she is currently working on a third monograph, tentatively titled "Imperial Coordinates," which engages a spatial reading of U.S. imperialism through Asian American writing about militarized zones, internment camps, and relocation centers.

Francis Tanglao-Aguas is a playwright, performer, director, producer, and teacher of theater, film, and dance. He graduated top of his class from UCLA receiving both his BA in Theater, Magna Cum Laude, and his Master of Fine Arts in Dramatic Writing. Diverse world theater traditions steeped in indigenous and folklore form the core of his international creative research work, taking him to field work and training in Indonesia, Japan, Thailand, The Philippines, Malaysia, Cambodia, Hong Kong, and Singapore. He is the author of "When the Purple Settles," winner of the Don Carlos Palanca Award in Literature, the Philippines most prestigious literary award. He is the founding Artistic Director of IPAX, International Performance Arts eXchange and UCLA Theatre Underground. He previously held teaching positions at Georgetown University, Kenyon College, and Ateneo de Manila University. He is a Fellow at Singapore Management University's Wee Kim Wee Centre for Diversity. In 2007, The College of William and Mary NAACP Image Awards accorded him the Outstanding Professor Award.

Dawn Lee Tu, received her PhD in cultural studies from the University of California, Davis, and is currently the Director of the Cultural Centers (The Intercultural Center and The Gender and Sexuality Center) at the University of San Francisco. She also holds an MA in American studies from New York University. Her research interests include Asian American youth and cultural production, diversity and social justice initiatives in higher education, neoliberalism in higher education, Asian American panethnicity, and cultural citizenship.

Ayako Yoshimura is a PhD candidate in folklore at the University of Wisconsin at Madison. Her research interests encompass ethnography, autoethnography, personal experience narratives, vernacular beliefs, the supernatural, material culture (foodways, arts and crafts, design), and public folklore (cultural exchange, community outreach). Her past awards include the 2006 Don Yoder Prize for Best Student Paper (Folk Belief and Religious Folklife Section, American Folklore Society). She contributed two entries ("Asian American Humor and Folklore" and "Ethnic Grocery Stores") to the *Encyclopedia of Asian American Folklore and Folklife*, ed. Jonathan H. X. Lee and Kathleen Nadeau. She is a recipient of a University of Wisconsin Chancellor's Fellowship in Engaged Research for the academic year 2012–2013.